Grammar of
the Shot

Grammar of the Shot

Third edition

Christopher J. Bowen

Roy Thompson

Focal Press
Taylor & Francis Group

NEW YORK AND LONDON

First published 2013
by Focal Press
70 Blanchard Rd Suite 402
Burlington, MA 01803

Simultaneously published in the UK
by Focal Press
2 Park Square, Milton Park, Abingdon, Oxon OX14 4RN

Focal Press is an imprint of the Taylor & Francis Group, an informa business.

Notices
Knowledge and best practice in this field are constantly changing. As new research and experience broaden our understanding, changes in research methods, professional practices, or medical treatment may become necessary.

Practitioners and researchers must always rely on their own experience and knowledge in evaluating and using any information, methods, compounds, or experiments described herein. In using such information or methods they should be mindful of their own safety and the safety of others, including parties for whom they have a professional responsibility.

Product or corporate names may be trademarks or registered trademarks, and are used only for identification and explanation without intent to infringe.

Library of Congress Cataloging-in-Publication Data
Bowen, Christopher J.
Grammar of the shot / Christopher J. Bowen, Roy Thompson.—Third edition.
    pages cm
ISBN 978-0-240-52601-0 (pbk.)
1. Cinematography—Handbooks, manuals, etc. 2. Composition (Photography)—Handbooks, manuals, etc. I. Thompson, Roy. II. Title.
TR850.T377 2013
777—dc23   2012038130

ISBN: 978-0-240-52601-0 (pbk)
ISBN: 978-0-240-52609-6 (ebk)

Typeset in Univers
By Cenveo Publisher Services

Printed and bound in the United States of America by Sheridan Books, Inc. (a Sheridan Group Company).

Contents

Acknowledgments   xi

Introduction   xiii

Chapter One – The Shots: What, How and Why?   1
  What to Show Your Audience?   3
  Choosing Your Frame   4
    Aspect Ratio   5
    Further Exploration – A Brief History of Aspect Ratios   5
    Further Exploration – Why We Might Like Widescreen so Much 7
  The Basic Cinematic Building Blocks – An Introduction to Shot Types   8
    Long Shot/Wide Shot   8
    Medium Shot   8
    Close-Up   10
  The Extended Family of Basic Shots – The Powers of Proximity   11
    Extreme Long Shot/Extreme Wide Shot   13
    Very Long Shot/Very Wide Shot   14
    Long Shot/Wide Shot/Full Shot   15
    Medium Long Shot/Knee Shot   16
    Medium Shot/Waist Shot/Mid   17
    Medium Close-Up/Bust Shot   18
    Close-Up   19
    Big Close-Up (UK)/Choker (USA)   20
    Extreme Close-Up   21
  Why Do We Even Have Different Shot Types?   23
  Pulling Images from the Written Page   25
    Scripts and Script Breakdown   25
    Shot Lists   25
    Storyboards   26
  Phases of Film Production   27
  Let's Practice   28
  Chapter One – Review   30
    Chapter One – Exercises & Projects   30
    Chapter One – Quiz Yourself   31

Chapter Two – The Basics of Composition   **33**

  Simple Guidelines For Framing Human Subjects   35

  Headroom   36

  Subjective Versus Objective Shooting Styles   38

  Look Room/Nose Room   40

  The Rule of Thirds   42

  Camera Angle   45

    Horizontal Camera Angles   46

    Vertical Camera Angles   54

  The Two-Shot: Frame Composition with Two People   62

    The Profile Two-Shot   62

    The Direct-to-Camera Two-Shot   65

    The Over-the-Shoulder Two-Shot   66

    The Dirty Single   68

    The Power Dynamic Two-Shot   69

  The Three-Shot   70

  Wrapping up the Basics of Composition   72

  Chapter Two – Review   73

    Chapter Two – Exercises & Projects   73

    Chapter Two – Quiz Yourself   74

Chapter Three – Composition – Beyond the Basics   **75**

  The Illusion of the Third Dimension   76

  The Use of Lines   78

    The Horizon Line   78

    Vertical Lines   80

    Dutch Angle   82

    Diagonal Lines   82

    Curved Lines   87

  The Depth of Film Space – Foreground/Middle Ground/Background   89

    Foreground   89

    Middle Ground   90

    Background   90

  Depth Cues   92

    Overlapping   92

    Object Size   92

    Atmosphere   93

The Camera Lens – The Observer of Your Film World   95

    Primes vs Zooms   95

    The Prime Lens   96

    The Zoom Lens   97

    Lens Perspective   97

    Lens Focus – Directing the Viewer's Attention   101

    Pulling Focus or Following Focus   103

    Chapter Three – Review   106

      Chapter Three – Exercises & Projects   107

      Chapter Three – Quiz Yourself   107

Chapter Four – Lighting Your Shots – Not Just What You See, but How You See It   **109**

    Light as an Element of Composition   110

    Light as Energy   112

    Color Temperature   113

      Color Balance of Your Camera   114

      Natural and Artificial Light   114

      Correcting or Mixing Colors on Set   115

    Quantity of Light: Sensitivity   116

    Quantity of Light: Exposure   117

    Quality of Light: Hard Versus Soft   121

      Hard Light   121

      Soft Light   122

    Contrast   124

      Low-key Lighting   124

      High-key Lighting   125

    Color   126

    Basic Character Lighting: Three-Point Method   128

      Contrast Ratio or Lighting Ratio   130

      Motivated Lighting – Angle of Incidence   130

      Front Lighting   131

      Side Lighting   132

      Lights from Behind   132

      Lights from Other Places   133

    Set and Location Lighting   135

    Controlling Light – Basic Tools and Techniques   137

Contents

Light … and the Light Years of Learning   138
Chapter Four – Review   139
   Chapter Four – Exercises & Projects   140
   Chapter Four – Quiz Yourself   141

Chapter Five – Will it Cut? Shooting for Editing   **143**
The Chronology of Production   144
Matching Your Shots in a Scene   146
   Continuity of Performance   146
   Continuity of Screen Direction   147
The Line – Basis for Screen Direction   150
   The Imaginary Line – The 180 Degree Rule   151
   "Jumping the Line"   154
   The 30 Degree Rule   155
   Reciprocating Imagery   157
   Eye-Line Match   160
Chapter Five – Review   162
   Chapter Five – Exercises & Projects   162
   Chapter Five – Quiz Yourself   163

Chapter Six – Dynamic Shots – Subjects and Camera in Motion **165**
Subjects in Motion – Blocking Talent   166
Presentation Speed – Slow Motion and Fast Motion   167
   Slow Motion – or Overcranking   167
   Fast Motion – Undercranking   167
Camera in Motion   168
   Handheld   168
   Pan and Tilt   169
   Shooting the Pan and the Tilt   173
Equipment Used to Move the Camera   175
   Tripod   175
   Dolly   176
   Steadicam   180
   Cranes and Such   181
Chapter Six – Review   182
   Chapter Six – Exercises & Projects   182
   Chapter Six – Quiz Yourself   183

Chapter Seven – Working Practices and General Guidelines   **185**

Slate the Head of Your Shots   186

Communicating with Talent   188

Safe Action/Safe Title Areas   190

How to Manually Focus a Zoom Lens   191

Always Have Something in Focus   192

Control Your Depth of Field   194

Be Aware of Headroom   196

Shooting Tight Close-Ups   198

Ensure an Eye Light   200

Try to Show Both Eyes of Your Subject   202

Be Aware of Eye-Line Directions in Closer Shots   204

Follow Action with Loose Pan and Tilt Tripod Head   206

Shooting Overlapping Action for the Edit   208

   Continuity of Action   208

   Matching Speed of Action   208

   Overlapping Too Much Action   209

Storyboards and Shot Lists   210

Aim for a Low Shooting Ratio   212

Frame for Correct "Look Room" on Shots that Will Edit Together   213

Shoot Matching Camera Angles when Covering a Dialogue Scene   214

Ways to Cross the 180 Degree Line Safely   216

Place Important Objects in the Top Half of Your Frame   218

Be Aware of the Color Choices Made Throughout Your Project   219

Keep Distracting Objects out of the Shot   220

Beware of Continuity Traps While Shooting a Scene   222

Use the Depth of Your Film Space to Stage Shots with Several People   224

In a Three-Person Dialogue Scene, Matching Two-Shots can be
Problematic for the Editor   226

Zooming During a Shot   228

Motivate Your Truck-In and Truck-Out Dolly Moves   230

Allow the Camera More Time to Record Each Shot   232

Allow Actions to Complete Before Cutting Camera   234

Use Short Focal Length Lenses to Reduce Handheld Camera Shake   235

Beware of Wide Lenses when Shooting Close-Up Shots   236

Shooting a Chromakey   238

Shooting B-Roll, 2nd Unit, and Stock Footage   240
Shooting a Talking Head Interview   242
During Documentary Filming, Be as Discreet as Possible   244
Chapter Seven – Review   245
   Chapter Seven – Exercises & Projects   246
   Chapter Seven – Quiz Yourself   247

Chapter Eight – A Few Words of Advice   249
Know the Rules Before You Break the Rules   250
The Reason for Shooting is Editing   251
Your Shots Should Enhance the Entire Story   252
Involve the Viewer as Much as Possible   253
Take Pride in the Quality of your Work and your Set Etiquette   255
Know Your Equipment   256
Be Familiar with Your Subject   257
Understand Lighting – Both Natural and Artificial   258
Study What Has Already Been Done   259
In Conclusion   260

Appendix A – Helpful Resources for the New Filmmaker   261

Appendix B – Essential Crew Positions for Motion Picture Production   265

Glossary   267

Index   289

Acknowledgments

I wish to thank the supportive team of publishing professionals at Focal Press who helped make this new and improved third edition a reality. I would particularly like to thank Carlin Reagan who walked me down the home stretch. I hope we continue to honor the legacy of Mr Roy Thompson who penned the first edition so many years ago. The goal we all share in producing this media manual is to get the pertinent information about shooting motion pictures into the minds and hands of the next generation of visual storytellers. I hope that this revised third edition continues to inform and inspire all those readers who are just beginning their creative journey into the world of motion media production.

As a professor of integrated visual media at Framingham State University, I benefit from being surrounded by fellow educators and a continuously refreshed supply of students in the communication arts. The environment fosters much innovation and new approaches to teaching and learning about our discipline. I wish to acknowledge the support of my colleagues and the helpful contributions from all of my students over the years. The same goes for my experiences while teaching at Boston University and at the Boston University Center for Digital Imaging Arts. A collective thank you to everyone who has added to my growth as an educator and filmmaker.

As a media professional, I wish to thank my many collaborators and clients who have helped me to continue learning and to explore new techniques in telling their unique stories.

I am also grateful to the third edition's proposal and manuscript reviewers for their helpful suggestions and critiques, with a special thank you to John Rosenberg.

Additionally, I would like to thank my on-camera talent for their time and cooperation: Rachael Swain, Caitlin Harper, Crystal Haidsiak, Olivia Lospennato, Jacob Cuomo, Elizabeth Lospennato, Rajiv Roy, Stacie Seidl, Timi Khatra, Wendy Chao, Hannah Kurth, Alexander Scott, Stacy Shreffler, Eliza Smith, Emily Klamm, and Tucker and Ghost. The majority of photographs are by the author, with a small but significant contribution donated by Miss Rachael Swain. The line art diagrams and the majority of the hand-drawn illustrations are also by the author. Once again I must offer my thanks and appreciation to Jean Sharpe, who donated her time and skills to illustrating much of the second edition – some of whose illustrations are reproduced here to relive their useful purpose.

Lastly, I acknowledge my family for their support and offer extra special thanks to Emily Klamm who has been there through the thick and thin of it all.

This book is for all people who wish to learn the basics about shooting film and video. I hope you have fun and enjoy the ride. If you would like to learn more about the topic, find additional resources, or contact the author, please visit the author's website www. fellswaycreatives.com.

For my #1 Mom

Introduction

For most of us living in the 21st Century, the majority of our daily experiences are inseparable from interactions with electronic or digital media. We are constantly *communicating with* someone or something or being *communicated to* by someone or something. Texting or speaking via mobile telephones, watching television, using the internet, listening to the radio, playing networked video games, reading books, newspapers and magazines, looking at billboards and advertisements, going to the movies, and on and on it goes. Our ability to understand these communications and gain further meaning from them is reliant upon our education – can we read, write, and speak a language, recognize images and sounds, decipher symbols, etc.?

This education, whether it is from schooling or just living life, helps determine how well we can compute what we take in, and there is a lot to take in. Collectively, over time, we have learned to codify our visual communications from pictographs to written words, to paintings, photographs, and now motion pictures. What we depict has a recognizable meaning. Viewers know how to decode the images that they are shown. Understanding, or clear interpretation of what is viewed, stems from the established grammar or rules of depiction that have evolved over time.

It is this concept of grammar – meaning gleaned from structure – that motion picture creators rely upon so heavily. Fictional narrative films, documentaries, news reports, situation comedies, television dramas, commercials, music videos, talk shows, "reality" programming, and the like, all use the same basic visual grammar to help communicate to the viewer. As a filmmaker, when you "speak" the common cinematic language, you will be able to communicate your story to a global audience. They will see it. They will hear it. They will get it.

This text, *Grammar of the Shot*, third Edition, has been redesigned and expanded. Most of the figures that illustrate the concepts have been replaced or refreshed. Each chapter begins with an outline of that chapter's contents. Each chapter ends with a detailed review section highlighting the main concepts covered by that chapter. New sections called Exercises & Projects and Quiz Yourself conclude each chapter. They present ways in which you can immediately put into practice the techniques and guidelines discussed in the chapter, and offer a gauge to see how well you absorbed the information. Many new topics have been added, and most recurring topics have been rewritten and restructured for clarity and flow.

Some of the major changes or additions are highlighted per chapter:

- Chapter One now contains information on the Master Scene technique of planning and shooting coverage for film scenes. You will read about script analysis and scene breakdown for shot lists and storyboard creation. A short practice script has been included for you to plan coverage, shoot, and edit. The three phases of film production are outlined.

- Chapter Two gets an overall rewrite and restructuring of expanded topics in camera angles, and shots covering multiple subjects (the 2-shot, Over-the-Shoulder, etc.).

- Chapter Three sees a new discussion of the use of diagonal and curved lines in frame composition. Sections on prime and zoom lenses, focal length, and lens perspective have been augmented. An all-over rewrite and restructuring has also been done.

- Chapter Four is a new chapter covering light and the art and craft of film lighting.

- Chapter Five is a refreshed and reorganized presentation of the Shooting for Editing topic. These sections inform you about the key issues within the visual material that face an editor during post-production. You are advised on how to think about your shots and see how they will cut together.

- Chapter Six finds a new section on slow and fast motion playback of your images. The moving subject and moving camera sections get a rewrite and restructuring.

- Chapter Seven, the largest and most diverse, is refreshed, totally reorganized, and contains many new topics and working practices to help you meet the challenges of production. The new photographic illustrations help clarify, visually, the numerous shooting guidelines and techniques discussed.

- Chapter Eight provides some concluding advice with rewritten and restructured topics that can apply to anyone working in motion picture production.

- Appendix A is an all-new listing of helpful resources and references found on the internet and in other book titles available from Focal Press.

- Appendix B is an all-new listing of the essential crew positions found on a film set and their brief job descriptions.

- The Glossary of Terms is expanded to reflect the new topics, and many of the existing terms have been rewritten or augmented for clarity.

This book is designed for those of you who are new to the realm of visual storytelling but who wish to be well acquainted with the basic rules, conventions, and practices of the global visual language of motion pictures. It will take you from the basic shape of the frame, to the different types of shots, to the ways to compose visual elements within those frames. You will be exposed to the basics of shot lighting, screen direction, depth elements, camera movement, and many general practices that make for a richer, multi-layered visual presentation. Most importantly, it will provide you with essential information to expand your visual vocabulary and help jumpstart your motion imaging career in this non-stop world of motion media communications.

Chapter One
The Shots: What, How and Why?

- Cinematic Language Defined
- Choose Your Frame Size
- Typical Shot Names and Definitions
- Master Scene Technique and Shooting Coverage
- Script Analysis and Breakdown
- Shot Lists and Storyboards
- Phases of Film Production

You can find moving images just about everywhere these days. Advancements in micro-processing, wireless transmission, and screen display technologies allow us to access time-based visual media on our mobile phones, tablets, and laptops. You can see motion imagery playing around the world in taxis, on planes, on billboards, on the sides of buildings, at bus stops, in the aisles of "big box" stores, at the malls, in museums, and, of course, on television and in the movie theatres. So many kinds of moving images, made by so many diverse groups of people for so many different purposes, are available via these numerous outlets. Yet we, the receiving audience, somehow know what all of these images mean. We may not understand the spoken or written language in these "movies" but we do understand, perhaps on a subconscious level, the visual language – the grammar of the shot.

It is this globally understood visual communication – in our case the cinematic language – that is the focus of this book.

Let's say you want to make a short film, or a funny web animation, or you need to interview someone for a school project. You, the filmmaker, are in a position of great creative power. You get to decide what the content of your video will be and how you will show it to a viewer. Your visual expressions (the pictures that show your story) need to be presented in ways that your audience can properly understand and interpret. If you do not "speak" the right language (use the proper grammar of the shot), then your message may not come across clearly. Think of this book as an introductory lesson in the visual language of moving imagery. It presents you with some of the core guidelines, commonly used tools, and accepted methodologies found in the art and craft of filmmaking.

If we are going to be discussing the grammar of the shot, then we are going to have to define what we mean by grammar and what we mean by shot. It should be understood that grammar in this sense of the word refers to the basic rules governing the construction and presentation of visual elements that are created for inclusion in a motion picture. These are the commonly accepted guidelines that define how visual information should be displayed to an audience. Viewers, all of us who have grown up watching films and television, have been trained over the years to observe, decode, and comprehend the various elements of the shots used in motion picture creation. In other words, we may not consciously express it, but we know what certain images mean and how they make us feel. An adept filmmaker uses this dynamic between the shots and the viewer to tell better stories.

We will explore what the basic types of shots are and what goes into their construction. We will also see what information and meaning the viewer can pull out of these shots when viewed in the context of your edited film. Remember, filmmaking is simultaneously a creative and a technical craft, and the extent of your success often depends upon how well you communicate your vision to your audience. If you confuse them with faulty film language or improper visual "grammar," then they will most likely not respond well to your work.

In order to keep things simple, we are, for the most part, using generic terms for discussion and explanation. For instance, the terms "motion picture," "motion imagery," etc. refer to any time-based media piece, work, show, animation, film, project, or program that is made up of individual images that, when displayed to our eyes very rapidly, provide the illusion of movement. The term "camera" will refer to any device that can record these moving images. The term "filmmaker" refers to any person undertaking the creation of a motion picture. At times, **camera person** or **camera operator** will refer to anyone who operates the camera that is recording the moving images.

What to Show Your Audience?

It may seem counterintuitive, but in filmmaking, if you are not sure where to begin, it can be very helpful to start at the end. Ask yourself some key questions. What is your goal? What are you setting out to make? What kind of story are you trying to tell and how do you wish to tell it? Who is the target audience? What purpose does this motion media piece have? What tools and other assets will you need to make it? Where and how will it be shown and viewed? Understanding what your end result should be will help inform where you can begin, and it will lead to many more creative and logistical questions for you to answer along the way. The best plan in media production (an often costly and time-consuming endeavor) is to have a plan. Our main concerns in this book are with the visual elements of your motion picture, so let's begin your planning there.

Movies, television shows, music videos, commercials, cartoons – all rely heavily on their visual elements. You have to decide very early on in the creation process what is important for the viewer to see and how should they, the audience, be shown those particular actions, events, or details. You have to develop a visual plan – one that incorporates both the overall style and look of your project and the technologies and techniques that can help you achieve that look. The decisions of what to actually photograph and how to photograph them can be the result of input from many people involved in the filmmaking process – from the writer to the director to the **director of photography**, actors or producers, and so on (see a list of film crew positions and their common job responsibilities in Appendix B). Regardless of who makes these choices, someone will, and for your initial projects it will most likely be you, the *filmmaker*.

Choosing Your Frame

The visual needs of your motion picture project are guided by the script of your fictional narrative story (discussed later in this chapter), or they are dictated by real-time documentary events. Knowing how you want to show your story can lead you to one of your first decisions regarding your visual plan – what camera and what lens? These two very important tools, the camera and the lens, work together to capture a particular horizontal rectangle of reality. This rectangle is only a small segment or cutout window of the total sphere of the physical world around the camera. This cutout has a defined and finite area and we call it the **frame** (see Figure 1.1).

Whatever is inside this frame is recorded as a two-dimensional (2D) representation of the actual world that exists in front of the lens. At present, because our video and film cameras can really only capture the two dimensions of width and height (frame left to right and frame top to bottom), they get displayed as flat images on a screen (projected movie, television set, computer monitor, tablet, or smart phone). The third dimension, depth, although present in reality, is only captured as an illusion on the actual 2D film or video. This concept is discussed in more detail in Chapter 2. We will not be discussing the technologies behind dual-camera 3D production – that goes well beyond the scope of this book.

Not to get too technical at the outset, but this next topic, frame size and **aspect ratio**, really should be addressed early on so that you can begin shooting your project with a solid understanding of the visual frame. It is the camera's format (the area of width and height of the imager) and the type of lens used that really dictate the shape and amount of space you get to record and what the audience may ultimately watch within the 2D rectangular frame. We will discuss lenses later, but we should address this topic of frame sizes now. Your choice of camera (**Video Format** or **Film Gauge** with

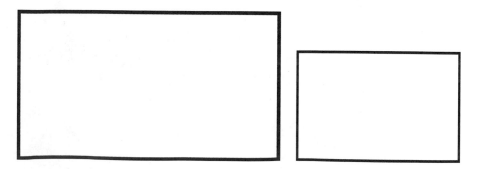

FIGURE 1.1 Basic widescreen 16 × 9 frame and ye olde tyme standard definition 4 × 3 television frame. Think of these as your empty canvases where you will get to "paint" the various elements of your shots.

variable masking) will lead to many other decisions in both the **aesthetics** of your motion picture (the grammar of your shots) and the **workflow** (or media pathways) used to complete it.

Aspect Ratio

The dimensions of a camera's frame (the active recordable image area) or the width-to-height relationship of that frame is often expressed as a ratio of that width to that height. This ratio is called the aspect ratio and, depending on the format of the medium, may be written 4:3, 16:9, 1.85:1, and so on. The first example, 4:3 (said "four to three" and sometimes written 4 × 3, or "four by three"), means that if the height is three units tall, then the width is equal to four of those same units. This is the aspect ratio for **standard definition** (SD) television in North America (NTSC, NTSC miniDV, and DVD) and Europe (PAL, and DV-PAL) [although the "standard" for 20th Century TV, SD has been rapidly phased out of both production and broadcast by HD – see below]. It can also be represented by the ratio of 1.33:1 (which is said "one-three-three to one"). The aspect ratio of all **high definition** (HD) video is 16:9, or 1.78:1.

Figure 1.2 shows several frame sizes and their aspect ratios from television and motion picture history. The size has evolved over the decades as technologies changed. At present, theatrical motion pictures, residual standard definition content, and high definition television all have different aspect ratios, which makes it rather confusing and complicated to get the images of one format to fit into the shape of another, but we will not worry about that now. We will simply select a single frame size and work with that. As SD has become a thing of the past, and professionals as well as amateurs have adopted Hi-Def or HD (of one flavor or another), we are going to use the widescreen 16:9 HDTV aspect ratio for our examples. If your project calls for using any gauge of film, NTSC-DV or PAL-DV, you have nothing to fear – the concepts we discuss, and our examples, will all translate into the shape of your particular frame. The beauty of film language is that no matter what camera or aspect ratio you choose, the shot grammar is still applicable, as many of these guidelines have remained relatively unchanged for the past one hundred years.

Further Exploration – A Brief History of Aspect Ratios

Theatrical motion pictures in North America have been widescreen (1.85:1) for a long time now. European widescreen theatres projected 1.66:1 images. Glass tube standard

FIGURE 1.2 Comparison of various frame sizes from the history of film and video. Note the tendency to move toward a wider rectangular frame.

definition television sets of the 20th Century (roughly 1.33:1 or 4:3) were more square-like in shape and less rectangular than Hollywood features and today's widescreen HDTV (roughly 1.78:1 or 16:9). There were several reasons for these differences, but the gist of it was that classical Hollywood 35-mm motion picture film had, for many years, used an aspect ratio of 1.33:1. This is overly simplistic, but when television became very popular in the late 1940s and early 1950s, the broadcasters needed material to play, and Hollywood could offer several decades of motion pictures to be displayed – thus the 1.33:1 television aspect ratio.

Television became more popular, and in order to compete with that popularity the movie industry began to create very wide or large-screen aspect ratio film formats such as VistaVision, Cinemascope (2.4:1), and, more recently, IMAX®. The less costly 1.85:1 was also popularized, and thus the standard North American widescreen aspect ratio was born. The problem was that the 1.33:1 frame size of television was too small to show the wider 1.85:1, 1.66:1, and certainly the 2.4:1 movies. A process called pan and scan was developed so that a smaller screen size could be extracted from the larger, wider original film's aspect ratio to show the television audience. The big downside to this was that the original composition – basically all of the hard work of the filmmaker's visual plan – was destroyed. Letterboxing (maintaining the original aspect ratio of the picture by placing black bars at the top and bottom of the frame) improved upon this, but TV audiences were never truly won over by this approach. Happily, the native wide-screen aspect ratio of HDTV more closely matches that of the feature films and there is not as much need for this "cutting off" of the original frame.

Further Exploration – Why We Might Like Widescreen so Much

It can be argued that the widescreen aspect ratios are a better choice for image capture because their display on the screen is more suited to audience appreciation. Longer, more horizontally rectangular in shape, the widescreen imagery appeals to our eyes (and brains) because the field of view (what we get to watch) is closer to what our eyes naturally see when we look at the world.

Try this – Stand in a well-lit room and stare straight forward. Hold your arms out at your sides, shoulder high but slightly behind you. With palms forward, point your fingers straight ahead and wiggle them quickly. Do you see your fingers moving? If not, slowly move your arms forward. Stop when you see your fingers moving in your peripheral vision.

Now, drop your left arm down towards your waist and raise your right arm straight over your head. Looking directly in front of you, do the same finger wiggle and slowly move your arms in front of you until you can see your fingers moving.

You should find that you are able to see a field of view much wider than it is tall. We see in widescreen.

Choosing Your Frame

The Basic Cinematic Building Blocks – An Introduction to Shot Types

You know the shape and size of your frame, but now you have to figure out how to fill it. Visual communication in the cinematic language starts with the most basic pictorial building blocks – the **shot types**. A shot is the recording of one action from one particular point of view at one time. Its imagery shows a discrete unit of photographic coverage of a person, place, or event in a motion picture from a unique distance and angle.

Typically, a shot is gauged by the power of magnification of its subject – meaning how small or how big the subject looks on screen. An audience member relates to the subject according to its apparent proximity – small is far away and less important, while big is closer and more personal. The "size" of the shot also helps show more or less information to the audience – or should we say different kinds of information. A successful filmmaker uses this connection between the viewer and the shot's perceived meaning and its visual information to create effective cinematic experiences.

Perhaps the terms long shot, medium shot, and close-up are already familiar to you, but let us take a look at an example of each shot type now. Although you may photograph or illustrate any subject matter in the world for your movie or animation, for clarity of discussion, we will first explore the shots through the simple framing of a standing human subject (static, **locked-off** shots). We will then build in complexity of content, composition, and execution throughout the remainder of the book.

Long Shot/Wide Shot

The **long shot** or **wide shot** (often abbreviated LS or WS) is a wide, encompassing shot that shows a large area (width, height and depth) of the film space. Physical, or spatial, relationships between or among subjects, objects and their actions are clearly visible from this apparently distant vantage point. The environment or location is the "star" and any persons or objects appear smaller within it. The long shot can establish place, time, and mood for an audience (Figure 1.3).

Medium Shot

The **medium shot** (MS) is the shot type that nearly approximates how we, as humans, see the environment most immediately around us. Typically there would be several feet of space between you and another person, which would most likely result in your viewing each other in medium shots – roughly from the waist up. A moderate distance

FIGURE 1.3   A long/wide shot with a single human subject.

then (let us say 3 to 5 feet) may lead to a medium shot. Other factors, such as actual object size and focal length of lens on the camera, can also come into play, but we'll explore those options later in the book. What it really comes down to, though, is how much of a person, object, or environment is included in the frame. A viewer watching a medium shot should feel comfortable with the proximity because the subject is near but not in their "personal space" (Figure 1.4).

FIGURE 1.4   A medium shot with a single human subject.

Close-Up

The **close-up** (CU) is the intimate shot in filmmaking. It provides a greatly magnified view of some person, object, or action. As a result, it can yield rather specific, detailed information to the audience. It also brings the subject inside the viewer's "personal space" – in a good way if the viewer likes the subject, and in a bad way if they do not (Figure 1.5).

These three major types of shot – LS, MS, and CU – will be the basic building blocks that you can use to start capturing your moving images. It will be up to you, the film-maker, which shot type you use to cover the various persons, objects, or actions in your visual story. To help you decide, you may find it useful to ask yourself, "If I were watching this motion picture, what would I want to be seeing right now?" Remember, it is the audience who ultimately watches all of your shots edited together, and their experience viewing your movie is based, in large part, upon the quality, variety, and appropriateness of shot types that you choose to present your story.

Next, we will list and define other derivations of these three basic shot families. So don't worry, you will have plenty of shot variety available to you for making your movies.

FIGURE 1.5   A close-up with a single human subject.

The Extended Family of Basic Shots – The Powers of Proximity

99.9% of motion imagery that is made is meant to be viewed by some audience of some kind in some way. A filmmaker should always be thinking about how to best show the "story" to the viewer. A key responsibility you have is to present the viewer with images that are engaging, informative, and efficient. The extended family of basic shots provides you with a larger vocabulary of visual expression.

The illustrative examples presented here are an introduction to the various magnitudes of shots that you will be able to create in each category. In order to keep things simple, the illustrations will depict a lone human subject in a plain environment. The recording camera is placed roughly at the same height as the subject's eyes. For comparative training purposes we will keep the subject centered in our frame, and looking straight to lens. As you continue to read this book, you will learn about more interesting ways to frame your subjects, but we have to start somewhere.

The following is a list of the basic shots (see Figure 1.6):

- Extreme long shot/extreme wide shot
- Very long shot/very wide shot
- Long shot/wide shot
- Medium long shot
- Medium shot
- Medium close-up
- Close-up
- Big close-up [UK]/Choker [US]
- Extreme close-up

Extreme Close-Up

Big Close-Up / Choker

Close-Up

Medium Close-Up

Medium / Mid Shot

Medium Long Shot

Long / Wide Shot

Very Long / Wide Shot

Extreme Long / Wide Shot

FIGURE 1.6 Examples of the nine shot types.

Extreme Long Shot/Extreme Wide Shot

1. May be abbreviated as XLS, ELS, EWS, or XWS
2. Also referred to as an extreme wide angle shot
3. Traditionally used in **exterior** shooting
4. Encompasses a wide and deep field of view, forming an image that shows a large amount of the environment within the **film space**
5. Often used as an **establishing shot** at the beginning of a motion picture or at the start of a new sequence or **scene** within a motion picture (typical of epic battle scenes, etc.)
6. Shows where – urban, suburban, rural, mountains, desert, ocean, battlefield, etc.
7. May show when – day, night, summer, winter, spring, fall, distant past, present, future, etc.
8. May show who – lone stranger walking into town, massive invading army – most often the human figures in the XLS are so small that details are not distinguishable – general, not specific, location information will be conveyed (Figure 1.7)

FIGURE 1.7   Example of an XLS.

Very Long Shot/Very Wide Shot

1. May be abbreviated VLS
2. Also in the wide shot family
3. May be used in exterior or **interior** shooting when enough width and height exist within the studio set or location building, such as an open warehouse, airline hangar, or sports arena
4. Environment within the film space is still very important as it fills much of the screen, but the human figure is more visible and limited clothing detail may be observed
5. May be used as an establishing shot where movement of character brings the figure closer to the camera
6. Shows where, when, and a bit more of who (Figure 1.8)

FIGURE 1.8　Example of a VLS.

Long Shot/Wide Shot/Full Shot

1. Abbreviated LS and/or WS
2. This is usually considered a "full body" shot, wide but in close to a figure with head and feet just visible in the frame
3. Interior or exterior shooting
4. Larger human figure should take attention away from the environment; however, the character's surroundings are still visible and still important for the audience to see
5. May still work well for an establishing shot, especially within a smaller interior space or a contained exterior space like a storefront
6. Shows where, when, and who – the gender, clothing, movements, and general facial expressions may be observed more easily (Figure 1.9)

FIGURE 1.9   Example of a long/wide shot.

The Extended Family of Basic Shots – The Powers of Proximity

Medium Long Shot/Knee Shot

1. Abbreviated MLS

2. First shot in increasing magnitude that cuts off a body part of the human subject – traditionally framed such that bottom of frame cuts off the leg either just below or, more commonly, just above the knee. The choice for where to cut may depend on costuming or body movement of the individual in the shot. If you cut off above the knee, it is sometimes referred to as the "Cowboy" because in American Western movies there was interest in being able to show the firearm in the holster strapped to the thigh of a cowboy

3. May be interior or exterior shot

4. Human figure is prominent; details in clothing, gender, and facial expressions are visible

5. Shows more of who than where and can still show when (Figure 1.10)

FIGURE 1.10   Example of a medium long shot.

Medium Shot/Waist Shot/Mid

1. Abbreviated MS
2. May also be called the "Waist" shot, as the frame cuts off the human figure at or just below the waist
3. Interior or exterior
4. Human figure is most prominent in the frame – eyes and the direction they look, clothing, hair color and hairstyle are all plainly visible
5. Subject movement may become a concern, as the tighter framing restricts the freedom of gesture – be careful not to **break frame** (have an actor's body part touch or move beyond the established edge of the picture frame)
6. Certainly shows who and may still provide generic detail about where (inside or outside, apartment, store, forest, etc.) and when (day or night, season) (Figure 1.11)

FIGURE 1.11 Example of a medium shot.

Medium Close-Up/Bust Shot

1. Abbreviated MCU
2. Sometimes called a Bust Shot or "two-button" for the tight bottom frame cutting off at the chest, roughly where you would see the top two buttons on a shirt. Definitely cuts off above the elbow joint. Adjust bottom frame slightly for men or women, depending on costuming
3. Interior or exterior
4. Subject's facial features are rather prominent – where the eyes look is obvious, as is emotion, hair style and color, make-up, etc. This is one of the most commonly used shots in filmmaking because it provides so much information about the character while speaking, listening, or performing an action that does not involve much body or head movement. Ideal for news broadcasts and "talking head" interviews in documentaries
5. An audience is supposed to be watching the human face with this framing, so actions or objects in the surrounding environment hold little to no importance – although these background objects should not be distracting, and blurring them helps
6. Depending on general lighting and costuming, you may discern general information about where and when (Figure 1.12)

FIGURE 1.12   Example of a medium close-up.

Close-Up

1. Abbreviated CU
2. Sometimes called a "head shot," as the framing may cut off the top of the subject's hair and the bottom of the frame can begin anywhere just below the chin or, more traditionally, with a little upper shoulder visible (costuming and hairstyle dependent)
3. Interior or exterior
4. A very intimate full face shot of a human subject showing all detail in the eyes and conveying the subtle emotions that play across the eyes, mouth, and facial muscles of an actor – health conditions and facial hair in men and make-up use in women are clearly visible
5. An audience member should be totally focused on the human face with this framing, especially the eyes and/or mouth
6. Who, but not so much where or when (except as indicated by lighting) (Figure 1.13)

FIGURE 1.13   Example of a close-up.

The Extended Family of Basic Shots – The Powers of Proximity

Big Close-Up (UK)/Choker (USA)

1. Abbreviated BCU – although many filmmakers may simply refer to it as a tight close-up or a choker
2. Human face occupies as much of the frame as possible and still shows the key features of eyes, nose, and mouth at once – however, the top of forehead and bottom of chin are cut off
3. Interior or exterior
4. Such an intimate shot puts the audience directly in the face of the subject. Because every detail of the face is highly visible, facial movements or expressions need to be subtle – very little head movement can be tolerated before the subject moves out of frame. An emotional connection is easy to make with this "in your face" framing
5. This shot is about who and how that "who" feels – angry, scared, loving, etc. (Figure 1.14)

FIGURE 1.14   Example of big close-up/choker.

Extreme Close-Up

1. Abbreviated ECU or XCU

2. Purely a detail shot – framing favors one aspect of a subject such as his/her eyes, mouth, ear, or hand only – OR a solitary object or magnified portion of a larger object

3. Lacking any points of reference to the surrounding environment, the audience has no context in which to place this body part or object detail, so understanding will stem from how or when this shot is edited into the motion picture. It may be helpful if the content of the XCU is first shown in its larger form in a wider shot so that context may be established for the viewer

4. This type of extremely magnified imagery can be used in documentary work, such as medical films or scientific studies, music videos, commercials, experimental art films, and may be used sparingly in fictional narrative, depending on the established visual style of the project (Figure 1.15)

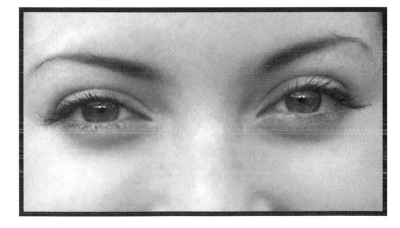

FIGURE 1.15   Example of an extreme close-up.

The Extended Family of Basic Shots – The Powers of Proximity

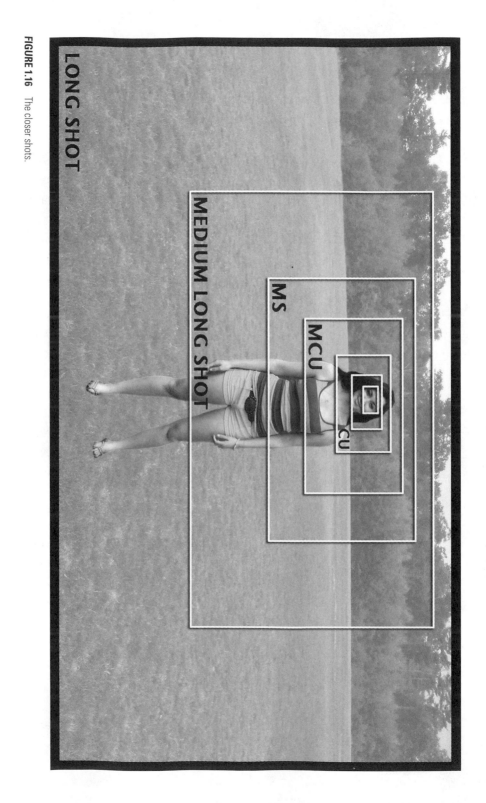

FIGURE 1.16   The closer shots.

LONG SHOT

MEDIUM LONG SHOT

MS

MCU

CU

Why Do We Even Have Different Shot Types?

The shot types just discussed were not all originally part of the visual language of film production when it began in the late 1800s. The first motion pictures often just documented actual events from real life, like workers leaving a factory or a train pulling into a station – almost exclusively filmed in a wide shot. Filmmakers then began to tell short stories from scripted material, but these too were photographed from a distance with a wide-angle view of the action. Much like a staged play in a theatre, the audience only got to experience the action from one vantage point. The sophistication of the camera (and lenses) and the storytelling devices evolved quickly and it wasn't long before an expanded visual vocabulary was forming. New shot types, like the close-up, and new editing techniques soon allowed for greater flexibility in showing an audience a more visually complex and emotionally engaging story.

What eventually developed was an approach to filmmaking that is still used by many today – the **Master Scene Technique**. A story is broken down into scenes, or events that take place at a certain time and in a certain place. The filmmaker initially records the entire scene from one, often wide, camera angle called the **master shot**. The actors say all of their lines and do all of their actions chronologically from the beginning of the scene until the end. The filmmaker then repeats the actions and records shots that show the events with closer and more magnified imagery – traditionally from the outside in or from wider shots to closer shots. The result is a selection of shots that depict all of the events in the scene from different angles and with different subject sizes within the frame. They call this shooting **coverage**.

On larger productions, a Script Supervisor takes notes on all coverage shot on each character for each scene. These notes, the script, and the video and audio media files of this production footage are later handed over to the editor. The editor takes all of these different views of the repeated action of the scene (the coverage) and stitches them together according to the script and notes – traditionally from wider to tighter shots. In its most simplistic assembly it might go something like this:

- A master (wide) shot opens the scene to establish the location and the subjects' placement within that environment – they begin their dialogue here
- CUT TO
- A medium shot that provides more detail of the subjects gesturing and speaking
- CUT TO

- A close-up that reveals the intimate detail of the emotional state of the subject at the most dramatic moment of the scene (typically near the end)

This process gets more interesting and elaborate when you add more shot types and subject/camera movement, etc. (see Chapters Two, Three and Six for more information).

The Master Scene technique, complete with shooting coverage using a variety of shot types, is a very thorough approach to filmmaking. You will be learning more about preparing your visual material for the editing process in Chapter Five.

Pulling Images from the Written Page

When you read a novel you get to create the look of the characters and the locations in your imagination. The descriptions on the written page help you conjure the imagery in your head. Making motion pictures involves a similar process. Whether you are creating a short film, an animation, a music video, or a how-to video, you are most likely going to start with a written script.

Scripts and Script Breakdown

The script for a project, even if just rough ideas for scenes or segments, provides the basic framework of your "story" around which you build your visual plan. Understanding the story you are trying to tell helps you figure out what shots you can use to show that story to your audience. This is often referred to as **script analysis** and **script breakdown**. You read over the scene and determine where it would be best to show the action from a medium long shot, a medium shot, a close-up, and so on. You analyze the content of the scene (dramatic dialogue, factual information, band performing a stanza from their song, etc.) and you break down the imagery into the necessary coverage for shooting that specific moment in your video.

Shot Lists

It helps to document these shot choices you decide upon during the script breakdown, so you should create what is called a **Shot List**. The shot list does what its name says – it lists the shots you need to record. Because you have done a scene-by-scene breakdown of the script, it makes sense to list your shots according to their chronology in the story. The first thing we see in the movie is Scene 1; the next major action at a new location is Scene 2, and so on. To be clear, the actual shooting of the film does not have to follow the chronology of scenes in the script. The shooting schedule is made around actor and location availability, etc. – so Scene 24 may be recorded first and Scene 3 may be recorded last. The goal is to record all of the scenes' coverage on your shot list.

Each individual shot type on your list that you need to record will most likely require a different physical camera placement. This unique camera position/framing is called a **set-up**. As each scene has a number, the first camera set-up for that scene, usually your master wide shot, would be noted as "Scene 1" or simply "1." The second set-up of that scene would then receive a letter starting with "A" as in "Scene 1, A" or, more typically, just "1A." The third camera set-up would be "1B" and so on. The English alphabet has 26 letters so you should be safe using this method, but on larger productions, repeats like "AA" or "BB" may be required.

If you have to record the action of a single set-up many times in order to get it just right, then these multiple recordings are called "**Takes**." The first attempt at shooting the first set-up of the first scene in your movie would be, "Scene 1, Take 1" or simply "1-1." If there was a flub then you would reset and shoot, "Scene 1, Take 2" or 1-2, and on it would go until it was recorded satisfactorily. Your goal should be to get the material recorded correctly in as few takes as possible in order to save time, energy, and money. Nobody wants to see "Scene 52ZZ, Take 117."

Storyboards

Beyond the shot list, another resource that will help you be efficient is a **storyboard**. If the written script is your framework, then the storyboards are the blueprints for your visual plan. You actually illustrate (draw) what each framing (shot type choice) will look like when you physically compose the visual elements for the set-up. Everyone on the film production crew will have a picture of what the visual goal will be when the time comes to record it (see Figure 1.17). On today's sets, with laptops or tablets so handy, the use of animatics has become more popular. Animatics are animated storyboards that can not only show framing, but animate the movements of subjects and cameras during each shot and may include voiceover and music. Regardless of how crude or advanced your pre-production "boards" are, their purpose is the same – to visualize what the final product will look like and help everyone get them set up correctly.

1. WS– Woman runs past glass doors w/ zombies just outside

2. WS– Woman runs into short hallway

3. WS– Woman runs past soda and candy machines

4. MLS– Low Angle Dutch Woman rattles locked doors and turns around in a panic

5. WS– DUTCH TILT, zombies in silhouette stumble up darkened hallway

6. MCU/OTS – Woman turns head toward candy machine and sees the candy bar hero

FIGURE 1.17 An example of a storyboard.

Phases of Film Production

All of this important preparation work should be accomplished before you begin the recording process. This initial phase of filmmaking is called "**pre-production.**" The script is written or acquired, your visual style is determined, you select your camera and other equipment, form the shot list, draw the storyboards, and do hundreds of other things like scheduling and budgeting and so forth. Which means that once you begin **principal photography** (the actual recording of the main shots of your story) you are in the phase called "**production**." Production continues until you have recorded all of your elements for the final version of your motion picture. All elements (picture and sound) are passed off to the editorial team and the "**post-production**" phase of film-making takes place. The shots are edited together to show the best story possible given the production materials submitted. The last steps in this chain are the distribution and exhibition stages – getting your finished product out to the world for people to see and enjoy.

Let's Practice

The following is a sample script that you may use to practice shot selection, storyboard creation, and coverage shooting using the shot type families (found in both Chapter One and Chapter Two). It is referred to as a "contentless scene" – meaning it is purposefully vague and does not follow strict screenplay formatting so that you may interpret freely and maximize your creativity. It may be helpful if you first read the script, make some choices about who these characters are and what their story is. Those choices will then inform how you may approach shooting the two brief scenes. Have fun.

CHARACTER A

Hey.

CHARACTER B

Hey.

CHARACTER A

How's it going?

CHARACTER B

Good.

CHARACTER A

Cool. Cool. Um, listen – I'm really

sorry about the –

CHARACTER B

Yeah. It's no big deal.

What are you going to do about it, right?

CHARACTER A

Right.

CHARACTER B

Well, I've got to get going.

CHARACTER A

Yeah. Yeah. Me too.

Character B exits – cut to new location. Character B enters followed by Character A.

CHARACTER A

Hey. Hey. Wait up. You forgot this.

CHARACTER B

That's not mine.

[A few hints about this particular script: it should happen in at least two different locations; Character A must be sorry about something that can be represented visually, in some way, in the scene; Character A must try to present Character B with some "forgotten" item, in either a literal sense or in a figurative or symbolic fashion.]

Let's Practice

Chapter One – Review

1. Visual "grammar" or film language is used and understood around the world.
2. The format of your camera initially determines the shape of your frame.
3. The aspect ratio describes the dimensions of your active recording area.
4. The three basic shot types are the long/wide shot, medium shot, and close-up.
5. The extended family of nine basic shot types comprises extreme long shot, very long shot, long shot, medium long shot, medium shot, medium close-up, close-up, choker, and extreme close-up.
6. Traditional approaches to the Master Scene technique encourage shooting coverage shots of the dialogue exchange between characters from different angles and with different "magnifications" of the subjects.
7. The written script or screenplay presents the bare bones of the story with brief descriptions of location and action and thorough inclusion of dialogue content. Filmmakers "break down" the scenes from the script into the shots that will best cover the action, and create a Shot List.
8. Having a storyboard, or drawings that represent the shot types needed for the project, is very helpful when you go to shoot the actual scene.
9. Pre-production, production, and post-production are the three main phases in the filmmaking process.

Chapter One – Exercises & Projects

1. Using your smart phone, tablet, video, or stills digital camera, practice capturing images of a person in all nine basic shot types. (Refer to Figure 1.6.)
2. In a similar fashion, practice location/object photography without any human subjects. Choose your own objects and your own locations, but shoot an example of each shot type.
3. Shoot and edit a shot type "training" video where you must teach someone who knows nothing about the nine basic shot types what they are called, what they look like and how they may be used in a short fictional narrative story. You should include illustrative video examples of the shot types (refer to Figures 1.7 to 1.15 for what to shoot, or use the images/video you shot for Exercise 1 above). Also, have clear examples of them "in use" in your own short movie you produce for this project. Titles/keyed graphics and voiceover will help clarify the educational points you need to make.

4. Create a shot list and storyboard for the script found at the end of this chapter.

5. Record the shots for the script based on your pre-production work from #4 above.

Chapter One – Quiz Yourself

1. If you need to clearly show the emotion in the eyes of your subject, which shot type might be best and why?

2. You're creating an animated cartoon that takes place in a dark, decaying futuristic city. You want to generate a wide view of this moody environment to show at the beginning of this story – what kind of shot would be good to use?

3. XCU is the abbreviation for what shot type?

4. What is the aspect ratio of HDTV?

5. Why might human beings respond well to widescreen motion picture imagery?

6. What is a camera "set-up" and how many would you need if you had to record an LS, MS and CU of only one subject?

7. What is "**principal photography**" and when does it occur?

Chapter Two
The Basics of Composition

- Headroom
- Shooting Style: Subjective vs Objective
- Look room/Nose room
- The Rule of Thirds
- Camera Angles
- The Two-Shot
- The Over-the-Shoulder
- The Power Dynamic Two-Shot
- The Three-Shot

Composition, as we are applying the term, is the purposeful arrangement of artistic parts selected for the "art form" being practiced. One can compose notes in music, steps in a dance routine, figures in a painting, elements on a web page, subjects within a film frame, and so forth.

Now that we understand how shots pictorially cover persons, actions, or events within a certain size frame, we have to look at how you can fill that frame with objects and information – meaning where, specifically, do you place the person's head in a close-up shot or where, specifically, do you place that tree in a wide shot? And it is not only where you place these compositional elements but also why you place them where you do. The arrangement of these visual elements and their placement within the overall frame is a big part of visual communication and should be a part of your visual plan for expressing your story. Object positioning helps establish traditional film aesthetics and can convey particular meanings to the audience. This is the power of picture composition. In this chapter we will explore ways to compose basic shots and see what those compositions can do to enhance a viewer's understanding of your visual story.

As the filmmaker, you decide what to capture in your motion picture frame, so let us go ahead and place a camera in your hands. Okay. Now what? Well, first you determine the shape of the frame for that camera's format. Knowing the active recording area and aspect ratio, you now understand the boundaries of width and height that are going to help you plan for the various compositional choices ahead of you. Next, figure out what you would like to shoot, point the camera at that thing, and record the images. Did you think about how you held the camera or where you placed that "thing" in relationship to other things or in relationship to the edges of your frame?

A new creative dilemma presents itself — you know the subject to be recorded, but you have to be equally aware of how you place that subject within the frame. It is this artful placement of objects around the frame that helps underscore meaning, provides **sub-text**, and, in general, empowers your imagery with an internal sense of beauty, balance, and order. This is the art of composition.

Simple Guidelines For Framing Human Subjects

Let us start with something simple that you will have to shoot many, many times: a medium close-up of a human subject. Perhaps you've already done this a thousand times, taking still pictures of your friends and family. We shall see that what at first seems rather simple will, in fact, require you to make many creative choices – choices that will help make your images better, stronger, and more understandable to a motion picture audience.

Here is a medium close-up (Figure 2.1).

FIGURE 2.1 Generic medium close-up of a single human figure.

What do you notice about this image? Does it look like one of those candid photos you took of your friends? The compositional elements are pretty simple, but where is the person's body located within the frame? Where is the head? Where do the person's eyes look? How much other visual information do we get from the rest of this image? A quick observation will tell you that the body is aligned down the middle, the head is very close to center frame and the eyes are looking directly at you, the audience member. This got the job done, but depending on the type of motion media project you are producing there are other choices you could make regarding this composition. We will first discuss the placement of the head.

Headroom

Within a given shot type (LS, MS, CU) there is a generally accepted guideline as to where the head of a person should be placed within the frame. This guideline applies much more to MS and CU shots because in these tighter shots you mostly see the person's body and head and much less of the environment. When communicating, human beings naturally tend to look each other in the face and, specifically, in the eyes. This "face focus" allows us to gain insight into the physical and mental health of an individual and to get a handle on their emotional state. Therefore, when an audience member watches a human subject on screen they will most often look at the person's face, particularly at the eyes and the mouth. Filmmakers know this to be true and they count on it when composing shots of people.

The placement of the head within the frame is very important, which is why we have the guideline of **headroom**. Headroom specifically refers to how much or how little space exists between the top of the subject's head and the top edge of the recorded frame. Because screen space is at a premium, it would be a shame to waste it, so we often set the top of the frame to cut off just above the talent's head in a tighter shot (Figure 2.2). In wider shots you should also consider how much screen space above the talent you allow (Figure 2.3). Unless the story or event calls for some extra room above the head, you let it go in favor of more information at mid-frame. Later, when we review examples of closer shots, you will see how it is appropriate to also cut off

FIGURE 2.2   Medium close-ups with too much, about right, and too little headroom.

FIGURE 2.3 Wider shots (VLS and LS) demonstrating proper headroom.

(or "frame out") the hair and tops of people's heads as long as you keep their eyes and mouths well within the screen space. There is no exact measure or global standard of what headroom needs to be for each shot. The amount allowed can vary from filmmaker to filmmaker, reflecting an individual style, but most will be very similar. In general, try not to give too much headroom as it wastes screen space and can throw off the overall composition.

Headroom

Subjective Versus Objective Shooting Styles

Now let us address how the subject's eyes are looking straight at you. What might it mean if the person being recorded by the camera looks directly into the lens? How does it make you, the viewer, feel when you are addressed directly by on-screen talent? Of course, it may depend on the kind of project you are watching or shooting, but it may make you feel "connected" to the person on screen or it may make them seem to be some sort of authority figure. If you were photographing a news reporter on location, then it would make sense for him/her to look straight into the camera's lens and deliver the factual report. The reporter makes a direct connection with you, the home audience, by looking you square in the "eye" and speaking directly to you. You see this all the time with game show, talk show and talent show hosts, sports analysts, and it is used quite a bit in music videos. These television programming **genres** have an accepted visual style that a subject may look directly into the lens and address the viewer. This style of camera work is often referred to as **subjective shooting or direct address**.

This is not so for scripted fictional narrative projects (at least for the most part – as you will grow to learn, there are often exceptions to the rules). With a fictional story you have actors playing roles in a pretend world. The camera is almost always an observer – a proxy for the audience – therefore it is not a direct participant, not something or someone to be addressed. The talent is not supposed to look directly into the lens – and often, not even near it. If an actor looks into the lens, or addresses the camera, it is called "**breaking the fourth wall**." This expression gets its origins from the theatre stage where the audience is always seeing the actors from the same direction – through this fourth "invisible" wall. If the camera were in a room recording the actions of a performer, the camera may see the back wall and the two side walls. The wall behind the camera, that is, the wall that should be physically in place where the camera is positioned, is the "fourth wall." It is the place from where the actions are being recorded and, ultimately, the place where the viewing audience is privileged to sit and observe the story. All on-screen talent behave as though the camera is not even there. This style of camera work is often called **objective shooting**.

For ease of demonstration, let us continue our medium close-up examples as though we are shooting for a fictional narrative film project where an objective shooting style is the goal. So let us take our subject's eyes off the **lens axis** (Figure 2.4).

This is a good start, but the face and body are still straight to lens. Depending on the focal length of the lens you are using, this can cause a flattening to the facial features

FIGURE 2.4   MCU of talent with eyes looking away from lens axis.

and is not always that interesting for the viewer. Let us put a small shift on how the subject is standing in relation to the camera (Figure 2.5). Now it appears that this person is looking at someone or something just out of frame. She is engaged by an unknown element within the film world. A viewer of this image will be curious about what she is seeing and will want to see that "thing" in the next shot. This is one of the key strengths of an objective filmmaking style. Rather than being told information directly by the talent, an audience is invited to get involved, to observe, to wonder, and to anticipate. They become invested in the story via the visual construction of the shots and how they are edited together.

FIGURE 2.5   Subject turns body and eyes off lens axis resulting in objective shooting style.

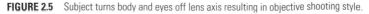
Subjective Versus Objective Shooting Styles

Look Room/Nose Room

Our composition of this individual is getting better, but the center framing may not work so well for our story. Notice how the face in the center of the screen is looking off to the side – at someone or something yet to be shown in another shot. A centralized framing like this is very solid and is often used in news reporting and hosted programming (with subjective or direct address), but perhaps it is too uniform or compositionally neutral for narrative fiction. Let us shift the image's balance and create more **look room** for our subject (Figure 2.6).

Look room (also called **looking room** or **nose room**) is the empty space that we have provided within the frame, between the talent's eyes and the edge of the frame opposite the face. It is this empty area or "**negative space**" that helps balance out this new frame where the weight of the object (the talent's head) occupies frame left and the weight of the empty space occupies frame right. In this case, the word "weight" really implies a visual mass whether it is an actual object, such as a head, or an empty space, such as the void filling frame right. This frame is now composed of two balanced masses. We will see later how the actor's gaze across this negative space causes an audience to also want to see what the actor is looking at, but for now, let us stay focused on where in the frame the head is placed.

What if we moved a subject's head to the opposite side of the screen but kept the face and eyes looking in the same direction (Figure 2.7)?

FIGURE 2.6 Placing head and body on frame left allows the subject to look across the empty space. The left and right halves of the frame are balanced.

FIGURE 2.7 No look room creates a void behind this subject crying out to be filled.

The look room in this composition is severely cut off on frame right and we have a large, empty space on frame left. Our weighted objects – the body and the void – still exist, but their placement just does not feel correct. We have not achieved a visual balance. The actor's face is too close to the near "wall" of the frame, making it look congested, claustrophobic, and trapped. Of course, this might be stylistically appropriate if the subtext for your character at this point is "up against it." Also, one gets the sense that the empty space occupying the majority of frame left is crying out to be filled with someone or something. That negative space behind the head can conjure feelings of suspense, dread, or vulnerability. An audience might expect that void to be filled by something, and they would call out, "Look out behind you!" So, unless that is your creative intention and it fits the mood of your story, it might be best not to compose your shot this way.

Our original MCU example with the head at the center of the frame is not wrong – it's a stylistic choice. It just may not always be as visually engaging to keep your objects of interest at the center of the frame. That may work well for still photographic portraiture and news broadcasting, but it lacks a certain punch for motion picture imagery recorded with an objective shooting style – especially when it comes to dialogue scenes. You will become quite adept at arranging important objects in your frame as you study and practice your visual grammar. We will discuss the direction of the look room in more detail later in the book, but right now let us introduce you to another rule or guideline that will help you place these objects within the composition.

Look Room/Nose Room

The Rule of Thirds

We moved the subject's head off toward frame left in our MCU example in order to generate a more balanced frame of weighted objects. Notice that we did not choose framing like the examples shown in Figures 2.8 and 2.9.

FIGURE 2.8 Back of talent's head is too close to frame left, breaking the frame edge.

FIGURE 2.9 Cutting the face in half may be considered "artsy" or "experimental" or useful in music videos.

We could create frames like this for particular reasons, but for the most part we are going to be following the accepted visual grammar, and the **rule of thirds** is definitely one of those points to follow. The rule of thirds is very easy to remember and very simple to execute. Take your frame and divide it up into thirds, both vertically and horizontally (Figure 2.10). Other art forms, such as painting, sculpture, and architecture, also have similar rules (often mathematically based) for the division of sections, etc. Feel free to explore those on your own to help expand your understanding of image composition and visual communication (see web and book references in Appendix A).

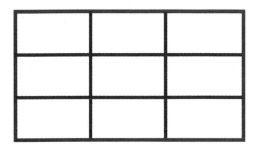

FIGURE 2.10   Frame markings along the 1/3 lines inside a 16:9 frame and a 4:3 frame.

Of course, these lines seen in our illustrations will never physically live on your frame (unless you want them to). You have to know their approximate placement on your particular viewfinder in your camera (although many digital video cameras do have a built-in grid overlay that you can make appear in your viewfinder or monitoring screen, often found under display settings). So, when searching for a rule of thirds composition, you may choose to frame your talent such that elements of visual interest appear at the crossing points where two of the lines intersect.

In Figure 2.11, the eyes within the head of our MCU figures are placed roughly at the upper left or right crossing point. The object in Figure 2.12 has been placed at the lower right intersection of thirds.

FIGURE 2.11   Subjects placed along the vertical 1/3 lines.

The Rule of Thirds

FIGURE 2.12 This object was purposefully placed at the lower right third intersection.

Camera Angle

So now you should feel comfortable composing simple subjects within your frame. The rule of thirds, good headroom, and appropriate look room provide you with some basic techniques for creating a well-balanced frame for use with an objective shooting style. Although we have stopped our actor from looking directly into the lens and the head is turned at a slight angle, we are still photographing the talent from a frontal camera placement. This makes some sense because you usually wish to place your camera at the most advantageous position to record the important details – in this case, the expression on the actor's face and the look in both of the eyes. There are times, however, when you need to move the camera around the actor and record the action from a different angle.

We will explore the "**angles on action**" from two separate circles that surround your subject. The "angles on action" refer to the angle from which you photograph a person, object, or event. The position of the camera and the view of our subject that that position offers to the audience will affect how much visual information is conveyed. It can also allow the viewer to glean certain meaning from the shot. First, we will work our way around the subject along a horizontal circle, where the actor is the center and our camera traces the circumference (see Figure 2.13). Then we will explore a vertical circle, where the actor is the center and our camera will move above or below a neutral height to show our subject from a low or high angle (see Figure 2.14).

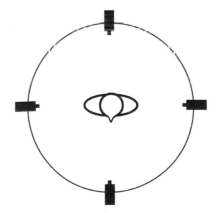

FIGURE 2.13 Bird's-eye view of camera's horizontal circle around the subject.

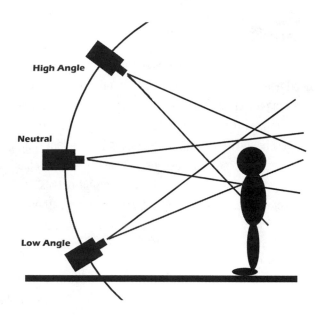

FIGURE 2.14 Side view of camera tracing path along vertical circle around subject. It is used to create high, neutral and low angle shots.

Horizontal Camera Angles

As mentioned earlier, when you photograph a person directly from the front of his or her face, it often yields a rather flat, uninteresting image (depending on lighting, which we will touch upon later in Chapter Four). An easy fix to this is to ask the talent to angle his/her face/body away from the camera lens. Keep in mind, however, that the camera can also be moved around the subject. Let us imagine that the talent is at the center of a circle, like the hub of a bicycle wheel laying flat. The camera, facing inward, can then move around that circle's center, showing the subject from any horizontal angle.

360 Degrees Method

As there are 360 degrees in a circle, let us use the degrees to help define how far along the circumference we can move the camera and what kind of shot that would create. We'll split the circle into positive and negative values up to 180 degrees (Figure 2.15).

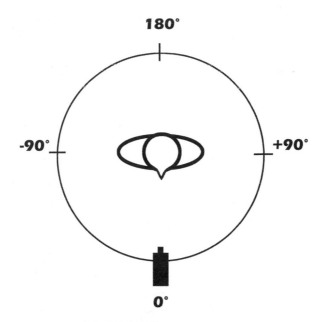

FIGURE 2.15   Camera's horizontal circle divided into degrees.

With the camera facing the talent at the zero degree mark, we would have a full frontal shot – flat and often uninteresting, but factual as in a news report. If the talent remains stationary and the camera begins to move around the subject along the arc of the circle to the talent's left side, then we go through the positive degrees (+45, +90, etc.) until the camera comes to the backside of the talent and sees only the back of the head at +180 degrees (Figure 2.16). The same type of arc can be made around the circle on the talent's right side and the degrees would progress the same but in negative values (–45, –90, –135, 180) (Figure 2.17).

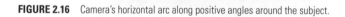

FIGURE 2.16 Camera's horizontal arc along positive angles around the subject.

FIGURE 2.17   Camera's horizontal arc along negative angles around the subject.

Clock Face Method

It might be easier to think of the degrees of the circle like the face of a clock where the subject is at the center of the hands and the camera is at the outer ring of numbers. In this case, you could use the callouts of six o'clock for full frontal, three o'clock for left profile, nine o'clock for right profile, and twelve o'clock for full back of head — which is sometimes called a Reverse (Figure 2.18).

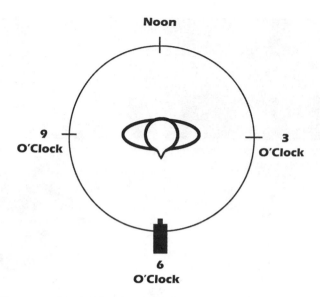

FIGURE 2.18 The numbers of the clock face can represent camera positions around the subject.

Camera Position Method

Many people simply use a family of rough camera positions around talent, such as frontal, 3/4 front, left or right profile, 3/4 back, and from behind or a "reverse" (see Figures 2.19–2.23).

The Frontal View

Remember from our earlier discussion that frontal shooting is used a great deal in nonfiction production (news reporters and talk show hosts, etc.), but you will also see it used often in fictional filmmaking when the subject is speaking or thinking, walking toward camera, or when they are driving (as seen straight in through the windshield). The difference lies entirely with shooting style – subjective or objective. The frontal view provides the audience with the entire face and both eyes. Much character information is visible. However, the overall image (depending on style of lighting and lens used) can sometimes seem flat and lacking a dynamic dimension.

FIGURE 2.19   Frontal camera angle.

The 3/4 View

The 3/4 front, or 3/4 profile as some call it, is probably the most common angle on talent in fictional filmmaking. It provides the audience with a clear view of the front of talent so that facial expressions, hand gestures, and the like may be plainly seen. It also provides the frame with an increased degree of dimension. In closer shots of the human face, it brings out the contours and depth of the facial structures (nose, mouth, cheek bones, brow, jaw, ear, etc.) and it still shows both of the subject's eyes. Note that the subject has swiveled around to achieve the 3/4 frontal view, and we have also placed the head and eyes along the line of thirds, yielding appropriate headroom and ample look room (Figure 2.20).

FIGURE 2.20   The 3/4 front left camera angle.

Camera Angle

The Profile View

The profile shot shows a person directly from the side. It quickly reveals the prominent facial features of the nose, lips, and chin, and can also help identify a character if they are known for a particular hairstyle, hat, or headdress (think superhero or cartoon character). In works of art and coinage, the profile was and is used to represent the portrait of a strong leader. The chiseled facial definition of this leader looks out and surveys all that she or he commands. Unfortunately, only half the information is visible. The viewer can admire this personality, but will not be privileged enough to see what the character might really be thinking or feeling. It is said that the eyes are the windows to the soul. Not showing your audience the eyes (and full facial expressions) of an actor (as with a profile shot) can generate feelings of duplicity, distrust, aloofness, or secrecy. Certainly there will be difficulty in making an emotional connection to someone you cannot fully embrace with your vision. Thematically, in your story's visual plan, if this is the desired result you seek, then by all means use the profile shot; otherwise, you may wish to reserve it for special compositions or for special characters (Figure 2.21). However, when you add another subject to the shot, as you will see later in the 2-shot, the profile view becomes a common and efficient way to show both characters interacting.

FIGURE 2.21 Subject shown in profile.

The 3/4 Back View

When used in tighter shots, the 3/4 back shot looks more like what is called an **over-the-shoulder** shot (OTS), which we discuss later. The camera gets to peek over the shoulder of our main subject and shows the audience what the subject is looking at (Figure 2.22). They get to see the film world from the character's **point-of-view** (POV). Granted, the face of the actor is hidden from view, so we do not know what he or she may be thinking or feeling from this particular angle, but the filmmaker probably has other angles of this character to cover the scene. The 3/4 back view still has the feeling of an objective shot and asks the viewer to share the experience along with the character in the story. The participating viewer is invited to do the thinking and feeling as if they were the character.

FIGURE 2.22   The 3/4 back camera angle on subject.

The Full Back View

180 degrees from the front view is the full back view. It is sometimes called a "Reverse," especially if used in a wider framing of the subject. Although you do not see the face of the subject, the usual rules of framing apply – headroom, look room, rule of thirds, etc. As you may have already guessed, this type of shot totally obscures the subject's face and therefore keeps hidden the real thoughts, feelings, and intentions of this character. If, however, this is a known character placed in a suspenseful situation in the narrative, then this type of shot takes on a very subjective point of view, as though someone or something were following our hero from behind and is just about to strike. Scary stuff (Figure 2.23)! When you add movement to the full back view (as in a

FIGURE 2.23 Full back camera angle on the subject.

tracking shot, discussed in Chapter Six) it becomes another strong method to have the subject lead the audience into a new scene or location, or to reveal new story information as the camera follows behind. On tighter shots, this view can generate mystery or suspense as the camera follows closely behind the subject without showing much of the environment to the curious audience.

Vertical Camera Angles

So far our camera has been on an even plane with the object of interest – our actor's head most often. In other words, if the head is four feet off the ground then our camera and its **lens** are also four feet off the ground (see Figure 2.24). We commonly refer to this value as the lens height. The lens height can also rise above or drop below the height of the subject, as we will see in the next section (see Figure 2.25).

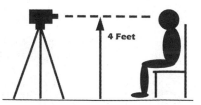

FIGURE 2.24 Camera height and angle of coverage traditionally fall at same height as subject's head for a neutral angle on action.

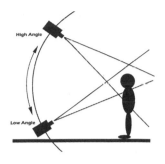

FIGURE 2.25 Vertical camera angles: high and low. Camera angles down or up to subject height.

Neutral Angle Shot

The general guideline to follow is that the camera and its lens should be looking at the subject from the same horizontal plane as the subject's eyes. This generates a neutral angle on action. The camera is positioned to observe the people, objects, or events from the same height as where the people exist or where the action takes place. The audience will relate to the characters as equals. Whether the subject is standing, sitting up in a tree, or laying stomach down on the ground, it is a good idea to place the camera at a similar height in order to maintain a neutral view (Figure 2.26). Once you raise the camera position above your actors or actions, or drop the camera below them, you begin to create a privileged point of view that deviates from how we might normally observe others in real life. These high and low angle shots usually result in a power dynamic within the frame and within the story itself. Let us explore both options.

FIGURE 2.26 Regardless of subject height (distance from ground), the camera observes from the same neutral, height.

Camera Angle

High Angle Shot

Shooting from a high angle means that you are covering a shot of a person or action from a higher vantage point. The camera is physically higher than the subject or the scene being recorded. Unlike a neutral shot, the lens is angled downward. Depending on the context of the shot in your story, there can be different implied meanings.

High Angle of an Individual

The grammar of a high angle shot of a character in a movie may be interpreted by the viewer to mean that who they are seeing on screen is small, weak, subservient, diminutive, or is currently in a less powerful or compromised position — perhaps both physically and thematically within the narrative. Through **foreshortening** and through "compressing" the character into the floor or ground underneath them, the camera's frame "contains" the subject and makes him or her physically appear small and "trapped" (Figure 2.27). Alternately, one will also find that a slightly higher camera angle down on a subject yields a more pleasing line of the nose and jaw (think about why most people hold their camera up high when taking a self-portrait picture for their social networking profile). As a filmmaker you will often strive to make your talent look as good as possible and this small angle down might do the trick.

FIGURE 2.27   A high angle view of the subject. The background enclosing the figure creates a claustrophobic feeling.

High Angle as a POV

What can it mean if the high angle shot represents a point-of-view from another character in the story? Literally, it simply shows that one character is physically up higher in the film space, looking down on the other character. Figuratively, this shot could mean that the higher character has the upper hand or does not think much of the other, lower character at this time. This POV may come from many entities such as a king, a giant, a judge, a dragon, or an alien spaceship. An up/down power dynamic is created. Of course, this scenario would require an **answering shot** up to the higher character and we'll discuss that in the next main section on Low Angles.

High Angle of an Environment

Whenever there is a vast expanse of geography to show within your frame (think XLS or very wide shot) it can be helpful to have the camera elevated above the space. You can establish the layout of the space and the events going on within it if you have a higher angle view. The parade, the concert, the crowded beach, the epic medieval battlefield can all benefit from being shown from above but still within the "human scale" of observation (Figure 2.28). Were the camera to be neutral in one of these environments it puts the audience in the scene as one of the players — only the immediate vicinity could be viewed. Drop the camera lower and angle up and you now have a victim, a child or someone vulnerable observing the scene from a compromised position within it.

FIGURE 2.28   A high angle view of an environment, shows more information in an objective style.

Camera Angle

If you place the camera very high, directly above the action, then you move into the realm of the **bird's-eye view** or **God view** (Figure 2.29). This angle down on action is not something that a typical viewer is accustomed to seeing in their real-world experiences and therefore it will stand out in your visual style – for good or for worse. Watching from directly overhead really compresses the subject into the ground, almost like a two-dimensional ant, and this unnatural vantage point can create feelings of being observed by otherworldly entities (ghosts, angels, aliens, etc.).

FIGURE 2.29   A bird's-eye view of a subject.

Low Angle Shot

Let us now go in the opposite direction and drop the camera and lens below the neutral point and shoot from a lower angle up onto our person or action.

Low Angle of an Individual

As you may have already guessed, this angle on action usually generates the reverse feeling in your audience member to that of the high angle. On a psychological level, the character seen from below appears larger, more looming, more significant, and more powerful. It is part of the accepted film grammar that a shot from below implies that the person or object you observe from that angle has a substantial presence, is considered "larger than life," or may, at that point in the narrative, have the upper hand (literally and figuratively) (Figure 2.30). Of course, this character may also

FIGURE 2.30   A low angle view up on to the subject.

simply be physically higher in the film space – running down a fire escape, climbing a ladder, etc.

Low Angle as a POV

The low angle as a POV shot also implies that the person (camera) doing that low angle observing is smaller, weaker, or in a more compromised position (think of a jungle adventure story where someone who fell into a pit trap is looking up at the person who set the trap for them – clearly a situation where the film space and narrative allow for the use of these shots). The low angle POV may also indicate awe or respect on the part of the observing character (think of a young person at the circus who longs to be a great aerialist one day looking up at the trapeze artist, or the bird watcher staring up at the majestically soaring birds in the sky). Again, it should be pointed out that sometimes a character is just at a lower elevation than other characters for the purpose of compositional balance in the frame. All of these views help to visually create a different energy and a different mood within the story and the viewing experience.

Low Angle of an Environment

Think of environments that could benefit from being seen at a low angle – perhaps a mountain range, a city skyline, or the interior of a giant cave. As a filmmaker, if you want to convey that a space is large and imposing then it can be helpful to show it from a lower camera angle (Figure 2.31). This can have greater effect if you incorporate

Camera Angle

FIGURE 2.31 A low angle view of an environment.

your characters in the frame, as in an XLS or VLS. Their diminutive size compared to the looming environment will further underscore the expanse of the location.

At this point, it would be wise to draw a distinction between a low angle shot and a shot that has a neutral angle but is taken from ground level. The tilt of the actual camera lens determines what the shot becomes and what the viewer experiences because of that angle. If you are making an animated cartoon about a family of worms, and you frame them neutrally against blades of grass, then we get to see them as equals — on their plane (Figure 2.32). Seen often in children's cartoons, the camera stays neutral

FIGURE 2.32 A neutral angle view of the worm family picnic.

to the height of the subjects (talking babies, cats, mice, etc.) and actually frames out the heads/faces of the adult humans – allowing the audience to make a connection with these smaller characters. But, if a giant boot heel looming over them suddenly imperils the worm family, then the camera could assume a low angle position shooting upwards on to the large foot overhead. This would yield a more diminutive POV from the worm's endangered position below (Figure 2.33). Similar treatments of the low angle could be used for babies or dogs or people among giant beings, etc. when you wish to stress the size differences.

FIGURE 2.33   A low angle view of the threatened worm family. Look out!

The Two-Shot: Frame Composition with Two People

So far our basic shot types have been composed around one person. What happens when you need to include two people in a single frame? Well, as you have probably already guessed, you follow similar guidelines as used for the single subject. Headroom, look room, rule of thirds, balance of weighted objects, and so forth all apply to a shot that must encompass two people having some interaction. The nature of the physical interaction, of course, also helps dictate what type of framing must be used and what type of **two-shot** will be composed.

The Profile Two-Shot

Perhaps the most common variety of two-shot, the profile two-shot, is used quite often to help set up a dialogue between two people in a scene. A long shot or medium long shot will most successfully cover all of the action during the meeting of the two characters. As the figures are smaller and the environment is more prominent, the setting can be established and larger body movements may be covered, particularly if one character must hand something over to the other character – the object could also be seen in this framing. There are innumerable scenarios where a profile two-shot may be appropriate. Some examples are a meeting of two friends (Figure 2.34), a confrontation between two feuding characters (Figure 2.35), or a romantic dinner for two over a small, candle-lit table (Figure 2.36).

FIGURE 2.34   Profile two-shot as composed for the long shot.

FIGURE 2.35   Medium shot brings the feuding characters very close together in this profile two-shot.

FIGURE 2.36   Profile two-shot as composed for the medium long shot.

When using a tighter framing to compose a profile two-shot (sometimes called a **50-50**), you alter the implied meaning of the encounter by enclosing the characters in a much smaller space. A medium close-up or a close-up will force the characters' faces together in an unnatural way, unless there is an obvious aggressive intention or an intimate overtone. On the basis of our previous examples, the confrontation (Figure 2.38) and the romantic dinner (Figure 2.39) may be good candidates for the medium close-up profile two-shot, but the meeting between the two friends may not be well served by that framing (Figure 2.37). Forcing the faces of two characters together in a tight frame, when there is no real reason to do so, can make the viewing audience feel subconsciously uneasy. For comedic purposes you could also unite two unlikely characters together in a tight frame, particularly if our hero is encountering a "close talker." We get to feel his discomfort.

The Two-Shot: Frame Composition with Two People

FIGURE 2.37 A casual meeting between two friends on the street seems a bit close in this MCU.

FIGURE 2.38 An aggressive confrontation works well in this tighter MCU.

FIGURE 2.39 An intimate occasion like this romantic dinner for two feels right at home in this MCU.

The Direct-to-Camera Two-Shot

Whenever two people stand side by side and face the camera, you generate a more subjective shot. Their attention is toward the lens and not necessarily toward one another. An example of a truly subjective direct-to-camera two-shot would be two news anchors or sportscasters sitting side by side, addressing the viewing audience directly. A less subjective example would be two characters walking side by side down a city sidewalk approaching the camera (often called a "walk & talk") (Figure 2.40), or perhaps two characters sitting in the front seats of a motor vehicle (Figure 2.41).

FIGURE 2.40   The medium long shot allows for ample room to move in this open to camera two-shot.

FIGURE 2.41   A very common type of direct to camera two-shot. The car's interior dictates the distance between and placement of the two characters facing the same camera. Here we see the storyboard frame, a front on and a reverse view.

The Two-Shot Frame Composition with Two People

These subjects have their bodies and faces "opened up to" (that means facing) the camera. The audience is privileged to observe what they do, what they say, and how they react.

Either way, the framing for this type of shot must be wide enough to accommodate the shoulder width of the two people. The 16:9 wide-screen aspect ratio of HD video will certainly help with this, but an MS or MCU may be the closest shot types that could be used to adequately frame a direct-to-camera two-shot. Attempting to frame any tighter will necessitate the use of overlapping one body in front of the other. This establishes a visual "favor" for the character in the unobstructed frontal position. In this case, "favor" may establish a more dominant character in the story, or it may just prove a convenient way of seeing a more intimate view of faces within one shot. Sometimes it is easiest to have the shorter talent in front and the taller one behind (Figure 2.42).

FIGURE 2.42   Achieving a two-shot open to camera in this tight MCU requires overlapping the subjects' bodies.

The Over-the-Shoulder Two-Shot

This shot looks like its name – while recording a dialogue scene you place the camera behind one character (A) and shoot over his shoulder to see the face of the other character (B). The backside of character A's head and shoulder form an "L" shape at either left/bottom or right/bottom of frame, depending on which side you have placed him (Figures 2.43 and 2.44).

This is a form of overlapping composition and is most often edited into a scene after the audience has first viewed an establishing shot and a wider profile two-shot. These preceding shots establish the location and the two characters involved in the dialogue.

FIGURE 2.43   Examples of over-the-shoulder shots for Character A.

FIGURE 2.44   Examples of over-the-shoulder shots for Character B.

An OTS shot allows the audience to focus more attention on the visible subject, what he says and his reactions to what the other character says. Of course, you would eventually shoot the matching OTS from character B onto A so you could alternate back and forth in the edit if needed. In both previous versions of the two-shot, an audience member could choose which character's face they would look at and when, but with the OTS the filmmaker decides that for them — for emphasis and/or for further character or story development.

An over-the-shoulder two-shot may be composed appropriately within a variety of shot types ranging from the long shot to the medium close-up and may or may not contain multiple characters (see OTS reference under 3/4 Back View in this chapter). Sometimes, as in Figure 2.45, the camera height is dropped and it shoots from behind the waist, hips, or thighs of a character, especially if they are carrying something of visual or dramatic interest at their side (a letter, gun, bouquet of flowers, etc.). The most commonly used framing, however, is the MCU (Figures 2.43 and 2.44). It allows for proper composition of the body, equal headroom, and maintains the screen direction of the "look" from one character to the other. The wider aspect ratio of 16:9 may allow for a tighter framing of an OTS, but it might run the risk of compromising good composition in favor of more facial detail — you won't know until you try it with your camera and your particular actors. A standard "clean" single close-up may be more appropriate.

FIGURE 2.45 Camera height has dropped in this modified over-the-shoulder shot. The foreground object is important to the story line as is seeing the look on this subject's face.

The Dirty Single

If you wish to get a small slice of character A in a shot of character B, but you do not want a full OTS or a "clean" single, you may compose what is called a "dirty" single (Figure 2.46). This slice of A in the shot helps keep the viewer oriented. As with any of these shots that incorporate a bit of head or body of the non-favored subject, you have to be extra careful with their placement and movement. Even the slightest gesture or head nod could disrupt the shot's composition. Be clear in your need for relative still-ness when you discuss the shot with your talent.

Additionally, as a filmmaker, you may have to ask your talent to stand unnaturally close to one another in order to achieve the two-shot framing you are seeking. This holds

FIGURE 2.46 Just a slice of Character A is visible in this "dirty" single.

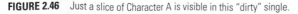

especially true for the over-the-shoulder shot or any tighter 50-50. For the actors it may feel strange, but on the recorded image the distance will look appropriate to the viewing audience. Also, depending on the scene, the players, and your camera placement/lens, you may have to ask the actors to stand or sit further apart, higher, or lower, in order to make the shot composition look correct for your needs. Just be aware that in cinematic language, proximity and grouping equate a unity between characters. The family of "two-shots" is an integral part of your standard scene coverage and the OTS may often be the best choice for recording different angles of the same conversation between two characters.

The Power Dynamic Two-Shot

We call this an "up/down" in a two-person profile shot. One character (A) is placed higher in the frame while the other character (B) is placed lower on the opposite side of frame (Figure 2.47). Even though the camera angle is neutral in this special two-shot, a power dynamic is created. As you will read further in Chapter Seven, the subtext of this shot tells us that the higher character has the "upper hand." The OTS coverage will clearly call for the use of high angle and low angle answer shots, further underscoring the significance of this composition within the story.

FIGURE 2.47   The character whose head is placed higher in the frame has control of this scene.

The Two-Shot: Frame Composition with Two People

The Three-Shot

Much as the standard two-shot works for two people, the "linear" three-shot can show three people standing side by side – especially with the widescreen aspect ratio of HD (Figure 2.48). The shot types capable of comfortably generating this framing range from the XLS up to the MCU. Think of the three contestants on a game show, three news anchors at the desk, or three friends walking down a school hallway. You may use similar guidelines for headroom and the rule of thirds. This shot could apply to both subjective and objective shooting styles.

FIGURE 2.48   The three figures fit comfortably in this "linear" three-shot.

If you were to put one person in the back seat of the vehicle shown in Figure 2.41, then you would have created another flavor of direct-to-camera three-shot. A triangle of connectivity is now present and the audience can play with the energy generated by bouncing attention from one to the others in this composition (Figure 2.49). You will find

FIGURE 2.49   The triangle shape created by the three heads generates energy lines for the audience to follow.

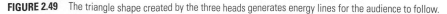

that geometric shapes (lines, triangles, squares, ellipses, etc.) are used quite often in visual communications. We discuss these more completely in the next chapter.

OTS three-shots are also possible when you are shooting coverage for a three-person dialogue, but generating two-shots can pose problems for the editor. A linear three-person OTS relies heavily on figure overlapping within the frame and can look rather "stagey" (Figure 2.50). A high or low angle three-shot OTS will create the same power dynamic as the triangular two-shot version (Figure 2.51).

FIGURE 2.50   Tight framing and tight talent blocking can generate this three person OTS.

FIGURE 2.51   Camera angle and triangular composition provide extra meaning to this OTS three-shot.

The Three-Shot

Wrapping up the Basics of Composition

The basics of frame composition are relatively simple. We have demonstrated them using several basic shot types covering one person placed "creatively" within the frame. The various two-shots introduce a second subject into the frame but still follow similar framing guidelines, and so it goes for the three-shot as well. The basics of composition will apply to any of the wide variety of shot types and to any objects that you need to record. When you create a shot of a vase with flowers, a cat, or a lone planet floating in space, you should consider the same guidelines of composition – headroom, look room, rule of thirds, camera angle, etc. Once you know the shot types, the basics of framing, and the power behind camera angles, you are well on your way to using our shared film language to make well-balanced images for your motion pictures – whatever the project may be.

Chapter Two – Review

1. Provide appropriate headroom for each shot type.

2. Decide whether a subjective (to camera lens) or objective (not to camera lens) shooting style is more appropriate for your project.

3. Create ample look room/nose room for your subject to balance the weight of the frame.

4. Follow the rule of thirds and place important objects along the one-third lines within the frame, both horizontally and vertically, and at their intersections.

5. Choose a horizontal camera angle around your subject for more meaningful coverage (the 3/4 profile being the most popular).

6. Shoot from a neutral, high, or low vertical camera angle to inform an audience about a character's "power dynamic."

7. Profile and direct to camera two-shots work best from long to medium shots, but over-the-shoulder two-shots may work best from the medium close-up.

8. A "dirty" single contains only a small portion of the other character in the scene. Good for audience reference but may pose a continuity problem for the editor.

9. A power dynamic can be generated while using a neutral camera angle on a profile two-shot if you place one character higher in the frame.

10. The three-shot can add a triangular energy pattern to your composition.

Chapter Two – Exercises & Projects

1. With whatever camera you have access to, practice framing a single human subject in all shot types, paying particular attention to your angle on action, rule of thirds, headroom and nose room, etc.

2. Shoot still picture storyboards of two people having a conversation:

   A) Across a table from one another

   B) Walking side-by-side down a street or hallway (either leading them or following them – for extra information on this, you may wish to skip ahead to Chapter Six, Dynamic Shots)

3. Find two actors of differing heights and shoot them in a standing profile two-shot and then try to figure out the best approach for getting matching over-the-shoulder shots of each. Or simply have one actor stand and one sit and shoot their matching OTS shots.

Chapter Two – Review

Chapter Two – Quiz Yourself

1. If you wanted to make a character in your story look subordinate or diminutive, where might you want to put the camera in relation to his/her body?

2. In a scene involving only one character, why might you choose to compose a frame shooting over that person's shoulder?

3. Why might you want to shoot a character in profile?

4. The cartoon you are animating starts where a little girl gets lost in a big jungle. In your shot composition, how could you visually indicate her feelings of being alone and small?

5. At what level, or height, would the majority of neutral shots of people be recorded? Why?

6. What possible scenarios would benefit visually from uniting the heads of two people in a profile CU?

7. What is the difference between a "clean" single and a "dirty" single?

Chapter Three
Composition – Beyond the Basics

- The Illusion of 3D
- The Lines: Horizontal, Vertical, Diagonal, Curved
- The Depth Factor: Foreground, Middle Ground, Background
- Depth Cues: Overlapping, Object Size, Atmospherics
- Lens Talk: Focal Length, Primes, Zooms
- Lens Talk: Focus

Up until now we have kept most of our compositions relatively basic – one or two subjects in a simple environment. By this point you should feel comfortable with your camera's aspect ratio, the families of shot types, the rule of thirds, headroom, look room, and camera angles on action. Chapter Three builds on these basic components of cinematic language and introduces new and compelling ways to compose your shots – increasing their visual information, meaning, and beauty.

The Illusion of the Third Dimension

There are many ways to use compositional elements to create the illusion of three-dimensional space within a still photograph, an animation, or a video frame. Many popular methods include diagonal lines, foreground and background objects, object size, atmospherics, focus, wide and long lenses, and lighting.

As we have said, the basic film or video camera captures a flat, two-dimensional image and the movie theatre, television, tablet and computer screens display a flat, two-dimensional image. So how is it that when we watch television and, more noticeably, movies on very large theatre screens the elements of the frame seem to occupy a three-dimensional space? Well, the simple answer is to say that this phenomenon is achieved through visual illusions and tricks for the human eye and brain. There are many more in-depth physiological and psychological reasons, but this is not the appropriate place to explore those topics fully. Feel free to do your own research on the human visual system and how we interpret light, color, motion, depth, and so forth.

What we will discuss briefly is how our human visual system differs from the visual system of a traditional camera. On the most simplistic level it comes down to how many lenses are used to create the image. Humans have two eyes on the front of their heads, and the eyes are spaced several inches apart. This configuration results in binocular vision (bi- meaning "two" and -ocular referring to the "eye"). Binocular vision allows us to establish depth in our visual space by causing us to see the same objects from two separate vantage points. Each eye, offset by those several inches, sees the same objects from slightly different horizontal positions and therefore "captures" a slightly different picture. The brain then unites those two separate pictures and generates one view of the world around us rendered with three-dimensional perspective (Figure 3.1).

Each eye's vantage point helps create the illusion of 3D depth. Test this yourself by holding any 3D object about 1.5 feet in front of your face, making sure that it is askew and not perfectly flat to your vision, then alternately open one eye and look at the object and then close that eye and open the other eye to see the same object – note how the two views of this close object are slightly different.

Technical Note – Relatively new on the market are consumer level 3D video cameras. Most have two lenses and record two separate images much as the human eyes do. The appropriate computer video editing software and display technologies will render

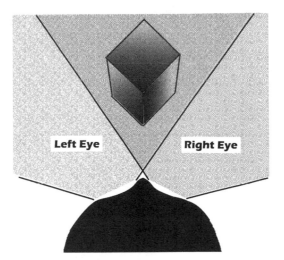

FIGURE 3.1   Each eye's vantage point helps create the illusion of 3D depth. The left and the right see slightly different versions of the same close up object. This difference in "angle" on objects does not apply to things further away from us.

a more "realistic" 3D viewing experience for the audience, although it is all still only seen on a two-dimensional screen.

Traditional film and video cameras, of course, only have one eye – the single lens – so they are unable to record the same type of three-dimensional space as the human visual system. Filmmakers must generate the illusion of multidimensionality. The following sections will give you some tools and techniques to help you explore ways to be a great 3D illusionist with your own shots.

The Illusion of the Third Dimension

The Use of Lines

In artwork, the use of lines – both straight and curved – helps us render patterns and shapes, direct attention and energies, and define sections. The filmmaker has to make many decisions about lines and how to incorporate them into the imagery of the motion picture. Just as in other works of art, film lines can do different jobs and generate different feelings. The following topics touch on some of their purposes and effects.

The Horizon Line

We are going to leave our human subjects aside for the time being and put our attention into shooting an exterior environment. Shot-wise we are talking about the long shot family, especially the extreme long shot (XLS) and very wide shot (VWS). Depending on the surrounding topography of your shoot location and your camera angle, this shot should result in capturing a large field of view of the world – the ground, the sky, and many things within those zones. For illustrative purposes we will keep the environment rather bare and start with just a **horizon line** (Figure 3.2).

The horizon line helps keep the audience grounded in an understandable spatial relationship with the environment depicted in the frame. In other words, it allows them to perceive a clear up/down and left/right orientation in the film world. Typically, a major goal is to keep your horizon line as level as possible and in alignment with – parallel to – the top and bottom edges of your physical film frame. You will see that Figure 3.2 accomplishes this goal, but let us add actual objects to help further discuss horizon line and composition (Figure 3.3).

FIGURE 3.2 A simple horizon line bisecting the vertical plane of the frame.

FIGURE 3.3   Adding visible objects to your horizon line frame helps establish place, time, and physical scale.

Now we can begin to appreciate what the level horizon line is doing for our picture composition. Figure 3.3 shows a frame cut directly in half – the horizon line bisects the frame, separating top from bottom. There is headroom for the volcano, sky, and clouds, but does the image follow the rule of thirds? Does it have to? Horizon lines may be placed across your frame wherever you see fit, but its placement will allow you to highlight more sky and less ground or less sky and more ground. If we tilt the camera angle down, we push the horizon line up in our frame (Figure 3.4). If we tilt the camera angle up, we push the horizon line down in our frame (Figure 3.5). Each of these examples shows the horizon line following the rule of thirds. To many, this is a more pleasing position within the frame, but it truly depends on what fits the visual needs of your story.

The Use of Lines

FIGURE 3.4   By tilting the vertical camera angle down, the horizon line now falls along the upper one-third of the frame, resulting in less headroom for the volcano and sky and more ocean.

FIGURE 3.5 By tilting the vertical camera angle up, the horizon line now falls along the lower one-third of the frame, resulting in more visible space for the volcano and sky and less ocean.

Designing your shot composition around your story is a key responsibility of any filmmaker, animator, or visual storyteller. After the rectangular border of your frame is set you should be planning the placement of the horizon line. Dropping the line towards the bottom of frame will expose more nighttime sky in your story about the possibility of invading aliens – the audience feels that they might be out there. Raising the line towards the top will expose a vast expanse of open ocean in your story about the possibility of sea serpents – the audience feels that they might be lurking just under the surface. Perhaps your story is about a long-struggling farmer during a drought. You can play it both ways with this. Push horizon up to show more dry, scorched barren fields, or pull it down to show the cloudless sky baking the thirsty earth below. Either way, the audience is feeling the farmer's plight.

Keep in mind that a horizon line exists in interior film spaces as well; it just may not be the actual "edge of the world." Interior spaces usually have strong horizontal lines such as where the floor meets a wall, window sills, tops of laboratory benches, tables or desk, and so on. The idea would be to keep these horizontal lines flat and level. Any narrative significance would have to be dependent upon the size of the set and the art direction, etc. Horizontal lines in general can imply stability, repose and order.

Vertical Lines

When your horizon is level, then all vertical lines in your frame should rise up straight, parallel to your left/right edges and perpendicular to the top/bottom (Figure 3.6).

FIGURE 3.6   Bold vertical "lines" like these trees accentuate height, strength and solidity.

Filmmakers use strong vertical lines for many purposes in their compositions. Just look around yourself and, depending on your location in the world, you are bound to see several strong vertical lines – doorways, corners of walls, edges of windows, edges of buildings, lamp posts, telephone poles, and trees, just to list a few possibilities. They are often associated with strength, height, loftiness, or even rigidity and staunchness.

A single vertical element can divide the frame into sections of different sizes depending upon where you place it. This serves to partition areas of your film world or separate characters from one another – both literally and figuratively. Doorways, or "frames" within your film frame, can do the same thing. Multiple vertical elements, like the posts in a fence, could symbolize the bars of a jail cell. Your wide horizontal rectangle of a frame can easily be cut down, blocked off, and recomposed by using verticals to create smaller squares and rectangles (see Figure 3.7). Beware of placing a single vertical background line directly behind your subject as it can appear strange on the screen and detract from the overall composition.

FIGURE 3.7   Vertical "lines" or objects can cut the frame into smaller pieces and can figuratively separate subjects in the narrative.

Dutch Angle

You will most often strive to keep your horizon line stable and level, thus ensuring an even viewing plane for your audience. A shift in your horizon line is also likely to cause shifts in your vertical lines – any tall building, tree, door frame, and so on will look tilted or slanted, not upright and even. When horizontal and vertical lines go askew it causes a sense of uneasiness and a slight disorientation in your audience. If this is done unintentionally, then you get people confused. Done on purpose and you have created what is called a **Dutch angle**, a **Dutch tilt**, a **canted angle**, or an **oblique angle**. When a character is sick or drugged or when a situation is "not quite right" you may choose to tilt the camera left or right and create this non-level horizon. The imbalance will make the viewer feel how unstable the character or environment really is – think of a murder mystery aboard a boat in rough seas; things tilt this way and then that, everyone unsure, everyone on edge. Once again, visuals underscore the story (Figure 3.8).

Diagonal Lines

The grid-like horizontal and vertical lines do a good job of partitioning the two-dimensional frame, but we need to begin our exploration of how lines help us achieve the illusion of depth. To get us started, let's look at Figure 3.9. This line shape could represent the slope of a hill. Depending on whether your energy is moving up the "hill"

FIGURE 3.8 Examples of Dutch angle or canted angle shots. Note how the slanted horizontal and vertical lines skew the balance of the image. Something is not quite right within the story at this point.

FIGURE 3.9 This bent line and small circle could indicate a "hill" and a "ball" rolling down the hill due to gravity.

or down it, the symbolic meaning of this ball shape within your story can be different. Implied "direction" and "movement" have been added, but we'll explore those topics in Chapter Six, Dynamic Shots. This example helps somewhat in understanding diagonal lines and how their varying thickness adds to an otherwise flat third dimension.

If we switch our example back to a horizon line and add two diagonal lines from the bottom that converge at the horizon, then we have made something new (Figure 3.10). Does this look familiar? To some of you with a studio art background, you may know that this example employs an artistic technique called the **vanishing point**. These diagonal lines may represent a road, a stream, a sidewalk, or, in our example, a train line (Figure 3.11). Railroad tracks have a consistent width and therefore should

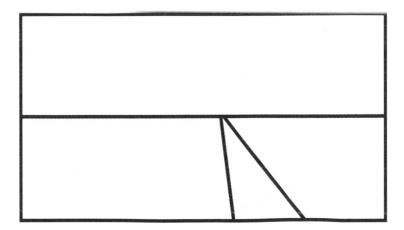

FIGURE 3.10 Two lines converge at a third. Where they meet is called the Vanishing Point.

The Use of Lines

FIGURE 3.11 A railroad track provides a good example of diagonal line perspective and the illusion of 3D.

be parallel to one another for as long as the tracks cover the ground. In reality, when observed across a large distance, the tracks seem to get closer and closer together until they appear to merge at the horizon. This place along the horizon where parallel lines appear to merge together is the vanishing point (see Figure 3.12).

This illusion, as perceived by our human visual system, signifies "distance" to our brains. When observed in reality, in drawings or paintings, and on a filmed image, we infer the existence of depth. This is related to foreshortening, as mentioned in our section on high angle shots, and is most noticeable on linear shapes (buildings, roads, even people) but is less effective on amorphous shapes of unknown mass (ocean, sky, rocks). The key thing to realize here is that the use of diagonal lines can bring that illusion of depth to your frame. So, whenever you can employ diagonal lines within your

FIGURE 3.12 The box indicates where the parallel tracks converge and appear to vanish at the horizon line.

composition (a road, a hallway, a line of people waiting for the bus) you are creating the impression of three-dimensional space on the two-dimensional film frame.

Staircases and their railings can generate a great deal of visual interest and energy when incorporated into your composition. They can rise up or down diagonally or recede into the depth of your shot straight on. Much like roads, paths, rivers, etc. they lead the eyes of the viewer in or out of the depth of your frame and they are useful for up/down power dynamics as well (Figure 3.13).

This does not mean that you must always use diagonal lines, however. Yes, they are compositionally bold elements within your frame, and yes, they can create depth, but what if your goal is to create a shot that has no depth? Your character is feeling trapped or not capable of moving in a dynamic direction at this point of the narrative. Composing her in a flat space, like up against a wall, could help visually underscore her state of being, reflecting the story's subtext and psychological messaging (Figure 3.14).

To achieve the shot in Figure 3.14, the camera had to be placed at the height of the subject and perpendicular to the wall itself. This frame, flat on to a wall, has no real sense of depth. The full frontal angle on action only shows some horizontal lines on the wall. The person is enclosed by the environment and can only move left or right, or potentially toward camera. In this instance, the absence of perceived depth adds to the mental or emotional state of the character. The composition of the shot underscores the state of being for the character recorded within it.

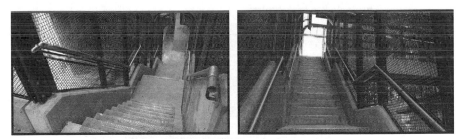

The Use of Lines

FIGURE 3.13 Examples of how stairs or railings can create depth into your shot composition.

FIGURE 3.14   The person, framed up against a flat wall, seems boxed in or trapped by the environment. Lacking indicators of depth, this shot can convey hidden meaning about the character in the story.

FIGURE 3.15   By recording the same woman by the same wall from a different camera angle, we now unlock the diagonal lines, which lead the eye into the depth of the "3D" shot. The meaning of the shot and the character's mental state may now be different — free and open.

A slight shift in the camera's angle on action (horizontal repositioning) yields a different image with a different meaning (Figure 3.15). It shows the same woman in front of the same wall, but now a diagonal line exists, as does a distant horizon. With the frame opened up this way, the character has more options for movement — left, right, near, or far — and she is pictorially and thematically freer. Depth is created because we can now see out into the world along those diagonal lines that draw the viewer's eye away from the main character and out into the deep space of the film world. So, in addition to helping create the illusion of depth, the presence of strong diagonal lines in a composition helps you direct the attention of the audience into that depth – to explore deeper inside your frame for more visual information about your story.

Curved Lines

Performing similar tasks to diagonal lines are curved lines, either enclosed like circles and ellipses or open like arcs and S-curves. Adding curves to your compositional arrangements can help lead a viewer's eyes into or out from the depth of your film frame, separate sections of your frame, conjure feelings of unity, or establish implied directions of the flow of movement or energy.

Curves may be fluid and smooth and subtle. These work well to help an audience feel relaxed by showing some natural connectivity (Figure 3.16).

Tightly kinked curves can generate feelings of anxiety or confusion (Figure 3.17).

Curves do not have to be physical lines either. They can be constructed, artfully, in your compositions by arranging people, objects, colors, and contrast (covered more in Chapter Four). The audience will "extract" the shape you "embed" in your shot (Figure 3.18). Humans are quite good at seeing patterns and shapes in our environment, and image makers (artists, film people, video game designers, etc.) count on this when they construct their images (Figure 3.19).

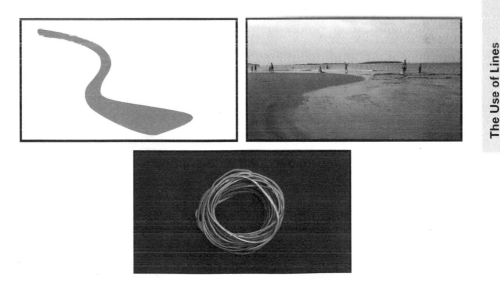

FIGURE 3.16 Relaxed or uniform curved lines help the eye stay calm and ask us to follow them.

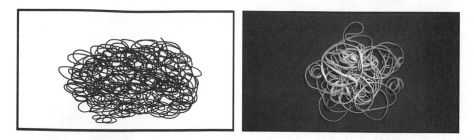

FIGURE 3.17 A viewer may just feel a mess while looking at these confused curved lines.

FIGURE 3.18 A viewer may sense the curved "lines" in this composition.

FIGURE 3.19 Do you see a familiar pattern in these "random" shapes?

The Depth of Film Space – Foreground/Middle Ground/Background

We have seen that diagonal and curved lines framed within a shot can help draw a viewer's eyes from objects close to the camera to objects further away from the camera, or deeper into the film's space. To help us understand this space better, let's first divide it into three sections based on the proximity to the camera's lens: **foreground** (FG), **middle ground** (MG), and **background** (BG). Together with the borders of the frame, these zones help form the film's three-dimensional space: height, width, and depth.

Foreground

As the name implies, the foreground is the zone between the camera's lens and the main subject being photographed. It is the space before, or in front of, the main area of interest. Nothing has to occupy this space and often it is simply filled with empty air. A creative filmmaker, however, can choose to place something in that space. Of course, a foreground element should enhance the composition of the shot and, if it is stationary, it should not obscure the zones behind it unnecessarily.

The object may serve to help set the environment (a tree branch), it may be an abstract shape (part of a lamp post or a park bench), and it may also carry meaning for the narrative (a stop sign at a crossroads) (Figure 3.20). Whatever the object and whatever the purpose, you should be judicious in choosing your treatment of foreground elements because they may distract your viewer from observing the more important details that are staged deeper in your shot. This type of overlapping or obscuration would work if your story involves someone "spying" on a character and the shot using excessive foreground elements is a POV (Figure 3.21).

FIGURE 3.20 The foreground elements help set up depth in the shots.

FIGURE 3.21   If used as a POV shot, the foreground elements create a sense of mystery or of spying.

Middle Ground

Regardless of the size of your shooting location, much of your important action may be staged in the middle ground. This is the zone where dialogue can unfold, a couple can dance, or a car can pull up to a stop sign. All or most of the physical action is visible within the frame. An audience member is likely to receive all of the information within the shot when the main action is staged here. Middle ground is much easier to establish in wider shots such as medium and long shots (Figure 3.22). With the close-up family of shot types it gets trickier to find the depth to show all three zones, but it is still possible if you plan well.

Background

You now understand foreground and middle ground, so it will be easy to guess what the background is — everything behind the MG out to infinity (Figure 3.23). Of course, if

FIGURE 3.22   The woman occupies the middle ground of this image 1. The addition of the FG element clarifies this in image 2.

FIGURE 3.23   The background is like the backdrop of a theatre stage. It sets the location for exterior and interior scenes.

you are shooting an interior location such as a restaurant then there will be no "infinity." The physical space behind the main action being recorded will be the background of your shot. The other patrons eating, the servers walking about, and the wall at the back end of the room all become part of the shot's background. The BG zone can be rather barren, like the dunes of a desert, or rather busy, like the commotion found along a city's avenue. When shooting on location, you may be limited by how much you can control the BG, but you should try to frame your shots so that the background does not overpower the main action in the middle ground. Later, we will discuss how focus and lighting can help direct the attention of your audience into the various depths of FG, MG, and BG – the OTS discussed earlier is a good example of this practice (Figure 3.24).

FIGURE 3.24   A traditional OTS represents all three "grounds" in the depth of film space.

The Depth of Film Space – Foreground/Middle Ground/Background

Depth Cues

Overlapping

The combination of foreground, middle ground, and background elements helps create the illusion of three dimensions on the 2D film frame through overlapping. The physical objects in your video frame accomplish this just like the layers in your photo editing or animation software. A tree branch in the foreground will partially obscure the elements of the MG and BG. The main action taking place in the MG will obscure visual elements found in the BG zone. So, just like in real life, when objects (static or moving) appear to be in front of one another it allows our brains to establish depth cues (Figure 3.25).

Object Size

The relative size of a known object will also trigger depth cues in your shots. Something large, like a mountain, appears in your composition. It seems comparatively small when viewed along with the other objects in your frame. From their real-life experiences the audience will understand that a mountain is not a small object, and for it to be seen as small in the image it must therefore be far away – somewhere deep in the background of the film space (Figure 3.26). Cartoonists and animators use this technique in their illustrations.

However, many filmmakers (especially those interested in special visual effects) have played with this optical illusion to create a false sense of depth where scale and

FIGURE 3.25   The layers of this simple animation overlap to help create depth cues.

FIGURE 3.26 Mountains are significantly larger than a tree or an ape, but their small size in this image indicates that they are far away.

FIGURE 3.27 This plane… is it real or a toy?

perspective were tricking the eyes and brains of the audience. Oversized props in the MG would look like normal objects in the FG. Miniaturized models of larger items placed in the FG or MG would have the appearance of existing as "normal" sized items (Figure 3.27).

Atmosphere

Another depth cue, found especially in wide or long exterior shots, is **atmosphere (or atmospherics)**. If you have ever looked up a long street in the city or stood atop a hill in the countryside and stared off toward the horizon, then you may have experienced the dissatisfaction of a less than clear view. Perhaps the distant hills or distant buildings seemed blurry or hazy or even totally obscured. This is often the result of what are called atmospherics — the presence of particulates suspended in the air (Figure 3.28). This is most often water vapor, but it may be smoke from a nearby fire, dust, pollen, or even pollutants.

When you stand in this atmosphere, it may not obscure your vision of local objects very much (unless it is thick ground fog), but when viewed across a greater expanse (as in an XLS) the cumulative effect of the particles in the air causes distant objects to be obscured. If you were to record a shot in such an environment, the viewing audience would immediately understand the depth cue. Fog machines are often employed for just such a purpose on film sets, in addition to the diffusion of light and the creation of mood (see Figure 3.29).

FIGURE 3.28   The atmosphere obscures the background alluding to greater distance.

FIGURE 3.29   Man-made "fog" on set helps create a mood in these environments and catches backlight.

The Camera Lens – The Observer of Your Film World

All this talk of frames, headroom, lines, and depth cues is great but there would be no grammar of the shots for us to discuss if there were no lens on the camera to record those shots. So, let us switch gears a bit and put some attention toward an extremely important piece of visual storytelling equipment – the camera lens.

For all of its complexity, the modern camera lens still performs the same tasks that it has done for a very long time:

- Collect light rays bouncing off the world in front of the camera (the scene you are shooting).
- Focus those light rays on to whatever recording medium you are using (emulsion film or a video camera's electronic sensor).
- Control the amount of light that hits the light-sensitive recording medium in your camera.

It can be that simple, yet the job of the lens, the types of lenses, and the quality of lens materials can vary widely.

It is through the lens that your frame is bound, your composition is created, the perspective is set, and the exposure is controlled. Depending on the lens you choose and how you use it, you can achieve very different and stylized looks for your story. Because we do not have the time to delve deeply into the history and current technology of film and video camera lenses, we will try to touch on the main points of interest that will help you make good decisions about your shots and about what the lens choice does for the grammar of those shots.

Primes vs Zooms

Camera lenses for motion picture creation come in two major categories: primes and zooms. Both types of lens are gauged by their ability to capture light rays (the **focal length**) and by their ability to pass more or less of those light rays through (the **f-stop** or **iris**). Filmmakers need to be familiar with both the technical differences and the corresponding aesthetics associated with each characteristic. This is not the place for getting deep into the mathematics and physics of optics and light energy, so we will keep the main concepts rather basic.

- Focal length (FL) is measured in millimeters
- Smaller FL numbered lenses (e.g. 10 mm) have glass elements that bend more light to a greater degree over a shorter focal distance and therefore capture a wider angle of view [you see more of the film space]
- Larger FL numbered lenses (e.g. 300 mm) have glass elements that bend less light to a lesser degree over a longer focal distance and therefore capture a narrower but seemingly more magnified angle of view [you see less of the film space but what you see is enlarged]
- F-stop is a calculated measurement in fractions of the lens aperture (iris or opening) at a particular focal length – used to help gauge exposure
- Small F-stop numbers (e.g. 1.4, 2, 2.8) signify a larger lens opening, allow more light into the camera, and let you shoot in slightly darker environments
- Larger F-stop numbers (e.g. 16, 22) signify a smaller lens opening, let less light into the camera, and let you shoot in slightly brighter environments

The Prime Lens

Historically, prime lenses came first. They are distinguished by the fact that they have only one focal length (e.g. 50 mm). A filmmaker would have to have several separate prime lenses in his or her kit in order to render different magnifications or shot type framings from the same camera position. If you had a camera with only one prime lens, and you wished to change the relative size of your subject in your frame, you would have to either move camera closer to subject or vice versa. Our initial shot type examples used this technique to generate the images.

Having few glass elements (lenses) built inside, they tend to be "sharp" and can render a very detailed image when properly focused. The basic construction of the prime lens also allows for it to be "fast" and yield maximum light transmission with lower F-stop numbers (larger apertures). Prime lenses tend to be smaller in size and lighter in weight than zoom lenses.

The prime lens is used a great deal in professional still photography and high-end motion picture production. They are less expensive than the more complex zoom lenses, but you would have to purchase or rent several prime lenses in order to cover your desired range of focal lengths. Most amateur filmmakers cannot consider using primes because their video cameras come with built-in zoom lenses (although the recent DSLR craze has changed this option of lens choice).

The Zoom Lens

Most likely you will be shooting your projects with some format of digital video (DSLR, HD, or less likely mini-DV). Your camera will probably have a built-in lens and that lens will most likely be a zoom lens. The zoom lens is very popular, especially with video camera manufacturers, because the one lens provides a large range of focal length settings (e.g. 28 mm to 135 mm). You can optically create a variety of frames – from a wide shot with a wide angle of view to a tighter, more magnified field of view without having to change camera to subject distance.

On your camera's zoom control, the wide end of the lens view is usually marked with a "W" (for wide) or maybe a "–" (for less magnified). The narrow angle of view or magnified end of the lens is usually marked "T" (for telephoto) or maybe a "+" (for more magnified). DSLR and other more professional video cameras can employ interchangeable "cinema" zoom lenses that use a focal length ring on the lens barrel (measured in mm) to manually change the magnification of the image.

The zoom lens is a complicated construction of many glass elements and telescoping barrels or rings that all work together to collect light. They can be expensive and heavy and, because of the numerous glass elements for the longer focal lengths, zoom lenses are often not as "fast" as prime lenses. Most of the less expensive ones cannot open to very wide apertures and therefore are not as good to use in low-light conditions. Due to the extra glass, zoom lenses may also not be as "sharp" – particularly around the edges of the image.

Until this point, our discussions of shot types, framing, and composition have all been based on camera proximity to subject. This means that if we had wanted to frame a CU shot we either moved the camera closer to the talent or moved the talent closer to the camera. This is just like your own eyes. If you want to see something in more detail you must move closer to it or move it closer to your eyes. The obvious point here is that we do not have zoom capabilities with our human eyes. We have one focal length to our vision, and that is relatively wide (recall the finger waggling trick from Chapter One). Because we cannot zoom with our own eyes, the zooming shot that moves quickly through a large range of focal lengths can feel very unnatural to an audience.

Lens Perspective

Having a fixed focal length lens in our human eyes, we get to see the world from a constant perspective. Camera lenses are manufactured to also have this "normal" field of view (in between the extremes of the wide end and narrow end of the zoom range). They appear natural or neutral in their perspective on the subject or scene shown, just as if the scene had been recorded through a pair of human eyes. Without getting too technical, the "normal" camera lens angle of view depends on the camera to subject distance when considering the focal length of the lens, the diameter of lens, and the size of the format imager (35 mm film, SD or HD video, etc.) (see Figure 3.31).

All this discussion leads up to one key point, and that is the feeling your shot perspective conveys to an audience. The normal or neutral field of view captures the shot as if we were there personally, observing the action rather than the camera. As soon as you move to the extremes of the zoom range, however, the optical illusions start to creep in.

A wide angle shot (from the short end of the focal length range) generates an illusion of perspective change between the near and far subjects in the shot. It appears to expand the depth of the shot and optically exaggerates the space between objects, therefore playing up the 3D perspective of the image (Figure 3.30). A wide angle lens is helpful if you want to make a small film space appear larger or deeper on screen (think closet, airplane bathroom, etc.). It is also good for shooting establishing shots of locations and broad vistas as in an XLS. Due to this illusion of expanded space, any moving object (either towards or away from the camera's wide angle lens) will appear to move quickly and cover a good deal of film space without much effort. This perspective illusion of quick movement can be used for certain stunt work and for comic purposes.

An image shot with a narrow telephoto angle of view (from the long end of the focal length range) appears to deemphasize 3D space. Through magnifying all subjects in the

FIGURE 3.30 Subjects seen through a wide angle lens. Note the apparent distance between subjects and background. The illusion of spatial expansion.

FIGURE 3.31   Subjects seen through "normal" lens perspective. Note the apparent distance between subjects and background.

FIGURE 3.32   Subjects seen through long (or telophoto) lens perspective. Note the apparent distance between subjects and background. The illusion of spatial compression.

foreground, middle ground, and background equally, an apparent compression of the depth of film space takes place (see Figures 3.30, 3.31, and 3.32). Objects in the frame have the appearance of being closer together on the screen than they actually are in real life. This illusion of space compression can help you safely record action sequences or stunt work and is used heavily in the coverage of sporting events when the camera cannot physically be located on the playing field. Be aware that this long lens magnification can make it more difficult to hold moving objects within the "tighter" frame.

Of course, the more extreme the focal length, the more the illusion of perspective distortion in the image will appear. This holds especially true for short focal length, very wide angle lenses (sometimes called "**fisheye**" lenses), which can really warp the depth cues of your shot and exaggerate the 3D space on close subjects (Figure 3.33). The grammar of shots like these tells your viewer that there is a warped or distorted view of the film world going on. Something is not quite right. Perhaps it is a nightmare sequence or a fantasy episode, or a character is thinking or behaving in an altered state of some kind. Whatever the creative visual reason, it certainly is not "normal." Much as in still portraiture photography, it may be advisable to shoot your subject's close-up shots with a slightly longer focal length lens from further away so that you do not exaggerate his or her features (enlarged nose, receding ears, etc.) (see Figure 3.34).

FIGURE 3.33 "Fisheye" lens distortion. An ultra-wide-angle lens very close to your subject can yield this sort of physical distortion within your image. A surreal, comical, or fantastical feeling may be generated by this lens choice.

FIGURE 3.34 Using a slightly longer than "normal" lens focal length combined with a further camera-to-subject distance often leads to pleasing portraiture of subjects in close-up framing.

When you combine a long lens with subjects further away from the camera, you get a more compressed perspective (see Figure 3.32). This compression can imply a "tight" or "flat" life being led by a character, or a place that is constraining or prison-like. The "slice" of background or environment around your subject is also small and confining. When you use a very long lens and you have a subject move from the depth of your shot to closer to camera it seems to take a very long time for that subject to cover a very small distance. This illusion is often used to give the impression that this character's movements are futile – he just cannot get anywhere no matter how hard he tries. Filmmakers use perspective optical tricks such as these as another tool in their visual toolbox – another part of their cinematic language.

Lens Focus – Directing the Viewer's Attention

We now understand that a big part of the "look" of a shot is established through camera format, proximity, angle, and lens focal length. Creating a composition of subjects that is interesting and appropriate to your story's visual style is a major goal. You will now be staging those visual elements with the rule of thirds and along diagonal and curved lines into the frame's "depth." The foreground, middle ground and background zones in your film frame also allow you to unlock an additional tool in your shot construction tool kit – **focus**.

Your eyes can only focus on one thing at a time. As you look from one object to another, your eye instantly changes focus to the new distance of the new object. The illusion of constant focus is achieved, but, in reality, you are only able to focus on one physical plane or distance from your eye at any one time. Go ahead and try it I look around you at things at different distances. What is in focus? What is out of focus?

A camera lens behaves in the same way. It can only generate clear, crisp focus at one distance from the camera at one time. This distance is called the **point of critical focus**. There is a zone around this distance of critical focus that may also appear to be in acceptable focus (not yet blurry), and this zone is called the **depth of field** (DOF) (Figure 3.35). Luckily for you, image optics follow certain scientific rules, so there are many charts and tables available to help you predict this changing depth of field. They allow you to creatively set what may be in focus within your frame [see internet and book references for DOF Charts in Appendix A].

Depending on the size of your production and crew, setting focus is the job of the camera assistant or the camera operator. Determining what important object within the

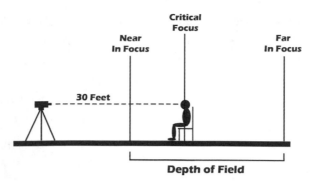

FIGURE 3.35 Critical focus set to main subject while depth of field occupies some distance roughly one-third in front of and two-thirds behind that critical focus plane.

composition of the frame gets treated to the primary critical focus is often the job of the director and/or the director of photography. As staging talent and set dressing deep into the shot are now possible, you get to determine where (what distance from the camera) the focus is set and can therefore control what the viewing audience will most likely pay attention to on the screen. Here's another bit of shot grammar for you: what is in focus in your shot is the important thing for the viewer to watch.

Again, the human visual system creates the illusion that all things at all distances are in focus all of the time. We are not accustomed to seeing things blurry (unless we need corrective lenses and choose not to wear them). A camera lens does not know what is or what should be in focus. Only you, the filmmaker, knows that. You set the critical plane of focus and the corresponding depth of field according to what you wish to have in proper focus. The audience will want to look at the objects within that zone of most clear and crisp focus. Anything outside the depth of field will appear blurry to the viewer's eye and therefore not be an attractive element to watch.

As you can see, selecting the focus object is a key component to directing your viewer's experience as they watch the elements within the width, height, and depth of your frame. Because the human face and eyes are usually the main objects of interest, you may wish to keep the DOF narrow on the face but blur out the possibly distracting BG. This way, the audience pays attention to the actor and not to the unimportant visual elements behind him. While shooting, check and recheck for proper focus on your subject. Large video monitors on set can help, as does instant playback of video mediafiles that are in question. The keen eyes of the viewer easily notice soft focus or slightly blurry shots, and unless there is an immediate correction or introduction of some element within the frame that comes into clear focus, the viewer will reject the shot and disassociate from the viewing experience. Bad focus remains one critical element of film production that cannot be "fixed in post."

Pulling Focus or Following Focus

A shallow depth of field allows you to place critical focus on your one subject in your frame – the foreground and background elements will blur out and the audience is left to pay attention to one thing. What if you wanted to have another subject enter the same shot but at a distance that is outside the established depth of field? The new character will be blurry – unless you shift the DOF closer to or away from the camera depending on the distance of this new subject in your shot.

This practice is called **pulling focus** or **racking focus.** If your goal is to keep focus on one moving object within your frame, then you may call it **following focus**. Many camera lens technologies allow only Auto Focus and focus shifts of this nature are harder to achieve. A camera with a Manual Focus setting unlocks this creative control for the film-maker and you can move the lens's focus ring in order to actually (optically) shift the focus from one distance to another in the depth of your shot. The current popularity of DSLR HD video cameras is partly due to this "cinematic" capability of the manually con-trollable still camera lenses. This shifting of focus within the depth of your shot is yet another technique to help you direct the viewer's attention around your frame.

The option to pull focus or to follow focus requires that not everything in your shot's FG, MG, and BG will be in focus at the same time. This scenario is the result of your manip-ulation of the depth of field. As you remember, the DOF is the zone around that point of critical focus that will appear to be in acceptable focus and it can grow larger to infinity or shrink smaller to just a few inches or centimeters. As a general rule of thumb, the DOF will be found roughly one-third in front of and two-thirds behind the plane of criti-cal focus (see Figure 3.35).

What determines your DOF is a combination of various factors involved in capturing the image. In order to keep it simple, we will just say that the focal length of your lens, the aperture (iris) set on the lens, the size of format (SD/HD video sensor or 16 mm/35 mm film), and the distance from the lens to the object of primary or critical focus all work together to determine the overall DOF. Let us explore the two extremes found in Table 3.1.

What this chart tells us is that when you shoot a daylight exterior wide shot of your subject with a short focal length (wide angle) lens, you will generate the largest

Table 3.1–Factors that control the depth of field without regard to size of format

	Large Depth of Field	Small Depth of Field
Focal Length	Short (Wide)	Long (Narrow)
Camera to Subject Distance	Far	Near
Lens Aperture	Small (High Number)	Large (Low Number)

possible DOF. Most likely a few feet from the camera to infinity will be in acceptable focus. Conversely, when you shoot a dimly lit interior XCU with a long focal length (telephoto) lens, you will generate the shallowest DOF. Perhaps only a few inches to a few centimeters might be seen in acceptable focus.

The lesson is that you can face difficulties in controlling your DOF in well-lit locations. Lots of light calls for a "stopping down" of your lens iris (closing to a smaller hole) to maintain proper exposure – which expands your depth of field. You can employ tools such as **neutral density filters (ND filters)** on the lens to help lessen the amount of light entering the lens on daylight exteriors. Some cameras handle this exposure limit electronically but still call it an ND adjustment.

A common problem with shooting low-light nighttime interiors is a DOF that is too shallow. Your subjects, especially if they are moving, will fall in and out of focus – moving in and out of the very shallow DOF. In order to get exposure, the lens iris has to be wide open. Adding more light will allow you to use a smaller aperture setting and therefore expand the depth of field – more of the important subject can then be in focus

FIGURE 3.36 A large depth of field allows all visual elements in the FG, MG, and BG to appear in rather sharp focus. This can often make it difficult for your viewer to know where to look for the most important visual information.

FIGURE 3.37   A shallow depth of field keeps the critical focus on the main subject and blurs the other elements outside the near and far distances of acceptable focus.

(Figures 3.36 and 3.37). If you do not have access to more illumination, you may try raising the video camera's electronic "gain" setting to increase sensitivity, but image quality will most likely degrade and not improve the DOF.

Chapter Three – Review

1. Understand how to create the illusion of 3D on a 2D image.

2. Horizon line – keep it level and steady. Raise or lower it in your frame for thematic reasons.

3. Vertical lines – indicate solidity, substance or strength and are good for dividing up the frame into smaller sections.

4. Dutch angle – skews horizontal and vertical lines to create imbalance. Implies that something is not quite right with this character or scene.

5. Diagonal lines – force perspective to vanishing point and create depth. Draw your viewer's eyes into the depth of your shot.

6. Curved lines – Natural and soft, they help your viewer move their eyes around and deep into the frame.

7. The depth of film space – foreground/middle ground/background – zones where you stage action and that exist at varying distances from the lens.

8. Overlapping objects – a depth cue that creates layers of objects and can highlight the importance of certain objects in the depth of the shot.

9. Object size – larger in frame means near, and smaller indicates far.

10. Atmospherics – great distance is implied via water vapor obscuration.

11. Prime lenses – only one focal length; often small, fast, and lightweight.

12. Zoom lenses – wide angle and/or telephoto – focal lengths capture a wide field of view or a narrow field of view of the film space, all in one lens housing. Often larger, slower, and heavier.

13. Focus – creatively shifting focus within your film's depth will direct the viewer's eye around the width and depth of your frame and keep them engaged – pull, rack, or follow focus.

14. Depth of field – only objects within the DOF will appear to be in acceptable focus to the audience. Expand/contract or shift that zone in order to achieve more creative compositions into the depth of your shots and generate energy and visual interest for the viewer.

Chapter Three – Exercises & Projects

1. Compose and record a long shot with a single human subject in the middle ground. Now recompose this shot with some overlapping visual element in the foreground. What object did you choose and where in the frame did you place it? How is the focus? What kind of distances did you have to spread between the camera and the foreground object and the subject in the middle ground?

2. If you have access to a video camera with a zoom lens, frame a wide shot of a subject and then recompose as you do a slow zoom through a medium shot and into a final close-up. Next, pick a "middle-ish" focal length on your lens and reshoot the same wide, medium, and close-up shots of your subject, but this time move the camera closer each shot to get the approximately similar framing/ subject magnification. Compare the video results. What differences do you notice? What similarities?

3. With any camera, go out into the world and record images that have differing horizon lines, strong verticals, diagonals, and curved lines. What physical elements did you use to create each kind of "line?"

Chapter Three – Quiz Yourself

1. What happens when you shoot in outer space? Where is the horizon line established then?

2. What might it mean if your horizon line is slightly canted or tilted on purpose?

3. What optical illusion (spatial perspective) seems to occur when you shoot with very wide lens focal lengths?

4. True or false: The "f/stop" is the place along the horizon line where two parallel lines appear to converge.

5. The depth of field surrounds what "point?" How much area of the DOF lives in front of this point and how much lives behind it?

6. How can you use diagonal lines in your composition to direct the visual attention of your audience?

7. How can you use "planes" of sharp focus and blurry areas in your composition to direct the visual attention of your audience?

Chapter Four

Lighting Your Shots – Not Just What You See,
but How You See It

- Light as Energy
- Color Temperature
- The Color Balance of Your Camera
- Natural and Artificial Lighting
- Quantity of Light: Sensitivity and Exposure
- Quality of Light: Hard vs Soft
- Contrast
- Color
- Basic Character Lighting: Three-Point Method
- Motivated Lighting: Angle of Incidence
- Set and Location Lighting
- Controlling Light – Basic Tools and Techniques

Unless you are using specialty cameras such as night vision, thermal, or infrared, you will need to illuminate your subjects, sets, and locations. Light allows us and our cameras to "see" and it will allow you, the filmmaker, to show your story to an audience – not merely with basic exposure, but also with creative purpose and intent. The lighting you design for your films and animations can guide your audience where to look, stress what information to process first, and influence how they feel. Light is a necessary and powerful tool and a key element in the grammar of your shots.

Light as an Element of Composition

In the last chapter we mentioned how creatively placing an area of crisp focus in the frame could lead the eyes of your audience around your shot. This chapter briefly explores how light can be used to do the same thing. Values of light and dark can generate a sense of depth in the 2D frame; create feelings of sadness, happiness, fear and so on; underscore themes about characters; and highlight or obscure the more important subjects in a scene. All of this and more fall within the capabilities of film lighting. It will often be the most powerful creative tool in your filmmaker's toolbox, but that does not mean it has to be the most complex or the most expensive. Learning about and using light effectively is a lifelong process, so let us move ahead and address some of the basics to help get us started on our way.

In daily life, our human visual system is programmed to respond to movement, light, and color. It stands to reason that while viewing a motion picture we would respond to these same visual stimuli, plus sharp focus. Knowing this physiological visual response of humans is a great creative tool for filmmakers to use in constructing engaging shot composition. It is very important for you to realize from the outset that well-planned and well-executed lighting can make or break the visual success of a motion picture project.

When you approach your lighting design for a particular project, you should be thinking about an overall look that fits the genre and works well with the messaging, purpose, and story. Can the lighting underscore or work against thematic tones? Does a character or the story require a particular color palette or quality of light? To what types of lighting equipment do you have access, and what techniques might achieve your lighting requirements? Any project can benefit from a solid lighting plan.

The art and craft of film and video lighting is a huge topic that is covered well by many qualified training manuals and film production text books [see internet and book references on film lighting in Appendix A]. We do not have the luxury of addressing all of the scientific, technical, and aesthetic aspects of light and film lighting here, but we will hit on some of the more important terms and practices involved with the discipline. The following list should set most of us on the right track:

- Light as energy
- Color temperature
- Natural or artificial light

- Quantity of light: sensitivity and exposure
- Quality of light: soft vs hard
- Contrast
- Colors
- Basic character lighting: three-point method
- Motivated lighting: angle of incidence
- Set and location lighting
- Controlling light

Light as an Element of Composition

Light as Energy

No matter what generates it, emits it, or reflects it, light is energy – energy waves of electromagnetic radiation that happen to live in a zone of frequencies known as the **visible spectrum**.

Light itself is invisible, but objects that reflect light can appear white, black, or combinations of colors or hues from violet, blue, green, yellow, orange, and red.

When white light (all color wavelengths combined equally) hits an object which then reflects all wavelengths equally, you see that object as white.

If an object absorbs all light energy wavelengths then the object is seen as black. It reflects no significant light energy for you to detect.

When an object absorbs all colors but reflects only one wavelength (like that of yellow) you see that object as yellow.

Not all light sources emit pure white light in a balanced spectrum, but luckily we have ways of measuring the color of light.

As with many forms of energy, light can dissipate across distances. A light fixture close to your scene or subject can deliver its light energy more efficiently and at an appropriate level for its intensity (wattage, lumens or lux). As you move that same fixture further from your scene or subject, the effective output remains the same, but the light energy that reaches your subject will be diminished. Be aware of this "drop off" when you place your lights and/or your subject in your shooting environment.

Color Temperature

Color temperature, along the scale of **degrees Kelvin**, helps us understand what color the invisible light is. It is measured in thousands of degrees (roughly 1000 to 20,000 degrees Kelvin). Without going into all the science behind it, you should just understand that there are two main colors of concern along the Kelvin scale for film and video shooting: amber/orange and blue. The numbers associated most commonly with their color temperatures are 3200 and 5600 degrees Kelvin, respectively. Film lights (with lamps or light bulbs manufactured specifically for use in motion picture production that have tungsten filaments) generally emit light that is at 3200 degrees Kelvin. Noontime sunlight is roughly around 5600 degrees Kelvin. The lower the number of degrees Kelvin (0–4000-ish), the more red/amber/orange the light will be. It is often described as "warm" light. The higher the number of degrees Kelvin (4000–10,000 and above), the bluer, or "cooler," the light will appear (Figure 4.1).

The terms "warm" and "cool," used above, do not refer to the actual temperature of anything. They describe the perceived psychological and emotional value given to those color groups by humans who experience them. Reddish/amber can conjure "warm" or "stimulating" feelings associated with firelight, candles, sunlight, natural brown leathers, etc. The "cooler" blue values tend to be seen as "calming" and are associated with overcast skies, moonlight, ice fields, and even morgues, etc. Audiences have grown to accept (and to some degree even expect) these color values in film scenes involving such elements. We will discuss more creative uses of color in film production in the Color section of this chapter.

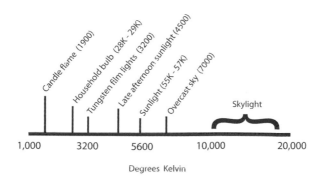

FIGURE 4.1 The Kelvin scale showing various examples of common color temperatures.

Color Balance of Your Camera

These values of degrees Kelvin are extremely important to motion picture production whether you are using digital video or emulsion film. Each, as a light sensitive medium, is balanced by the manufacturer to want to see either 3200 degree light as "white" or 5600 degree light as "white." For emulsion films, the balance toward 3200 is referred to as **tungsten balanced**, and the film that seeks 5600 degree light as white light is called **daylight balanced**. The digital light sensors in most video cameras and mobile phones [either **charge-coupled devices** (**CCD**s) or complementary metal oxide semiconductor (**CMOS**)] are also calibrated to record tungsten (3200) or daylight (5600). Older video cameras often have a setting for both, but modern cameras can usually calibrate across the entire range of color temperatures.

Some video cameras require that you "white balance" or "neutral balance" the light entering the camera. This can be accomplished by placing a white card under the light sources you are using, zooming the lens in on this white card until it fills the frame, properly setting the exposure and then setting the "white balance" (usually a button found on the camera body or under the menu settings). Whatever the color temperature the light is that you are using, it will now be seen as "color neutral" by the camera — blues will be blue, reds will be red, and whites will look white, etc.

Natural and Artificial Light

Tungsten lighting is so called because tungsten is the chief element in the metallic filament inside the light bulb (or lamp) that glows "white" hot when electricity is run through it. Many people also refer to this kind of light as film or quartz lighting and it is used chiefly in film and video making. To clarify, however, any kind of light source generated by a man-made device can be called an **artificial light** even though it is not emitting 3200 degree Kelvin waves. Examples could include neon lights, a household incandescent or CFL, overhead fluorescent lighting, a computer or TV LCD screen, **LED**s, street lights, car headlamps, a flashlight, and so on. Because artificial lights produce a wide range of color temperature light, try to use the special film lights for your shooting or use all the same kind of lamp in multiple fixtures so you at least have consistent color output on your scene.

The daylight calibration derives its name from its chief supplier, daylight, and it may fall under the category of **natural light**. Natural light sources include the sun, the moon (reflected sunlight), and flames, and they too can all have different Kelvin temperatures.

However, there are man-made film lighting fixtures (**HMI**s and new LEDs) that also emit light waves around the 5600–6000 degree Kelvin ballpark. These lights can be used to augment or replace natural sunlight/daylight. When shooting outdoors, an easy way to add to your light levels is to bounce or reflect the free and available light (more on this technique later).

Correcting or Mixing Colors on Set

You must be careful, however, which light sources you use with which color tempera-ture-balanced film or video. If you give tungsten-balanced media (film or video) daylight energy waves, it will record with a bluish tint. If you give a daylight-balanced medium tungsten light, it will record as reddish (Figure 4.2). Generally, you should match the color temperature of your light source with the color temperature sensitivity of your film or video medium. There is also a wide range of colored gelatin sheets that you can place on the lighting fixtures to alter or correct the color output of the raw lamp so that it matches your camera's balance and other light sources.

It is also possible to mix natural and artificial lighting for creative or dramatic purposes. Often you will see a nighttime interior scene with warm household lights juxtaposed with cooler "blue-ish moonlight" coming in the windows. There are many ways to play with the camera's balance and the artificial or natural light color temperatures on your set. And you should not rely on them during production, but there are also some very capable software tools you can use to help your video color balance in post-production – a process called color correction or grading.

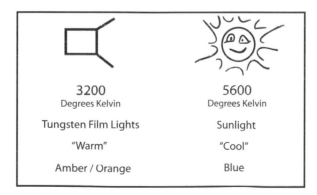

3200	5600
Degrees Kelvin	Degrees Kelvin
Tungsten Film Lights	Sunlight
"Warm"	"Cool"
Amber / Orange	Blue

FIGURE 4.2   The two main color temperatures for video and film.

Color Temperature

Quantity of Light: Sensitivity

How well do you see during the daytime? How well do you see at night? Our vision is quite good in daylight, and, when given an adequate adjustment period, pretty good in darkness as well. The light receptors in our eyes (rods and cones on the retina) do have a wide range of "exposure" sensitivity. Of course, just detecting light is one thing but forming a good image is another. We have a particular minimum threshold for reacting to light energy – a bias towards needing more light to see properly in both luminance (brightness) and chrominance (color) values. The majority of emulsion films and video sensors are modeled after our own vision capabilities – they are also biased towards needing a fair amount of light to create a quality image.

Unlike our eyes, most light-sensitive material is manufactured to have one "recommended" or "best performance" light sensitivity rating or "speed." We say "recommended" because although the technology is calibrated to this rating for best results, you are free to creatively deviate from this suggested value. It is most often represented by a number calculated by the International Organization for Standardization (ISO rating), or it is noted in the form of an exposure index (EI) or perhaps even an ASA or ANSI rating. These light sensitivity ratings are a scale of numbers. Lower values (50, 64, 100, etc.) indicate a large amount of light needed for proper imaging, while higher values (400, 800, 1600, etc.) require less light to react and form an image. Many digital video sensors are built to a moderate/fast sensitivity of 320. DSLRs and other more "processor-based" imagers can dial in a very wide variety of ratings that you get to choose in the settings.

Quantity of Light: Exposure

With this sensitivity rating in mind, you can provide your camera's light-sensitive medium (CCD, CMOS, film) with the manufacturer's recommended quantity of light and yield a good image. This is known as achieving "proper" **exposure**. You have exposed the imager to the "right" amount of light. We've gone quotation happy in this section because so much of this practice is subjective – relative to the technology's abilities and your story's creative visual needs. Traditionally, a "proper" exposure represents an image with a wide-ranging **gray scale** (dark areas to bright areas, see Figure 4.9) and a faithful depiction of color values. However, what is appropriate for one project may be totally inappropriate for the visual mood or tone of another.

Keeping things simple, the basic exposure for your camera's sensitivity settings is affected by several factors:

- Quantity of light on your scene – Are you using very bright, direct sunlight, many large film lights, or just a single candle flame? The amount of light you place on your actors, set and location helps determine how your image is created in the camera. Typically, more light is better than less light because it is easier to lessen the amount of light you have but it can be difficult to add to it.

- Camera aperture – How much light do you let through your camera lens? The iris (often related to the f/stop scale) controls the quantity of light entering the camera to expose the image sensor. "Opened up" (larger aperture) lets in more light, while "stopped down" (smaller aperture) lets in less light (see Figure 4.3).

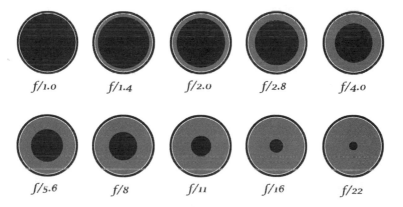

$f/1.0$ $f/1.4$ $f/2.0$ $f/2.8$ $f/4.0$

$f/5.6$ $f/8$ $f/11$ $f/16$ $f/22$

FIGURE 4.3   The iris scale, or aperture settings of a lens. Note that the larger openings seem to have lower numbers, but, in fact, all f/stop numbers are fractions under "1/" so 1/2 is indeed larger than 1/16.

- Shutter speed/Exposure time – Some cameras are set to 1/30th of a second for each frame, others are 1/60th, and still others have a variable electronic shutter speed to control the "length of time" the sensor is exposed to the light. Higher shutter speeds create more exact renderings of the image in motion, but require more light on the scene to do so. Lower shutter speeds require less light for exposure, but can cause motion blur between frames.

Except for the amount of light on your scene, most video cameras have auto settings and take care of these choices for you. Certain models have manual settings where you get to control your iris, shutter, and so forth. Either way, you most likely have a **light meter** built into the video camera which, when calibrated to your medium's light sensitivity rating, is used to help measure the quantity of light reflecting off your scene and recommends the appropriate iris setting given the shutter speed. With manual options you have greater creative control over how the lit scene gets recorded by the camera. If you recall, **neutral density** filters (some built-in to camera electronics) will help you lessen the amount of light hitting your sensor. **Gain** control is also present on many cameras, allowing you to increase the amount of electronic processing the video signal receives. Although it may appear to help make a darker scene brighter, it comes at the cost of image quality.

If you provide too much light to your camera, by flooding your filming environment with large quantities of light energy, by opening up to the largest iris setting, or cranking up your ISO setting, you can **overexpose** the image. You shift the gray scale up to show only middle gray and white and there will be no black values (deep shadows, etc.) in the frame. The resulting image will be too bright and have "blown out" high-lights (Figure 4.4). Of course, your story may call for such a visual treatment of a scene. Filmmakers have used overexposure to indicate being in Heaven, a flashback or dream sequence, a POV from a character who has been drugged, and so forth. Overexposure is also used a great deal in music videos. Be aware that most video cameras do not react well to large amounts of light and will not record proper details in those bright areas of your frame. If your video image has serious overexposure (burn out in the highlights) then it will stay that way forever because there is no fix for this lack of image data in post-production color correction.

If you do not provide enough light to your image sensor, either by shooting in a very dark environment or by stopping down your iris, you will **underexpose** the image. It will be, overall, too dark. The gray scale shifts down to mostly dark and only up to mid-gray without having any bright or white areas in the image at all (Figure 4.4). Details in the dark areas of the frame cannot be recorded and color values suffer as well. You

FIGURE 4.4   The range of exposures. A – Overexposure blows out highlight regions of the image. B – Averaged exposure should represent all portions of the gray scale. C – Underexposure loses details in the shadow regions. Proper exposure is whatever the story calls for. Creatively speaking, you may wish to severely under- or overexpose a few shots in your film due to story requirements, but most shots should be in a moderate range of exposure.

may decide that a certain scene for your story could benefit from being underexposed, but be aware that video cameras will often produce "video noise" (like film grain) when you do not provide enough energy to make the imager react properly. The image can look muddy with speckled, muted colors popping around the dark areas. It may be better to provide plenty of light to the subjects you do wish to see and stop down the iris. The brighter things you care about will be exposed well and the darker areas can reveal more detail but retain a truer representation of "black values."

Achieving basic exposure of the visual elements within your frame is just the beginning. Achieving creative control over how much light you put on your film set, where you place it, and what quality of light you use is your real goal. As you have seen, light affects many other creative choices.

One easy lesson to remember about the quantity of light and exposure is that the more **illumination** you have available on set, the larger your depth of field (DOF) can be (think daytime exterior). You would have to "close down" your camera's iris to block out more of the available bright light, which, in turn, increases your DOF. The less light you have, the more shallow your depth of field will be when you "open up" your iris. So purposefully limiting the light used for your scene's exposure can not only illuminate certain areas as needed, but it can also creatively alter what is in or out of focus in your shot (Figure 4.5).

Quantity of Light: Exposure

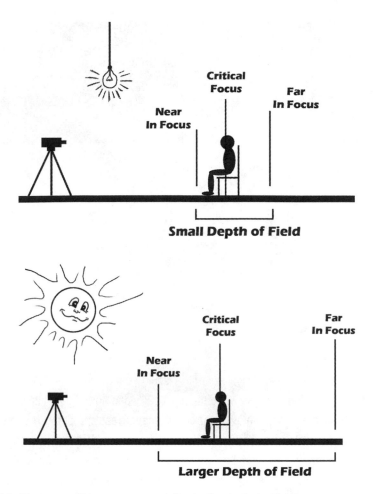

FIGURE 4.5 The amount of light on your scene can directly affect the depth of field focus range.

Quality of Light: Hard Versus Soft

Beyond the color temperature and the quantity of light, most filmmakers are also concerned with the quality of the light. Not how good or how bad the lighting looks, although that is extremely important, but how hard or how soft the beams of light are that illuminate the actors and the set.

Hard Light

If you have ever stood outside on a cloudless day you no doubt noticed how distinct your shadow was. A hard-edged shadow is the primary giveaway that you are using a **hard light** source. The sun, as a single **point source** light, sends its light waves to Earth and, for the most part, they are parallel to one another. They create a single, deep shadow with well-defined edges (Figure 4.6).

These parallel light waves are very **directional**. As they leave their source and encounter some physical object, they will illuminate that one near surface brightly, get blocked by that object, and cause a hard-edged shadow on the background. This does not mean that hard lights (with parallel rays) are brighter than softer lights; they are just more focused. Hard light can cause objects in your frame to "pop" off the screen or stand out from other objects. Because it is so directional and therefore more controllable you can pinpoint your light beam to strike very precise areas of your set. When placed at the side or back of your film set they can create rims, halos, or kicks of light around people or on surfaces. Hard light, depending on its application, can also create scary, dangerous, harsh, or mysterious environments (think film noir, horror, etc.). It is often less pleasing on the human face and can cause harsh eye socket shadows (top light), highlight skin imperfections (think the surface of the moon), and, from the front, flatten features, and so on.

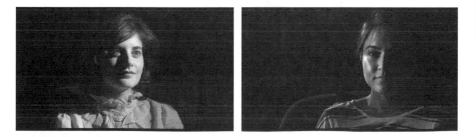

FIGURE 4.6   Examples of hard light

The biggest and most readily available hard light source is our sun (on a cloudless day). It is free to use, so take advantage of it during your shooting as much as possible – just be aware of a few factors. Consider the sun's direction (angle from up in the sky) and where it puts the shadows. What is the actual exposure/iris setting and your resulting depth of field? How long will it take to shoot your scene coverage versus how much time is left in usable sunlight? Did you look at the weather forecast? Is there impending cloud cover that can change your lighting look?

In addition to the sun, hard light sources include the open face, the enclosed Fresnel unit, HMIs and new LED spots.

Soft Light

Soft light is very diffused light. If you were to go outside on a very cloudy, overcast day (with no direct sunlight visible) you would not easily see your shadow at all or, if you did, it would be very faint and not hard-edged. The hard, parallel rays of sunlight hit the clouds in the atmosphere and then get all jumbled up and diverted into many different directions and bounce around our atmosphere. This diffused light of multidirectional energy waves comes at objects from many sides and therefore it illuminates more evenly all around – not hard and directional from one side but soft and diffused from several sides.

Almost any light source can be made into a soft light by diffusing it or bouncing it off bright or white walls or ceilings (Figure 4.7). Soft light sources tend to be more flattering to the human face because they cause little in the way of deep shadows. The light seems to wrap around the curves, bumps and contours of the facial structures (brows, nose, cheekbones, etc.), smoothing out the surfaces. For interior scenes, soft light may feel more natural because most light fixtures in reality (in homes, offices and stores, etc.) emit non-parallel rays. Because of this, soft lighting can imply a sense of warmth, friendliness, or romance when used in motion pictures (Figure 4.8).

Soft film lighting fixtures include fluorescent lights, anything with a frosted lamp, and any light housing that diffuses the light energy either by passing it through a diffusing material or bouncing it off curved, internal surfaces. Actual hard light fixtures can be softened by bouncing their directional beams off a bright but marginally textured surface or by passing the beam through a diffusion gel sheet or white silk flag before it falls on the subject.

FIGURE 4.7   Reflecting or Bouncing light off of bright or white matte finish surfaces (like bounce cards or acoustic tiled ceilings) will diffuse the light rays and soften the light falling on your subject. An easy way to also get usable Fill light from your Key source.

FIGURE 4.8   Examples of soft light.

Quality of Light: Hard Versus Soft

Contrast

The relative differences between light areas and dark areas within your frame are referred to as the image's **contrast**. Most often, the image creator's goal is to have a well-balanced contrast within the frame where there are bright regions, dark regions, and a good representation of "gray scale" tones in between (Figure 4.9). An image with good contrast is said to have "snap." A **high contrast** image is one that contains areas that are both very bright and very dark, but it lacks middle gray values in between the two extremes. High contrast images can be described as "moody." A **low contrast** image contains more even lighting levels across the whole frame such that the delineation between light and dark regions is not well defined. Mostly shades of middle gray, the low contrast image can look flat and bland.

FIGURE 4.9   The gray scale from black, through mid-gray, up to white.

Low-key Lighting

High contrast, snappy or punchy, lighting schemes can make for more dramatic or suspenseful imagery, but they also yield more depth to your frame. The interplay of light and areas of deep shadow across the foreground, middle ground, and background of your shots helps create a layering effect within the set's deep physical space. The irregularity of objects in the frame, including the human face and body, gains a relief or modeling from these pockets of light and dark, which helps them achieve a three-dimensional appearance on the two-dimensional film frame. This type of lighting design is often called **low-key lighting**. Hard, directional beams of light (from one or several directions) striking precise locations or objects in your scene can help create this visual style (see Figure 4.10).

FIGURE 4.10   Examples of low-key lighting schemes. Strong areas of darkness and brightness.

High-key Lighting

Low contrast, flat or even, lighting schemes can make images seem more open, friendly, or "brighter," but they also yield a flatter, less visually separated frame. Often, the point of low contrast, or **high-key lighting**, is to provide overall even illumination so that all elements of the frame are visible to the viewer. Talk show, news broadcast, and situation comedy sets are often lit in a low contrast fashion. This way, the multiple cameras that record the events can all receive proper exposure without the need to continually adjust lighting levels on the set. What you gain in even visibility you lose in dramatic flavor. Additionally, the 2D frame, including all objects in it, will appear flatter and, in the opinion of many, less visually interesting (Figure 4.11).

FIGURE 4.11   Examples of high-key lighting schemes. More evenly lit overall.

Contrast

Color

Color is another great creative tool for a filmmaker. Your visual plan for your motion picture project should include color considerations from the outset as there are many color choices to be made during production and post-production. This is especially true if you are creating an animation, and you have to be aware of every color of every character and background.

The quality or "look" of your recorded color imagery is related to many factors. The type of camera you are using (image sensor color sampling, compression processing, bit depth, etc.), the quality and quantity of light energy you use for exposure, and the actual colors of the wardrobe, set dressing, exterior environment and so forth all play a role. We will not dig into the numerous technologies and processing algorithms here, but instead we will touch on some of the basic characteristics of color and how you might use them in your films.

As we know from our talk about light energy and color temperature, the colors of light have particular wavelengths. These energy wavelengths are interpreted as electronic voltages in both video cameras and on computer editing systems and show as particular **hues**. Color **saturation** is directly related to how much light energy you have on your scene and the "color reflectance" values of the object being recorded. If you have very little energy on the scene you will generate low color voltages and the colors will render as muted or de-saturated. If you have a larger amount of light energy the voltages are higher and the colors will be more saturated.

Saturated colors (deeper, more vivid) in combination with a higher contrast level will make the image "snappy" and more vibrant. Children's programming, cartoons, commercials, music videos, and musical theatrical films can all use highly saturated color palettes. They generally make an audience feel happy, bright, energized, and so forth. Low contrast, low energy images can appear more de-saturated, muted or grayish. Images with this look lack that visual "snap" and can seem somber, dull, or low energy to an audience.

Colors can be used as symbols or identifiers as well. Countries have colorful flags, sports teams have colorful jerseys, and film environments can have colors associated with them as well. The "soulless" financial executive sits in his modern, high-rise office depicted as steely-blue-gray, while our small town hero is shown around lush green lawns and warm/brown natural woods. The nuclear bunker is a jaundiced yellow-green.

The Princess's rooms are deep reds and warm golden hues. The color palettes of these places not only help orient the viewer as to where, physically within the film world, they are, but also help them feel a certain way towards the people or events seen in those environments. Additional subtextual information is being conveyed to the audience through these color choices. [see color theory reference book in Appendix A].

Similar color treatments can be done for a character's wardrobe. The angel on Earth, whom no one knows to be an angel, always wears a white suit. The possessed little girl in your horror film always has a red ribbon in her hair. Or it could be a very subtle choice and you withhold a particular color from a character throughout the story.

Beyond the basics of accepted color treatments (blue for moonlight and cooler temperature locations, such as a meat freezer or the Arctic Circle – or amber for warm, safe places, such as a family home or a candle-lit dinner for two) a filmmaker can use colors to underscore a story's themes or represent a character. The important thing to remember is that you should always be conscious of the colors in your frame, whether you are using them creatively or not.

Color

Basic Character Lighting: Three-Point Method

How one uses hard light and soft light to gain selective exposure on talent and on set is the fun part of creative lighting for composition. There are innumerable ways for you to place light on your actors, and hopefully, over your career as a filmmaker, you will have the opportunity to experiment with many of them. Starting off on solid ground is useful, however, so we are going to explore the most basic standard in subject illumination — the **three-point lighting method**.

The three points actually refer to three distinct jobs that lighting fixtures perform when put into particular placements around the film set. Rather than describing the light's properties, these terms define their purposes.

> KEY—**Key light** is the one light source around which you build your lighting scheme. It provides the main illumination to your film set or location. You "key" your other lights (quantity and quality) off this main source. The key light may live anywhere around your subject, but it traditionally is placed 45 degrees (horizontally and vertically) off the axis of the camera's lens and above the height of the talent's head.
>
> FILL—**Fill light** is a light source used to help control contrast. The light energy that is used "fills in" the shadows often created by the brighter key light. The traditional physical placement of the fill light is on the opposite side of the subject from the key light, roughly 45 degrees (horizontally) off lens axis.
>
> BACK—**Back light** is the light that defines an edge, or halo effect, around the backside of the subject. Because it lives behind the subject (opposite side of the film set from the camera's lens) and provides a light "rim" to the outline of the subject, the back light serves to separate objects from the background and enhance the illusion of depth within the film frame.

The quantity of light from these three light sources must be enough to achieve exposure on the scene. Clearly, the key light will provide the most illumination. The fill light will contribute varying degrees of additional illumination, depending on how low or how high a contrast difference you would like to have (how much or how little shadow). The back light need only apply enough glow to the edge of the subject to "read" or be recorded by the medium (Figures 4.12 and 4.13).

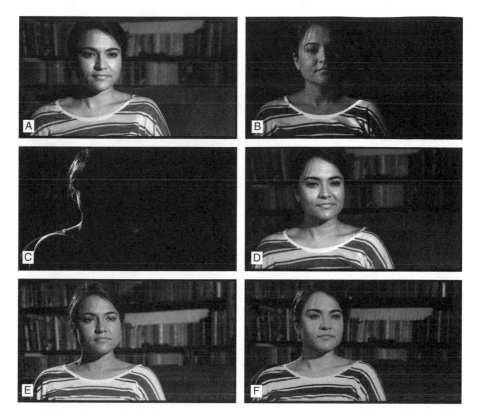

FIGURE 4.12   The evolution of the three point lighting method in several combinations. A – Key only. B – Fill only. C – Back only. D – Key + Fill. E – Key + Back. F – Key + Fill + Back.

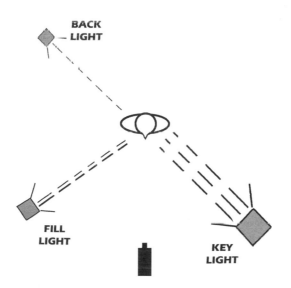

FIGURE 4.13   An overhead schematic of the three point lighting fixture placement in relation to subject and camera.

Contrast Ratio or Lighting Ratio

The lighting contrast specific to the human subject is a relationship known as the **contrast ratio** or the ratio of the key + fill side of the face to the fill side of the face only (often shown as Key+Fill:Fill). The quantity of light can be measured with a handheld light meter, but you really should develop your "eye" to gauge the relative amounts of light on each side of the face – is there more or less shadow present? Even light levels on each side would be a 1:1 lighting ratio and would create a high key scene of even and flat lighting. Differing quantities of light on each side may yield a higher contrast ratio, such as 4:1 or 8:1, and would be described as a low key scene with more deep shadow regions on one side of the face (Figure 4.14).

Motivated Lighting – Angle of Incidence

In fictional narrative cinematography, the lighting you see is generally **motivated;** meaning it is supposed to be generated by some source within the "reality" of the film world you are watching. A desk lamp, a computer screen, a lantern, even the sun itself are all examples of objects that can motivate light on a film set. This does not mean that these "sources" actually contribute to the illumination of your scene (although they can). It is the film lighting fixtures job to add light to your frame and make it look as though the motivating sources are actually providing the exposure.

FIGURE 4.14   A – Image with 1:1 lighting ratio. B – Image with "average" lighting ratio. C – Image with high lighting ratio.

Where you place your film lights around your set is partially dictated by the location of these motivating light sources within the film's world. The point of origin for a beam of light determines its **angle of incidence.** If the light is supposed to be coming from a light fixture in the ceiling, then the film light must have an angle of incidence from higher than the subject's head – from above, or top lighting. If someone stands next to a campfire, then the film firelight effect must have a lower angle of incidence and come from below the level of the subject's head.

Front Lighting

Just as you know that the camera can be placed around the subject along imaginary horizontal or vertical circles, lighting fixtures can be placed in similar ways – in this case, think of them more as hemispheres above the subject's waist and below it. When the lamp head is in the upper hemisphere and near the recording camera's neutral angle on action (or lens axis), it is called **front lighting**. If the subject's face is open towards camera, this lighting tends to flatten out the features by evenly illuminating all surfaces. This technique is used in fashion portraiture of women because it diminishes the presence of the nose while fully informing the details of the eyes and mouth. The loss of shadow across the face and body can also limit the perceived dramatic impression of the audience and reduce the illusion of 3D in your composition (see Figure 4.15).

Depending on the height of the lamp head in this scenario, you may also cause a shadow on any visible surface behind the subject being front lit. Upper hemisphere lamp heads with a higher angle of incidence force the shadows down along the floor. Any lights at or below the talent's physical height will throw shadows across and up

FIGURE 4.15   Example of even, flat front lighting. Notice how it smoothes out the bony features of the face.

the set, which can be visible to the camera lens and are often not visually pleasing nor part of your visual plan. In general, shadows of actors are not welcome on film sets, unless you place them there on purpose because they fulfill a creative or thematic purpose in the story.

Side Lighting

If we continue our way around the imaginary circle and place a lamp head 90 degrees away from the camera, it is called **side lighting.** This holds especially true if the light source is at the same height as the talent's head. Examples might be a bedside lamp, a window, light coming through a doorway from another room, sunrise and sunset. Hard sidelight can generate a half-bright half-dark face split along the bridge of the nose (Figure 4.16). Without any fill light, this lighting style makes a bold statement and can conjure feelings of mystery, half-truths or a split personality. The higher you raise the lighting fixture the more it will resemble traditional upper hemisphere lighting from above.

Lights from Behind

When the light is behind the subject, opposite the circle from the camera lens, it is often called a backlight. As discussed earlier under three-point lighting, the backlight helps separate the subject from the background. Traditionally it has a higher angle of incidence. If the lamp head is placed between 90 degrees and 180 degrees it may be called a **kicker** or a **rim light** – highlighting the edges of the hair, shoulders, and sometimes the jaw bone (see Figure 4.17). A hard light source may work best for this

FIGURE 4.16   Example of hard side lighting.

FIGURE 4.17   Backlighting can rim a subject and add highlights to the ground or set dressing.

"hot kick" lighting glint, as softer backlights tend to yield a more even halo effect with less punch. Backlighting is also used to illuminate water vapor from a "fog machine," falling rain, and wet pavement or shiny polished floor coverings like marble, hardwood, and linoleum.

Lights from Other Places

Most light sources in the real world, and subsequently in the film world, come from above and slightly away – somewhere in the upper hemisphere. Many lights in our public and private spaces come from above and sometimes from directly overhead. This light that comes from directly above (**top lighting**) is not always replicated exactly in film lighting. Either hard or soft, the top light causes the brow ridges on most faces to block the light from the eye sockets, putting the eyes into deep shadow. A small "moustache" shadow will also be cast on the upper lip by the nose. By keeping the eyes of the character in deep shadow you take away one very important visual means for the audience to relate to the character. If you can't see the eyes, you probably cannot trust this person (see Figure 4.18).

Conversely, if you light from below, you are creating a rather unnatural lighting effect, as very few lights actually exist below the level of our heads in daily life. **Under lighting**, as this is called, causes the structure of the human face to take on a scary or ghoulish appearance and, therefore, is often used in horror films (see Figure 4.19).

FIGURE 4.18 Top lighting can obscure the subject's eyes.

FIGURE 4.19 Under lighting can turn good people into evil people.

Set and Location Lighting

Placing light on your set or location (on the walls, furnishings, floor, trees, cars, etc.) is often just as important as lighting the faces of your subjects. Certainly you need to add light to your set for general exposure, but placing light on specific areas of the set or location can add to the ambience of the scene, and change its tone or mood. When shooting dark environments or night scenes, placing lights in the deep background can also help create an illusion of 3D space by drawing your viewer's eyes into the "depth" of the shot. They can also "rim" a subject and help further separate them from the darker background and so forth.

If you have a lighter background on your film set and only illuminate that background and not your subject in the middle ground, you will create what is called the **silhouette** effect (Figure 4.20). Exposing your camera for the well-lit background, and leaving your talent's face in darkness (with no fill light), you force the silhouette. The camera is told to see the bright background as "normal" and that shifts the exposure on the dark face into the underexposure values of blackness. Use this for a sense of mystery, intrigue, or to protect the identity of an informant.

Any light fixture on your set that actually works and emits light that helps toward exposure and the overall creative lighting design is called a **practical**. Its job is to appear within the frame and provide light to the scene. Most often practical lamps are not bright enough to generate good exposure levels of light, so they are usually accent lights that provide points of visual interest around the set or act as motivators for other

Set and Location Lighting

FIGURE 4.20   Whether you are protecting the innocent or creating an air of mystery, the silhouette keeps the subject in constant shadow while the background remains visible.

(off screen) larger film lights that raise exposure levels on the set. These augmenting film lights would need to be of matching light quality, color, and angle. Practical lights can also be a good source of motivation for creative color usage, as in "warm" amber firelight, "cool" blue refrigerator interior light, deep red neon light, and so forth.

If you are making a **period piece** from the days before electricity, or your story involves a power outage, then you may use light sources such as lanterns, candles, firelight, flashlights, automobile headlamps, mobile phones, or any light that is battery or solar powered or run off a back-up generator. Most recent digital video cameras can get a decent exposure with lower light conditions. If you cannot or choose not to augment the practical source with film light illumination, then it helps if you shoot most of your shots in medium to close-up framing with minimal camera to subject distances. Light energy "falls off" in its intensity over distance, so a faint light source will just look more faint from further away. Keep it close to faces and to camera for best results in exposure (see Figure 4.21).

Almost any other light-emitting or light-reflecting source can be used as a practical in almost any other film story situation. The important thing to remember is that effective output, intensity of light, may not actually be enough for exposure, so additional film lights will be needed to add levels but maintain the illusion that the light is coming from the practical fixtures. You should also be aware that color temperatures of these practical lights can vary widely and some color balancing may be necessary.

FIGURE 4.21   A practical. This functional lighting source on set actually helps give the image exposure.

Controlling Light – Basic Tools and Techniques

A film lighting fixture is rather like a big bucket of light. Set it up, plug it in, point it to where you want the light to go and turn it on. If your goal were to just get exposure levels on your subject, then you'd be done with your lighting. Fortunately for all of us, there is more to it than that – or at least there should be.

Sculpting with your lights – applying their energy where and how you want – is often the best approach to creating great-looking images. There are many tools and techniques to help you do this (far more than we could list in this book). **Grip equipment** will be your best friend to help control your lights on set. You'll become familiar with such things as C-stands, solid flags, nets, silks, and the ever-popular cucoloris. If you do not have access to grip equipment then there are things that you can do just with the film lights you might have.

Most hard light fixtures have "barn doors" (metal blades) that close over the output hole and knock down the amount of light coming out of the unit. These doors can also help sculpt the light. Hard lights also typically have a knob for Flood/Spot that spreads the beam out over a larger area or focuses it in to a small "hot" spot. Hard lights, in general, being more directional, are easier to control, cut, block off, and so on. As mentioned earlier, hard lights can also become soft light sources by using diffusion gels, **bounce boards**, **bounce cards**, or **shiny reflectors**.

Soft light, being less directional, is not as easy to control. You will need larger "blockers" to keep the diffuse soft light off certain areas of your film set [see Internet and book Grip references in Appendix A].

Controlling Light – Basic Tools and Techniques

Light ... and the Light Years of Learning

This chapter has covered just some of the basic concepts in the art, science, and craft of film lighting. It is hoped that as you develop your overall skills with shot composition you will be expanding your abilities in the use of creative lighting as well. You cannot have one without the other. As you will grow to understand more and more, everything in filmmaking is related to everything else. Light relates to lens optics, aperture, CMOS/CCD/film sensitivity, exposure, ratios, color, emotional audience reaction, thematic/character interpretation, and so on and so on. Let us just say that you should always be conscious of how you are lighting your shots. Your lighting and compositional choices need to serve your "story" and not fight against it or leave it wanting or incomplete. What you choose to reveal to the audience or hide from them will yield more or less information, more or less understanding, and more or less enjoyment of your project.

Chapter Four – Review

1. Lighting is one of the most powerful and creative tools available to the filmmaker.

2. Light is energy – energy waves of electromagnetic radiation that happen to live in a zone of frequencies known as the **visible spectrum**.

3. The color temperature of light is measured in degrees on the Kelvin scale. Film lighting is approximately 3200 degrees Kelvin and noontime sunlight is roughly 5600 degrees Kelvin.

4. A camera set for tungsten light color balance will see daylight as bluish. A camera set for daylight balance will see tungsten film lights as amberish.

5. Most manufacturers build their video cameras to have a particular exposure index or ISO rating for sensitivity to light levels (e.g. EI 320). Some cameras can have a wide range of ISO settings (e.g. 100–6400). Lower numbers mean more light is needed for the imager to react. Higher ISO/EI numbers mean less light is needed for an acceptable exposure on the image.

6. Image exposure is affected by the amount of light on the subject, lens aperture, sensitivity rating of the recording medium, and the shutter speed or time of exposure.

7. Neutral density filters lower the quantity of light hitting the camera's imager, but they do not alter the quality of light (color, etc.).

8. Hard light comes from sources with very directional, parallel beams of light waves, like the sun on a cloudless day.

9. Soft light comes from sources with very diffused or scattered beams of light waves, like a cloudy day.

10. Contrast is a reference to the amount of very dark, mid-gray and very bright areas in your image. High contrast is mostly black and white with very little gray. Low contrast is mostly gray tones with very little pure black or pure white in the image.

11. Color refers to a particular hue or a palette of hues (ROYGBIV), and to the associated saturation or intensity of that color wavelength.

12. Choosing a certain color palette for your film will help show your story on a thematic level.

13. The traditional three-point lighting scheme for video is: Key, Fill, and Back. Each light does a job and can be placed in many regions around your subject.

14. The placement of a lighting fixture (or light source) and the placement of the subject in relation to that light fixture dictate the light's angle of incidence. High angle for top lighting and low angle for under lighting. The standard key light is 45 degrees above the subject's head and about 45 degrees off axis from camera lens. In reality, you may place the key light wherever you wish provided it suits the "look" of your scene.

15. Practical lights are light sources on the film set (like a desk lamp, computer monitor, etc.) that actually emit light and add to the overall exposure and "look" of the image.

16. Grip equipment (C-stands, flags, nets, bounce boards, etc.) help you control the quantity and quality of light used on your film set.

Chapter Four – Exercises & Projects

1. Take two series of photographs with any digital still camera. Series 1 – Find any interior space that has a window to the outside. Photograph this interior space from an angle where you do NOT see out the window – in the morning, in the mid-afternoon, and at dusk. Series 2 – Record images of any exterior space in the morning, in the mid-afternoon, and at dusk. Compare the quantity of light and the quality of light from each location at the three different times of day. What do you notice?

2. Acquire at least three or four different subjects (a mix of male/female, young/old, etc. would be good). It would be best to perform all of the following during one session.

   If you have access to film lights of some kind, set up a standard three-point lighting scheme and make it look as good as possible on the first subject. Record some video of that set-up. Then, without changing anything about the lights or camera, sit your next subject in the same place and record some video of that person. Do this process for all subjects. Watch your video and note what worked and what didn't for each subject.

   Return your camera to the same position if you moved it for image review, sit your second subject again and tweak the lights to improve the look. Do the same process for each remaining subject; sitting, tweaking, recording improved "look." Take note of what was different about each subject and what you had to do to the lights in order to get the best look.

3. Set up an MCU on a subject in some room where you can control the lighting. With your camera in place and your subject seated, darken the room. Have an assistant hold a desk lamp or powerful flashlight and move it slowly around your subject from different heights (above/below) and angles (front/back/side). Review the recorded video results and take note of how the light from different angles of incidence interacted with your subject's facial structures (nose, eyes, brow, chin), hair, and clothing.

Chapter Four – Quiz Yourself

1. What is the color temperature (Kelvin scale) for most manufactured film lights?
2. If you are shooting under direct sunlight, typically what color temperature would you need to set on your video camera?
3. What do the terms "white balance" or "neutral balance" refer to?
4. What factors can affect the exposure of your recorded image?
5. How does light quantity affect your recorded image's depth of field?
6. What could you do with a hard light source in order to make it appear as soft light on your subject?
7. What do you call a functional light fixture on a film set that is part of the set dressing or art direction but also contributes light to the set and subject, helping both the exposure and the "look" of the scene?

Chapter Four – Review

Chapter Five
Will It Cut? Shooting for Editing

- Continuity and Performance
- Continuity and Screen Direction
- The 180 Degree Rule
- The 30 Degree Rule
- Coverage with Matching Shots
- Eye-Line Matching

It is important to remember that the planning and recording of your shots is only one part of the visual storytelling process. No matter what type of motion image project you need to create, the scripting stage is the basis for the content – the "story." The careful filmmaker will generate shot lists and storyboards from the script – think of these as the "paper edit." He or she will have a vision of what the final project *should* look like. Production yields the actual picture and sound files that can be accomplished in the reality of shooting. It is during post-production – during the edit – that the story can actually be told – as completely as possible given the production materials that were provided.

There is a certain degree of "psychic" ability required of the filmmaker to pre-think the needs of the edit team. When using the master scene technique or other means of capturing events or actions, the filmmaker must shoot the appropriate coverage of the material and deliver a variety of shots that will best show the story. This is called shooting with editing in mind. What will the editor need to cut to at this point? What would the audience like to see next? How can this information be shown at its best? What shot framing will engage and inform the viewer? Which shot is new, exciting, or cool? Etc., etc., etc.

By recording a variety of shot types (coverage of the scene, event, etc.), you provide the editor with more choices. The editor can then decide at what point the viewing audience will desire fresh information and how much or how little information to show. A scene is created when the editor stitches together all of the important and usable information found in the shots you provided. If the planning went well, and the shot lists were followed, then the editor should have enough valid material to work with and the audience should be able to understand what is going on in the "story." To learn more about the editing process, feel free to review the contents of our companion book, *Grammar of the Edit*.

The Chronology of Production

Production can span days, weeks, or even months, but the resulting images recorded during this time, when edited together, will need to appear as though they were all captured at the same exact time with fluid movement, matching actions, and seamless continuity.

Depending on the availability of locations and people or the quality of weather and so forth, the shooting schedule for a project can be erratic. You may shoot the wide shot of a scene on Monday, but you may not get to the close-up of a supporting actor until the following Thursday. The look of everything (camera positioning, eye-line, costuming, action, etc.) will have to match to be useful to the editor. This also holds true for coverage of exterior and interior shots for the same scene recorded on different days – or even whole scenes shot at different times that must follow one another in the movie.

The individual shots you create on set are just parts of a greater whole. They are pieces of a bigger visual puzzle. In the end, they will have to work with one another, intercut with one another, and show an entire visual story together. Based on the chronological events of the script, the shots (usually recorded out of sequential order) are assembled to make a scene, the scenes can become sequences, which cut together to make an **Act**, and the acts cut together to make an entire motion picture (Figure 5.1). Maintaining consistency in your visual elements is very important and we have a few ways to help you stay aware of the potential glitches.

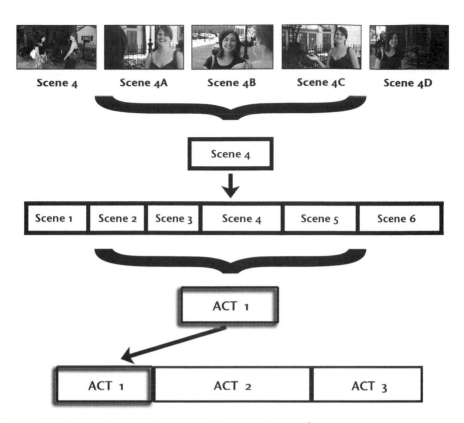

FIGURE 5.1   The evolution of a motion picture's building blocks. Shots > Scene > Act > Motion Picture.

Matching Your Shots in a Scene

When using a single camera to shoot Master Scene coverage of scripted dialogue between multiple characters, you will most likely need to run through the action several times. Start with the wide, run through one character's shots into the close-ups, turn it around and shoot the other character through to close-ups. Recording each pass from a different angle and with a different shot type in your camera set-up will help ensure that the editor has the right material to assemble a meaningful and visually interesting scene. The performances of your actors and the framings of your shots all have to maintain some consistency throughout these repeated runs of the same dialogue and actions.

Continuity of Performance

Having the actors repeat the same actions and dialogue from shot to shot requires that you pay attention to **continuity**. Continuity of performance is the consistent repetition of movement, action, and dialogue by the actor from one camera set-up to the next. If you plan a wide, and a two-shot and then an MS, OTS-MCU and clean single CU for each actor, you will have eight camera set-ups for one simple dialogue scene. That becomes a lot of repetition of dialogue delivery, expressions, body actions, etc. for each actor – and then multiply that by the number of takes you have to do in order to get all of those variables the way that you want them. Yikes!

This gets tricky to follow even when you are paying attention. Recording fewer takes can save time and money and keep your talent fresh. Continuity of performance is often overruled by the quality of performance when an editor assembles the visual material from a scene. A way around some of these performance issues is to use the long-take style of filmmaking. All of the dialogue and action of a scene unfolds in one long master shot, but you shoot no coverage angles of details. There is no need for a cut because there is nothing to cut away to. This style is more like recorded live theatre. The majority of films and television programming, however, does rely on differing shot coverage to visually construct a scene – and continuity will need your attention.

Continuity is not just making sure an actor moves his hand the same way in each take of each shot. Continuity, on a cinematic language level, involves a much wider range of planning and attention to detail as well.

Continuity of Screen Direction

As we know, the camera occupies the "**fourth wall**," allowing the audience a privileged view of locations and actions within the film's "space." It invites them to observe the actions and events that happen inside this other world. As a result, filmmakers have a responsibility to the audience to present a knowable world that conforms to some consistent, and familiar, attributes of the physical world such as up, down, left, right, near, far, and so forth. This prevents the audience from getting spatially confused while watching the motion picture. The horizon line mentioned in Chapter Three is a stabilizing device, but there are other ways that you can keep your audience grounded (Figure 5.2).

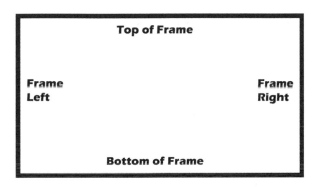

FIGURE 5.2   The motion picture frame has four edges and corresponding areas of interest: frame left, frame right, top of frame, and bottom of frame.

The frame itself is a useful tool. The top, bottom, left, and right edges of the frame act as references of direction for the audience. The character looks off frame left – the car exits frame right. The viewer associates the edges of the frame with the directional attention of a character or the movement of subjects in the film space. It should be clear then that **screen direction** – the left/right or up/down movement of a subject – must be maintained from one shot to the next. Figures 5.3 and 5.6 should help illustrate this concept of continuity of screen direction.

Matching Your Shots in a Scene

FIGURE 5.3 Action shows a person walking toward and exiting frame left.

FIGURE 5.4 Holding on empty frame for a bit just after the person has exited.

FIGURE 5.5 Cut to new shot of new location, but the subject has not arrived just yet.

FIGURE 5.6 New shot plays and the same person continues their walk, but this time they are entering the shot from frame right. Action follows a continuity of screen direction.

The audience member viewing these recorded actions on the screen (Figures 5.3 to 5.6) assumes that there is a larger "film world" just beyond the four edges of the frame. Because this film space exists in its own version of reality, the rules of physical movement (the concept of directional space) should be followed as in reality. (Please keep in mind that cartoons, science fiction/fantasy, and even video game cinematics can take their liberties with this guideline.)

If a person moves away to the left they must keep moving away to the left until we see some change in their movement happen on screen. That is, if, during a shot, a person walks out of frame left, and we don't see them turn towards a new direction, then we could assume a continuation of movement in that established direction – which is to the left. Logic dictates that if that character is still moving to the left when the new shot cuts onto the screen, then they should enter this new shot from frame right. The continuity of screen direction for movement within the film's space has been maintained across the cut.

The Line – Basis for Screen Direction

Not all screen direction is based on large, physical movements. A good deal of important narrative information and spatial relationship data can be discerned by the viewing audience just through their observation of the directions of **attention**. This concept plays a major role in engaging the audience and keeping them actively involved in the images and in the story. Fortunately for filmmakers, humans are "programmed" to watch other humans – for all sorts of cues. One big one is to draw our attention to other things in our shared environment, such as a source of danger. Have you ever been walking down the street when someone near you, someone you don't even know, quickly looks over at something? What do you do? If you're like most people, you look over to see what the other person is looking at. Maybe it's a safety mechanism or maybe it is just curiosity, but we are very good at picking up on connections between people, objects, and patterns in general.

Most often, each subject within the film space pays attention to some other subject or object within the same film space. The couple look at one another (Figure 5.7) – the pool player aligns her shot (Figure 5.8) – the hungry woman eyes the juicy apple (Figure 5.9). The audience is keen on observing these attentions (what some film folks call "the **gaze**"). They use these connections between people and people, people and objects, and so on to establish **lines of direction**, which are also called **sight lines**. Good filmmakers know that an audience wants to follow these lines of attention, so they use this phenomenon to compose shots, help establish narrative meaning, and reinforce spatial relationships within the film's world.

FIGURE 5.7 The young couple look at one another. A line is created.

FIGURE 5.8 The player aligns her pool shot. A line is created.

FIGURE 5.9 The hungry woman spies the best apple. A line is created.

The Imaginary Line – The 180 Degree Rule

The lines of attention need to be understood, established, and respected by the production team. As the audience relies upon these lines to receive and maintain spatial cues, it is very important that they remain consistent throughout the editing of a scene. To help maintain lines of attention and screen direction from shot to shot there is a popular filmmaker's concept known by several names: **180 degree line**, **imaginary line**, **action line**, or **axis of action** (Figure 5.10). As some of the names imply, it is an imaginary line drawn through the shooting location, roughly where all of the main action occurs, and it is established by tracing the sight line of the subject within the shot.

The Line – Basis for Screen Direction

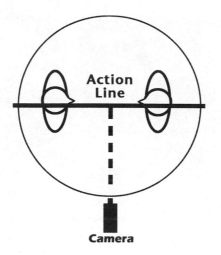

FIGURE 5.10   Bird's-eye view of the action line.

This concept's other name, the **180 degree rule**, will surely help clarify how this all works the way it does and why it is considered important. Much like we discussed the horizontal camera angle circling around your stationary subject back in Chapter Two, we will once again imagine that your subjects are at the center of a large circle. For your first shot, a wide two-shot, the camera is once again positioned at the outer ring of the circle, facing in toward the center where your action is occurring. Now superimpose in your mind the action line cutting across the diameter of the circle from frame left to frame right (Figure 5.11).

Once you have established this first action line, it stays in place for as long as these characters maintain this same attention between themselves. Of course, to shoot the coverage of your subjects you will have to move the camera around the film space, but now you will have to respect this initial axis of action. The line has cut an arc out of the

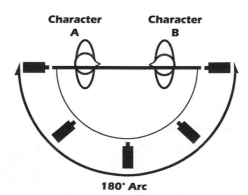

FIGURE 5.11   Keep your camera setups within the 180 degree arc on the near side of the established action line.

imaginary circle that is 180 degrees around from side to side. Your camera must now operate within that 180 degree arc when you set up for your new camera angles and coverage shots (Figure 5.11).

In our example, the first wide shot establishes frame left and frame right and also establishes the line of attention through the film space. Character A is talking with character B. A is sitting frame left and his sight line is traveling from frame left to frame right. B is sitting frame right (receiving A's attention) and is looking back at A (sending a sight line from frame right to frame left). When you frame your shot for a CU single of A you will need to maintain screen direction and continuity. A is still frame left with his attention pointing frame right (even though B is no longer physically visible within the frame). The matching coverage of B in her CU would necessitate a similar treatment. B is framed toward the right, looking over to frame left. The series of shots and overhead diagrams in Figure 5.12 should help clarify this practice.

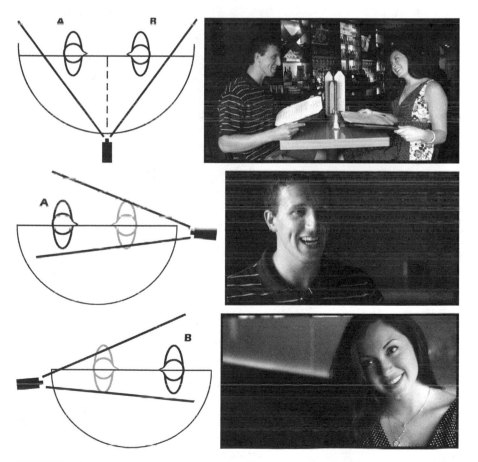

The Line – Basis for Screen Direction

FIGURE 5.12 Respecting the imaginary line and staying within the 180 degree arc will result in correct continuity of screen direction across the coverage shots for this dialogue scene.

"Jumping the Line"

This happens a lot with new filmmakers, but most do not notice it until they get into the editing process. To "**jump the line**" or "**cross the line**" means that you placed the camera on the opposite side of the established action line and recorded coverage shots from the wrong side of the 180 degree arc. This effectively reverses the established directions of left and right and flops the film space on the unaware viewers when they watch the shots edited together.

In the series of shots shown in Figure 5.13, the first two are repeated from our example given earlier, but the third shot is taken, by mistake, from the far side of the arc. The result is a nice CU of character B, but the real mistake is not apparent until the three shots are edited together. B's screen direction and line of attention are reversed and therefore the cuts make no sense. It now appears that both A and B are sitting frame

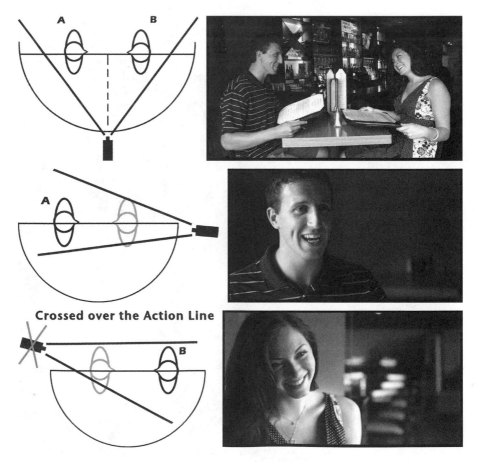

Crossed over the Action Line

FIGURE 5.13 Only when edited together does one see the incorrect screen direction of character B's attention in the close-up. The camera had jumped the axis of action.

left looking off frame right, rather than looking back and forth at one another which was established in the wider two-shot.

Crossing the line is acceptable under certain circumstances that involve moving talent and camera, but these are explored in more detail in Chapter Seven. For now, just think of how you would have to cover a couple slow dancing cheek to cheek on a dance floor. You would have one face on one side of a head and the other face on the opposite side, with the axis of action cutting through each. In order to see the faces in coverage, you would have to cross the line to set up your tighter shots.

As you may have picked up by now, there are very few absolutes when it comes to the guidelines and "rules" presented in this book. If you have creative reasons to execute a certain shot or group of shots in a certain way, then do it, even if it flies in the face of convention. Just make sure that your shot choices show your story best.

The 30 Degree Rule

Grounded in the execution of the 180 degree rule is another important guideline called the **30 degree rule**. Simply put, when you are seeking various angles on action for a variety of shot coverage within your 180 degree arc, you should ideally move the camera at least 30 degrees around the semicircle before you begin to frame up a new shot of the same subject. A focal length change would also be necessary (Figure 5.14).

The angle of view or perspective on the same subjects is then considered "different enough" when the camera is moved away from the previous set-up by at least 30 degrees. Each shot or view of the action is supposed to show new information to the audience. It makes sense that you would not wish to create two separate coverage shots with very similar framing. No one expects you to have a protractor on set measuring the 30 degrees – just get a good feeling about eyeballing it (Figure 5.15).

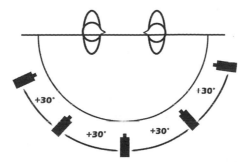

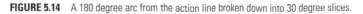

FIGURE 5.14 A 180 degree arc from the action line broken down into 30 degree slices.

The Line – Basis for Screen Direction

FIGURE 5.15 The same subjects as seen through the camera at five 30 degree slices around the 180 degree arc. The first set has no focal length changes and may not cut that well together. The second set incorporates angle and FL changes. This maintains the action line and achieves a new framing and angle on action appropriate for the edit.

Following the 30 degree rule can help avoid what is known as a **jump cut.** A jump cut occurs when you edit together two shots of the same object that have very similar framing and composition. The similarity in object placement causes a visual "jump" for the viewer in either space or time (Figure 5.16).

FIGURE 5.16   Taken from within 30 degrees of one another, these shots (even with different object sizes), when cut together, cause a visual jump on screen due to their very similar but not exactly matching compositions.

Reciprocating Imagery

Our recent example of shots cutting from a wider two-shot to two singles in a medium close-up serves well to illustrate our next point. Whenever you shoot one type of shot to cover one character in a scene you should create a similar corresponding composition for the other character in the scene. They call this **matching shots** or **reciprocating imagery** or the **answer shot** (Figure 5.17).

Tradition holds that an editor might normally show a scene from the outside in, where the shots of the action start off wider to show environment and characters and then, as the action progresses, cut together tighter and closer in order to show more intimate detail by the end. Each new camera setup with new framing should match for object size and object placement. Of course, you may have to make allowances for actual subject size, hairstyle, hat, or other accessories that may require slightly different framing. Your main goal in most cases will be to provide the editor with equal numbers of shot types and matching compositions for each character. When the time comes to edit the scene, the editor can progress through shot types as needed – from the outside in or in whatever order of shots the scene or the visual style of the project calls for.

The same can be said for the camera angle itself. Generally speaking, when you cover two separate characters with single shots from the same scene, you should take care to match the camera height, camera angle (tilted up or down or neutral), the lens focal length, and especially the quality and quantity of lighting. The overall camera angle on action is tied in with the 180 degree rule, so the associated geometry really helps keep

FIGURE 5.17   Shooting matching shots for medium close-up coverage is best. Providing an editor with an MCU of one character but only a BCU of the other may cause issues during the edit. The shot types do not match.

everything organized. Of course, because you must take your storytelling needs into account, not every aspect may match exactly.

If you shoot character A from several angles around your established 180 degree arc during his cycle of coverage for the scene, then you should reset camera around your arc, tweak lighting if needed, and shoot character B from the corresponding angles for her cycle of coverage. Provided that you keep the same camera height and lens focal length, you should be able to easily generate the reciprocating images or answer shots of the second character that will match the framing of the first character's shots (Figures 5.18 and 5.19). A camera log or notebook will help maintain all of this metadata for reference.

When two subjects appear in the same frame, the same matching shot rule applies. For example, the **over-the-shoulder** shot allows the audience to keep track of the physical placement of each character in the scene. Lines of attention and screen direction

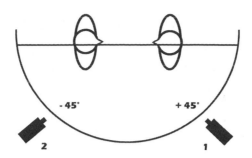

FIGURE 5.18   Camera setup 1 records MS of character A from 45 degrees on the arc. Camera setup 2 records MS of character B from –45 degrees on the opposite side of the same arc.

FIGURE 5.19   The resulting matching MS shots of characters A and B.

are still required to maintain spatial relations. When you establish a frame that favors character A's face, you include a portion of the backside of character B's head and shoulder. For consistency in editing purposes, the reverse shot, favoring character B's face, must also be recorded. The audience will often expect that reverse shot to be matching in subject size, subject composition, camera height, angle on action, and so forth, unless you are providing purposefully altered framing for storytelling reasons. When cutting from one OTS to another, any differences in these image factors will be very apparent and the mismatch will cause your audience, perhaps just on a subconscious level, to have an unfavorable reaction to the scene (Figures 5.20 and 5.21).

FIGURE 5.20   Matching over-the-shoulder shots for characters A and B.

The Line – Basis for Screen Direction

FIGURE 5.21 Mismatching over-the-shoulder shots for characters A and B. Note how the subjects framing, size, and angle are not consistent.

Eye-Line Match

Another important consideration associated with shooting for editing is the concept of **eye-line match**. This takes the line of attention or sight line from one shot and ties it directly with an object in a new shot after a transition or cut. Eye-line match usually involves a character isolated within a frame (perhaps illustrated most easily with an MS or an MCU shot) when his/her attention is directed somewhere outside the four edges of that frame. The audience traces an imaginary line from the character's eyes to the edge of the frame where she is looking. The audience wants to see what the character is looking at.

The filmmaker is aware of this impulse "to see," and may choose to show the audience what the character is looking at. The next shot would then be that object of interest revealed to the audience. And it's not just revealed in some arbitrary composition. It should be shot from a similar direction, angle, and height that closely match what the perspective would be from the vantage point of the character observing the object in the previous shot. This does not have to be a direct, subjective POV shot, but it does have to maintain and respect the eye-line established with the observing character so that the audience feels adequately informed that they, too, are seeing the same object as the character in the film.

Eye-line match is a "set up and pay off" scenario. The first shot sets up an expectation and then the second shot fulfills that expectation. The important thing is to frame the second shot from a corresponding vantage point. The illusion of connectivity to the character and the "realities" of continuity are maintained in the mind of the audience (Figure 5.22).

FIGURE 5.22   The first shot sets up the subject and the eye-line of interest. The second shot, presented from a correspondingly subjective viewpoint, reveals the object of interest.

Chapter Five – Review

1. The shots you create must be edited together, so plan for that process.
2. Watch for continuity of action in performance.
3. Maintain continuity of screen direction from one shot to another.
4. Let the line of attention connect objects for the audience.
5. Use sight lines and the action line to maintain proper screen direction while shooting coverage for a scene within the 180 degree shooting arc.
6. Move the camera at least 30 degrees (or more) around your shooting arc and change your focal length so that no two shots of coverage seem to come from the same angle on action.
7. Match your coverage shots for framing, angle, focal length, and lighting when shooting a multi-character scene, unless you have a creative motivation to do otherwise.
8. An eye-line match across a cut keeps your audience informed and grounded. Expectations are set up in one shot and paid off in the next.

Chapter Five – Exercises & Projects

1. Plan and shoot coverage of a simple two-person dialogue scene. What helped you maintain screen directions? What would happen if you added a third or fourth character to this same scene?
2. Create a scenario where two characters occupy one film space, but at opposite sides and with one sitting and one standing. They talk about and look at an object just off screen. Record the MCU of that object that both characters are looking at from different locations within the same environment. How are you going to address the eye-lines and angles on the object of interest?
3. Record a subject entering and leaving frame at five unique locations. Did you manage to keep screen direction consistent in all five shots? If you changed the subject's screen direction from shot to shot, how did you handle that?

Chapter Five – Quiz Yourself

1. What is the "fourth wall?"

2. What are "attention" and "sight lines" and how do they work into shooting coverage?

3. How does "jumping the line" mess with the coverage shots when they are edited together?

4. You are going to move your camera around your 180 degree shooting arc to get more coverage of a subject. How many degrees around that arc will you have to move the camera until you get a frame that looks dissimilar enough from the previous set-up so that a jump cut will not be created in the edit when these two shots are cut together?

5. Why is it important to have matching "answer" shots in your two-person dialogue coverage? What shot attributes should be reciprocated in order to get the shots to match?

6. What factors should you consider when you are shooting an insert shot of an object of desire? Think of this shot as the reveal of what a subject in the preceding shot is looking at.

7. What is the "axis of action" and with what common film "rule" is it associated?

Chapter Six
Dynamic Shots – Subjects and Camera in Motion

- Subjects in Motion – Talent Blocking
- Slow Motion/Fast Motion
- Handheld Camera
- Pans and Tilts
- Dolly Moves and More

We have been talking about basic guidelines for shooting motion pictures, but we have not really discussed the motion part yet. Presenting the illusion of moving objects on a screen has been the main attraction of movies and television since they were first introduced. Beyond still photography and live theatre, motion imagery (film, video, 3D computer animations) has been able to successfully engage audiences and show them virtually any information or entertainment that can be imagined.

In this chapter we will explore the basic approaches to handling subject and camera movement during motion picture production.

Subjects in Motion – Blocking Talent

The human visual system responds well to brightness, color, and movement. The movement of subjects within a static frame is a great way to give your shots visual energy. The term **staging** is often used to describe the physical placement of subjects on the film set and within the borders of the recorded frame. The term **blocking** is often used to describe the physical movement of subjects on the film set and within the same frame. Creating interesting blocking can engage the viewer's eye and keep them involved with the imagery and in the story. We like to watch things move around on screen. So, talent blocking across the screen (left to right or vice versa) helps reinforce direction. Talent blocking deep into the set or location adds to the illusion of a three-dimensional film space and draws the viewer's attention into the depth of the frame (Figure 6.1).

Static shots and stationary subjects, when arranged in compelling compositions, can have a visual energy and power all of their own, and can serve as contrast to moving shots when edited in sequence. It depends on the type of motion picture project that you are creating. Talent movement, when blocked creatively, will also add dynamic physical energy to your shots. In some schools of film theory, even the direction of movement can have meaning within the narrative. As an example, in an American frontier story, characters on a long journey to the territories may always have a screen right to screen left movement, perhaps implying that the right is East and the left is West – "civilization" is ever marching westward. Maybe a character is always moving from the foreground of a shot into the background – perhaps this means that he is running away or is too mysterious to be captured up close within the frame for very long.

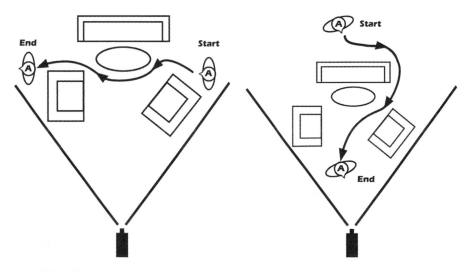

FIGURE 6.1 Talent blocking may be across the frame, deep into the frame, or both.

Presentation Speed – Slow Motion and Fast Motion

When it comes to the presentation speeds of "normal" motion, the two key numbers to remember are 24 frames per second (**fps**) for emulsion film and high-end video productions and 30 frames per second for most other video. Technologies surrounding image capture are changing all the time, but a basic rule still applies – changing the standard capture frame rate of your medium while preserving the presentation frame rate of that medium will create a change in the perceived speed of objects in motion.

Slow Motion – or Overcranking

Capturing images at a higher frame rate than "normal" (24/30) will yield the appearance of objects moving slower than normal when displayed at the normal frame rate speed. Basically, the movement of an object (athlete, racehorse, bursting water balloon, etc.) is broken down into many more representative "slices" or frozen frames by increasing the frame rate/shutter speed of the camera. The more frames you can capture in one second, the slower the objects will appear to move. When you have many more frames of motion to display but you show them at the normal rate of delivery, each shot (not frame) plays on screen for more time than the original action took to complete. The audience will therefore see movements in slow motion.

Scientific films and sports playback have used slow-motion imagery for motion analysis for many decades. Fictional narrative and animation films have also used slow motion cinematography to great effect. Watching events play out in slow motion can be very dramatic, moving, powerful, and sometimes comedic experiences for a viewing audience.

Fast Motion – Undercranking

Capturing images at a slower than "normal" (24/30) frame rate will yield the appearance of objects moving faster than normal when displayed at the normal frame rate speed. This method is used to create time-lapse motion images, such as speeding traffic flow or sunrise or sunset and cloud movements across the sky. It condenses events that take a longer time to unfold and displays them at a much faster rate for the audience to watch.

Fast motion is often associated with the silent comedy movies of the early 1900s. It is used in educational films, scientific visual studies, industry promotional videos, and fictional narrative and music videos – just about any motion image project that seeks to condense actions across time.

Presentation Speed – Slow Motion and Fast Motion

Camera in Motion

If having your subject move within a static frame puts energy into your shot, then imagine what will happen once you start moving the camera while recording your images. Because the camera is the proxy for your audience, a moving camera will really take them on a ride. Gauging just the right kind and amount of movement is one of your creative and technical decisions. Does a slowly moving camera match the energy of the scene? Does a quickly moving and shaky handheld camera match the tone of a scene depicting a chess match? Does it have to? In order to figure this out, it would be helpful if we explore the various ways in which the camera can move.

Handheld

Perhaps the best place to begin a discussion of camera movement is with the most basic yet most challenging approach – going **handheld**. You may find it convenient to hold a smaller camera in your hand, but just because it is a readily available mode of shooting does not mean that it is appropriate and it certainly does not mean it is easy to do well. The first factor involved is a technical one: the camera you are using to shoot your project. Modern digital video technologies have allowed cameras to be quite small and quite capable; they can weigh a few ounces to just a few pounds. If you are working on an emulsion film motion picture, the nature of the medium requires much heavier and much more substantial camera equipment, often weighing in at 20 to 40 pounds or more. This is not necessarily conducive to handheld shooting, although they do have specially designed cameras and support (like a Steadicam™ or a Glidecam™) for just such a purpose.

The smaller, more lightweight handheld camera is simultaneously a blessing and a curse. It allows for easy movement, but that often leads to too much movement. Having and using a tripod is always encouraged, especially if you are new to shooting motion pictures. Remember, everything you do with your shots should have a purpose. Shooting handheld should not happen because you lack the appropriate **camera support**, but rather because you know that your story will benefit from the kinetic energy that a well-controlled handheld camera can bring to motion imagery.

Due to the spontaneous and uncontrolled nature of the shooting environments, documentary and news recording will often use a handheld shooting style. When replicating similar real-life events – a riot, armed conflict, natural disaster, etc. – fictional narrative filmmakers will also employ a handheld camera to lend that feeling of reality to the experience on screen. Amateur videos are mostly shot handheld and, for similar reasons, filmmakers will use this style to mimic "amateur" content in their professional films. Handheld camera is also used when shooting action sequences, or any scene with quickly rising drama, to lend them a visually frenetic style. This can enhance feelings of tension and suspense in the audience. Reality TV programming (and spoofs of reality shows) also employ handheld; again relying on an audience to assume that handheld camera coverage means real and immediate events unfolding (unscripted) right before their eyes. Music videos use a fair amount of handheld camera coverage as well.

Perhaps it would be best to compile a brief list of advantages and disadvantages for the handheld camera option.

Advantages

- Easy to readjust framing on the fly
- Creates sense of personal immediacy within the scene (subjective POV)
- Allows operator to move freely around the set or location
- Infuses shots with a lot of energy from motion
- When it's wanted, can easily make an audience think of documentary/news/amateur video

Disadvantages

- Easily becomes too wildly shaky or causes swaying on the horizon line
- Difficult to manage focus with narrow DOF
- Difficult to cut with static camera shots
- Too subjective, may be inappropriate for neutral voice of the motion picture
- Generally limits focal length usage to wider angles of view because the more environment visible within the frame, the more "stable" the image will appear

Pan and Tilt

Pan and **tilt** refer to the horizontal and vertical repositioning of the camera lens. A pan (or panoramic shot) keeps the camera anchored to the center of an imaginary circle but rotates or swivels the camera lens horizontally left or right (see Figure 6.2). A tilt rotates or swivels the camera's lens up or down during the recording of a shot. If a balloon floats out of a child's hand and drifts up to the clouds, the shot can start with the lens pointing down toward the ground and end tilting up toward the sky in order to follow the path of the balloon (see Figure 6.3).

There is also a combination shot that combines a pan with a tilt where the camera lens is simultaneously panned across the film space and tilted up or, conversely, the camera is tilted down while panning across. Either way this results in a diagonal motion through the film space in front of the camera. An example could be two people walking through a sculpture park: as they pause (frame right) to look up at a tall sculpture (currently out of the frame), the camera sweeps up and across the location to the left in order to end the shot on the sculpture itself. An upward diagonal **tilt-pan** has been executed to cover both the people and the taller work of art (Figure 6.4).

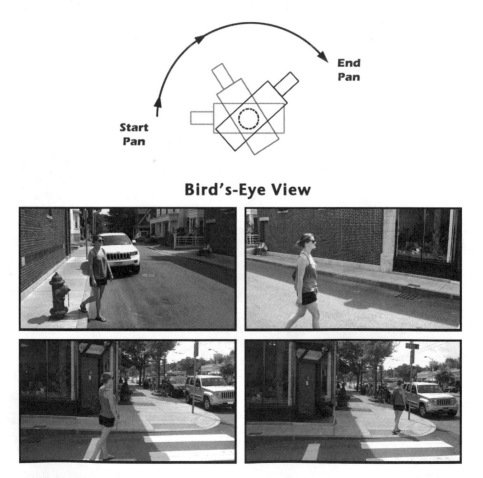

FIGURE 6.2 Overhead of camera panning horizontally during a shot. The camera pans right to follow the subject's actions.

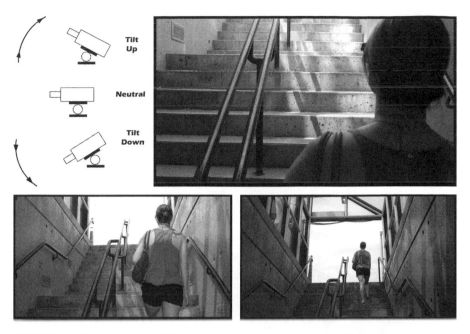

FIGURE 6.3   Profile view of camera tilting from neutral position to up or down positions. Example of a tilt up shot.

FIGURE 6.4   These are frame grabs from one continuous tilt-pan up and across this location. One shot provides the audience with multiple pieces of visual information through this tilt-pan movement.

Camera in Motion

The action of a pan or a tilt is actually an unnatural experience for the human visual system. Our eyes and brains do not make smooth pans or tilts while viewing our surroundings. Instead, the eye travels along the horizontal or vertical path locking onto points of interest, registering with the brain, and then darting along quickly to the next point of interest. It becomes a very rapid series of starts, stops, starts, stops, with the resulting illusion that we have panned along the city street or tilted our eyes up the building or mountainside. Because a motion picture camera lens is not as selective, everything that it "sees" throughout the duration of the pan or tilt gets equal treatment. The smooth execution of a pan or tilt and the speed of that execution directly affect how the human audience receives the information within the movement of the shot.

To help the audience accept the camera's panning or tilting movement, it is often good to motivate the move. In our examples so far we have provided these motivations. The upward movement of the lost balloon motivates the camera to follow the action and it tilts up toward the sky. The audience would like to see what happens to the balloon so they would naturally wish to follow its motion upward. Then we have the two characters who stop and stare up at the interesting sculpture. Their eye-line from frame right across to upper frame left motivates the diagonal camera tilt-pan up to **reveal** the taller work of art. All of the important narrative information is delivered in one continuous moving shot. The camera fulfills the expectations of the audience by showing the object of the characters' interest without having to cut to a new shot.

Recall that an audience member often places him- or herself in the position of your camera, which is showing the audience the story. When the camera moves, it then takes on a sort of intelligence, following action or seeking information. Motivating your camera moves (pans and tilts especially) helps keep the flow going and feeds the inquisitive nature of the viewing audience. The movement of a subject or object provides a reason for the camera to pan or tilt along with it.

There are times, however, when you have no visible motivating action for the camera to follow on a pan or a tilt. Perhaps you wish to shoot a long, slow pan of displayed photographs depicting several generations of a family, or maybe there are many different pairs of shoes in the front hallway of a home you would like to record. There is no motivating movement of these subjects, but the camera takes on a "mind of its own." It becomes a narrator or an "unrepresented" observer showing the audience things that are important to the story. The camera can pan or tilt slowly or quickly. The pacing is set by the tone of the scene – slow for languid, emotional moments or quickly for fast, energetic scenes.

Shooting the Pan and the Tilt

Traditionally there has been a preferred method of accomplishing a good pan or a good tilt shot. When you first start out operating a camera on pans and tilts they should have three components: the **start frame**, the **camera movement**, and the **end frame**. A pan or tilt composed of all three elements will be able to be edited into your scene more easily than if you had just movement alone.

1. The Start Frame

Almost every pan or tilt shot should begin with a static camera position. Your starting frame of the shot should be well composed — it could stand alone as a good still image. It is from this start frame that the subject that motivates the pan or tilt begins its action. Keep the camera still, let the action begin, and then begin the camera's panning or tilting. We do not discuss editing much in this book, but a quick word to the wise: cutting on movement, either into a shot already in motion or out of a shot once in motion, is a visually complicated thing to do and often poses an editorial challenge. Your editor will thank you when you begin your pan or tilt shot with several seconds of a static start frame.

2. The Camera Movement

Once the subject's motion has begun, your camera movement also begins. The camera's motion should ideally be smooth and steady and actually "lead" the movement of the subject. By this we mean that proper headroom, look room, and pictorial composition should be maintained throughout the life of the pan or tilt action (see Figure 6.2 or Figure 6.3). Any individual frame extracted from the shot during the camera movement phase would be able to stand on its own as a well-composed still image. Because the camera is leading the subject's progress, the camera would naturally reach the end of its horizontal or vertical arc prior to the subject completing its movement.

3. The End Frame

As the camera has already come to a rest before the subject completes the movement, the end frame has been reached successfully. This end frame should, once again, be a well-composed static shot that can complete the pan or tilt action in a visually compelling fashion. You should linger on this end frame, recording several seconds of it while there is no camera movement. The editor now has a steady, locked-off frame to cut out from at the end of your pan or tilt if the edited story calls for it.

As you become a more experienced filmmaker, you will be in a better place to experiment with a moving camera on pan/tilt shots without static frames at the head and the tail, especially if they cover a series of very fast action shots. The easiest visual test to see if static head and tail frames are required for a panning or tilting camera move is to record it twice – once with and once without. In your editing software, create two versions of your sequence of shots. One version will use the video clip with static start and end frames while the other version will just have motion. Most often the static start and end frames will help during the edit process.

Equipment Used to Move the Camera

Pan and tilt shots require no equipment to be accomplished successfully. They can be done with a handheld camera. One of the problems inherent to using a handheld camera is the lack of consistently steady control over the movements. No matter how steady you try to keep your hands and arms, the camera, especially the smaller, light-weight video cameras, pick up on each step, bump, and even breath. And no matter what you think may be a cool or popular style of crazy camera movement, nothing can take the place of smooth, steady shots that engage the audience rather than alienating them. It is almost always advisable to use some sort of camera support that will not only steady the camera, but also allow it to do more well-controlled, precise movements and help maintain proper focus. The following section discusses some of these devices.

Tripod

The camera should always have a companion piece of support equipment to keep it stable and level when you need it. The **tripod** is the ideal tool for this job. Tripods come in different sizes and weights, depending on the camera that needs to be supported, but they all have three legs. The three-leg design allows for solid balance and leveling on most surfaces. You attach the camera to what is called the **tripod head**. On most models, the tripod head is designed to provide pan and tilt movements, so it is often called a **pan and tilt head**.

Attached to the head is a stick that allows you, through the use of torque, to execute rather smooth pan and tilt movements by grabbing this arm and swiveling the tripod head on either the horizontal or the vertical axis. This stick is called the **pan handle** and is most often positioned between the camera operator's body and the back of the tripod head itself. Many tripod heads control their axis movements through either plate friction or fluid pressure. The tighter the settings, the more rigid/slower the movement — the looser the settings, the freer/faster the movement. Advanced tripod heads for professional motion picture work are called **geared heads** and use two wheels to pivot the camera through pans and tilts and there is no pan handle per se.

A level, locked-off tripod allows you to record extremely stable static shots. Many models of tripod have a built-in "bubble" level on the head, but you can also align any vertical objects (trees, walls) or the horizon line to the edges of your frame to achieve a useable "level." A tripod with the pan lock loosened allows for very smooth and level horizontal pans. The pan lock engaged and the tilt lock loosened allow for very accurate tilting movements up and down without any drifting to the left or right. One would have to have both pan and tilt locks disengaged in order to maneuver the tripod head to execute a smooth and stable diagonal pan-tilt. Tripods will generally sit directly upon the floor or the ground, and will have either spiked or rubber cup feet. A device called a **spreader** (that attaches to all three legs from the center) keeps them from spreading too far apart and dropping the camera too low to the ground. Many place a **sandbag** on the spreader for extra weight and stability. Tripods are also commonly referred to as **support**, **legs**, or **sticks**.

Dolly

The original motion picture cameras had a hand-cranked film transport mechanism, which meant that one hand (often the right) of the camera operator was constantly engaged in turning the crank motor during the actual recording of the shot. The camera was mounted on a tripod and the entire apparatus did not move during the shooting. The desire for camera movement quickly led to experiments where the camera and tripod were attached to a four-wheeled cart. The operator would stand on a platform, cranking the camera, and other crew members (now called **grips**) would push or pull the entire apparatus around the film set or location. This, in essence, evolved into the modern-day film **dolly**.

At their roots, all dollies are wheeled platforms. Some have three wheels, some have four wheels, and some have many small ball-bearing wheels like those on a skateboard. Many dollies have thick rubber or air-filled wheels that allow it to be pushed or pulled around relatively flat surfaces like a gymnasium floor or along the tiled hallway of a school building. Other dollies have grooved, hard rubber wheels that fit on tracks on the ground. These tracks (or rail) are like small railroad tracks and come in straight or curved sections and you can assemble different lengths to create a path for the dolly to follow (Figure 6.5).

Each of these different dolly types has different ways of mounting the camera. Some simple ones are just flat beds that let the tripod and the operator sit on top. Others have a built-in pedestal that can be raised (ped up) or lowered (ped down) via hydraulics. Still others have a **boom arm** that sits atop the pedestal and the camera and head are mounted to the end of the boom, allowing for wheeled movement and camera height and angle changes all at the same time. In a pinch, a hospital wheelchair, a skateboard, a wheeled office chair or a blanket being pulled over the polished floor can act as an impromptu dolly as well. Currently, **sliders** (or mini-dollies) are very popular with moving small form-factor DSLR HD video cameras.

The basic job of the dolly is to smoothly transport the camera across short distances. You can follow or lead or move alongside a subject and record its movements across the film space. Slow movements can be less noticeable to an audience, but they can be more difficult to accomplish on set. The faster dolly movements help instill a dynamic energy or sense of urgency in the shot. Just as the pan and tilt had three components, so too does a dolly move have the static start frame, the camera dolly movement, and finally the static end frame.

Always use extra caution when performing dolly moves or whenever camera and camera operator may be in motion. Personal safety is always more important than getting a good shot.

Let us take a look at the two major movements of direction that can be accomplished with a dolly.

Crab

Much the same as a crab on the seashore walks sideways, a dolly can be pushed left or right parallel to the action being recorded. In this case, however, even though the dolly is physically moving parallel to the subjects, the camera is perpendicular to the action. Traditionally, during the **crab dolly**, the camera moves at the same pace as the walking talent.

Picture a man walking down the sidewalk of his urban neighborhood greeting the many people he encounters along the way. The camera and dolly would be set in the street and pushed along the street at the same pace as the actor as he progresses down the sidewalk. Parked cars may make up the foreground, the man and the neighbors would make up the middle ground, and the storefronts and stoops of the apartment buildings would make up the background. The man and the dolly both move in the same direction and have similar pacing (see Figure 6.6).

Truck

If you need to push the camera into the set or in toward a subject being recorded, then you are "**trucking in**." If you need to pull the camera out away from the set or the subject being recorded, then you are "**trucking out**." These movements may also be referred to as **tracking in** and **tracking out**. This type of dolly move usually entails

FIGURE 6.5 Various styles of camera dollies and booms. (Photos courtesy of Chapman-Leonard, Inc., J.L. Fischer, Inc., Matthews Studio Equipment.)

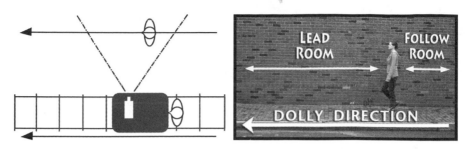

FIGURE 6.6   Although the crab dolly rides parallel to the action's direction, the camera lens is most often aligned perpendicular to the movement.

that the dolly and the camera are pointing in the same direction. The one axis glides deep into the set or out of the set in a straight line (Figure 6.7).

When done slowly, this achieves a barely noticeable change in shot type: a long shot becomes a medium shot and a medium shot ends as a close-up. This is a way to alter framing or shot type without having to perform a change in focal length or have the editor add a cut to the scene. You basically alter the framing and composition of the shot over space and time during the recording of the shot. Unlike a zoom, which alters magnification and perspective on objects, this movement appears much more natural to an audience member as the moving camera lens acts like our own visual system and maintains perspective on the changing field of view. When done slowly enough, the dolly movement is barely apparent to the consciousness of the viewer – things have

FIGURE 6.7   Overhead showing the dolly trucking in to the set along the tracks. The movement of the subject motivates the move in

Equipment Used to Move the Camera

just changed somehow but no one "saw" how. Some refer to this extremely slow dolly movement as a "creep."

One can certainly combine several of these movements discussed so far in order to create a more complex shot that is sometimes called a developing shot. You could have talent move through a set as the camera dollies along the ground to follow the action and have the camera boom up the pedestal to alter the lens height during the shot. A focal length change could also be introduced during a developing shot. The movement of the dolly and the possible pan or tilt can help disguise the zoom factor as the focal length change occurs. These types of developing shot can be very difficult to execute, but they can show a lot of story action in one shot and be very visually interesting to the audience.

We have not really mentioned it during any of this discussion on movements, but it should be made apparent once more that **focus** is going to be a major concern of any filmmaker engaged in these sorts of movement shots. Camera-to-subject distances will change where focus falls on the set and it is the job of the camera assistant and camera operator to keep these consistent throughout the duration of the shot. This can become quite difficult and requires a great deal of preparation and organization on the part of both talent and crew. It is often best to run through the action for several rehearsals so that talent, camera operator, camera assistant, and dolly grip all understand what the timing of the shot is going to be like. The crew will use a measuring tape for camera-to-talent distances and set marks on the lens or follow focus wheel. These complex developing shots that involve talent movement, camera movement, focus changes, and possible focal length changes can eat up a lot of time on set, so be careful with your scheduling on that shoot day.

Steadicam

For the most part, dollies are limited in the direction of their movements (left, right, in, out, and sometimes around). Handheld camera work can be liberating but you constantly run the risks of bad framing, bad focus, and too much shaky movement (unless your story calls for such a visual treatment). Luckily, a device called the Steadicam was invented in the 1970s that allows a camera to be mounted to a spring arm that mounts onto a body harness that is worn by a walking camera operator. This clever device makes it possible for a camera to achieve dolly-like smoothness as it is maneuvered on foot – in essence "hand held." Focal length and focus are controlled remotely by an assistant, but composition and movement are controlled by the operator wearing the vest harness. Because the camera is freed from having to follow dolly tracks, the Steadicam allows for rather long and intricate tracking shots where talent moves into and out of sets or locations, up or down stairways, and over rough terrain.

In the film industry marketplace, there are many similar devices available. They vary in complexity, size and expense, but they all balance a "handheld" camera for smooth moving shots.

Cranes and Such

Sometimes your motion picture project calls for a grand, sweeping shot of an exterior location. A camera at ground level, regardless of how wide your lens is, just cannot encompass as broad a section of your film space as you would like to see. This is where the use of **cranes** comes in. Just as large cranes allow construction equipment to work up high, cranes employed for film use allow the camera to work up high. There are many different types and sizes of cranes, but the general idea is to lift the camera (and sometimes the camera operator as well) up in the air over the set or location to achieve a very high angle view down on the action. Many crane-like devices called **jibs** also have the ability to "boom" the camera from ground level up to a higher elevation during the actual recording of the shot. This movement, although not a natural move, is fluid and graceful and can add visual power to a scene. Crane shots will help you show a lot of information from a high angle or even a direct overhead bird's-eye view. You will often see crane or jib shots used as establishing shots to open a scene, or summation shots that close a scene.

Equipment Used to Move the Camera

Chapter Six – Review

1. Blocking is the plan of movement for your talent around the set.
2. Slow motion results from the use of higher frames per second than in normal recording of action. Fast motion results from fewer than normal fps.
3. A handheld camera should serve a narrative purpose. Beware of shaky cam syndrome and questionable focus. Handheld is often used in news gathering and documentary.
4. Horizontal pans and vertical tilts should ideally begin with a static start frame, move smoothly through the camera motion, and finish on a well-composed static end frame.
5. The tripod is the best way to secure smooth, level, stable shots that will cut together.
6. A wheeled dolly or a smaller slider, whether on tracks or just the floor, helps achieve smooth gliding camera shots in either crab mode or trucking mode.
7. The Steadicam device combines the best qualities of smooth dolly work with the ease of movement of handheld photography.
8. Cranes, booms, and jib arms help you get sweeping upward or downward moves that add large areas of information and a sense of grandeur to your shots.

Chapter Six – Exercises & Projects

1. Practice panning/tilting with a handheld camera. Did you create a motivation for the camera movement?
2. Shoot pan and/or tilt shots as part of a scene but do not have static frames at the beginning or end of the move. Edit the scene. Do the pans/tilts work without the static frames? Why or why not?
3. If you do not have a dolly, improvise one out of a rolling chair or skateboard and record a short tracking shot that ends on a close-up of a subject. Recreate the same shot but do not move camera – zoom in to get the CU. Review the two shots and note any differences and similarities in the imagery.
4. Practice recording a "crab" profile shot (either dolly or handheld) of a person walking slowly, and then once again walking quickly. Was it easy to keep pace with the moving talent? Were you able to maintain lead room, headroom, and focus?

Chapter Six – Quiz Yourself

1. True or False?: "Blocking" refers to the focal length settings involved in a long zoom shot.

2. What type of image creation is the term "overcranking" associated with? What is the basic concept behind it?

3. List three advantages and three disadvantages to handheld camera operation.

4. What are the three main components of performing a pan or tilt shot?

5. How is tracking in on a dolly different from zooming in during a shot?

6. Why does a tripod not have two legs or four legs?

7. What does a Steadicam (or similar rig) offer that a traditional handheld camera cannot?

Chapter Seven
Working Practices and General Guidelines

We have come a long way with our understanding of the grammar of the shot. We should all be more familiar with the types of shot and the guidelines covering framing and composition. We have seen how lens choices, focus, lighting and camera movement help to show your stories with richer visual meaning. And we know that all of our hard work during production pays off when we pre-think the editor's needs and deliver the appropriate goods.

The grammar you are learning and putting into practice is a well-established and proven set of principles that will help your audience understand your visual intentions. In filmmaking, as with any discipline or craft, there are many different ways of approaching the material. Finding solutions to the challenges that confront you is part of the learning process and part of the fun. Although not an exhaustive list by any means, the content of this chapter is designed to help bolster your understanding of cinematic language. It offers tips, tricks, and suggestions (both general and specific) that may enhance your work habits and lead to a stronger and more effective visual presentation – and they may also prevent some headaches down the road.

Slate the Head of Your Shots

Organization is a key factor in successful filmmaking. Even a small project can produce a large amount of video and audio files and keeping track of them through post-production is a big deal. It is very beneficial to identify the beginning of each take, and a **slate** can help with this process (see Figure 7.1). These devices used to be made of actual slate way back when and a camera assistant would write important information on them with chalk. Today they are more like a "white board" and you can use dry-erase markers to pen down the pertinent information. When you record the slate at the beginning of the shot it identifies what the title of the project is, the scene/shot/take being recorded, the director, the DP and the date of production. Being able to see this information on the screen at the head of each shot helps the editor organize the material during post.

Beyond the written information, the slate board also helps with the syncing process. Syncing or synchronization is required on emulsion film or video productions that employ dual-system recording. The film or video captures the picture information and a digital audio recorder captures the sound. Although the video camera could also capture sound data, the quality of the audio is often superior this way. The picture and sound files are synchronized (or married together) during post with the aid of the slate board's clap sticks. When a clapper/loader voice slates the start of a take, s/he also physically closes the striped sticks on the slate board, which makes a loud "clack." S/he has marked the take. The picture file for that take has only one frame where the sticks are shown at the moment of closing. The audio file for that take has only one "frame" where the sound of those sticks closing is heard. These two matching frames are paired together and the picture and sound files will then play in sync during the editing process. On high-end film productions, **timecode** syncing makes this process a bit easier.

When shooting video projects without a separate digital audio recorder, your camera captures both picture and sound information. The captured files on your editing system are already married together on the basis of their **timecode**; there is no need to "sync" them. It is still a useful practice to "head slate" the shot on video because the visual and auditory shot identification will make shot organization that much easier for the post-production team. If you do not have the physical slate to write on and record, then you should at least **voice slate** the head of the shot so that everyone will still know what the shot is (stating project, scene, shot, take, and date).

There are occasions, especially found in documentary shooting, where you do not have time to head slate a shot because the real-world event begins so abruptly. You can perform what is called a **tail slate**, where you identify the shot after the event has transpired but before you cut the camera's recording. The physical slate is held upside-down for the tail slate (Figure 7.1).

Sometimes you will be shooting material that has no usable audio associated with it. When you are recording with emulsion film and you do not "roll" audio for a take it is called filming "MOS." This anagram has several possible origins, but the meaning is the same – do not look for an audio file during post-production because one was never recorded. The slate is still used to add the visual information to the picture track, but the clapper/loader holds his/her fingers inside the clap sticks so they cannot possibly close – confirmation to the editor that no corresponding audio file should be looked for with this particular picture track.

However you handle the slate, your main goal is to help identify the shots for easier post-production workflows.

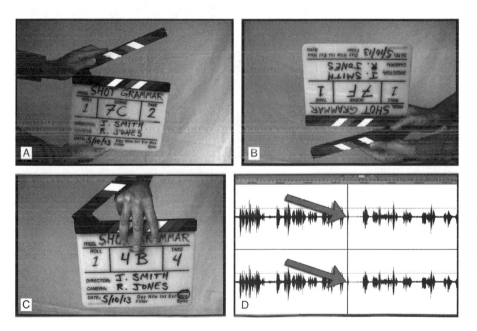

FIGURE 7.1 A slate is used primarily on film sets when two separate devices record picture and sound information. A – a traditional headslate; B – Tail slate; C – an MOS headslate (where audio is not recorded); D – audio waveform of slate sticks clapping.

Slate the Head of Your Shots

Communicating with Talent

Communication is the name of the game. Your motion picture project may be trying to convey a message or information, or evoke a thought or feeling in the audience – communication is happening. Crewmembers must share their production plans and make the project happen efficiently – communication is happening. The on-camera talent needs to be guided toward delivering the best performance – communication is happening. All too often with novice motion media producers, this last need for communication is overlooked.

Trained actors as well as amateurs need help in understanding the limitations of your framing of the shot – how much room do they have to look, move, gesticulate, and so on before they encounter the edges of the frame? Interview subjects need to be advised where to look near camera. Band members need to know what action to perform during a shot from a music video, and so forth. So many technical and logistical things are happening on a set that it becomes all too easy for newbie filmmakers to forget about the talent, or assume that they "get it." Getting lights, camera, and sound ready for a take only counts if the talent is on the same page. When everyone understands what the shot is about, it has that much more of a chance at being done successfully.

When you do communicate with the talent, try to keep the interaction brief, clear, and professional – after all, they are trying to do their job, too. Above all, you should be using language that makes sense to them. Remember that as you sit behind the camera facing the talent, they are facing you and your worlds' directions are mirrored. What is to their right will be to your left and vice versa. In order to keep things simple, provide stage directions that fit with the talent's alignment to the set or location. Some people actually use theatre stage directions on a set. If the talent is not familiar with that terminology and you need them to slide over to your frame left a bit more, say something like "Please slide to your right by an inch or two." This method makes it immediately clear in their mind in what direction they are to move and by how much (Figure 7.2).

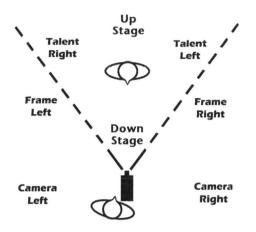

FIGURE 7.2   The camera's frame left and frame right are rarely stage left and stage right for the talent. Speak in their terms and directions will be easy to follow.

Safe Action/Safe Title Areas

Technologies are changing rapidly. The traditional 4:3 "tube"-based television set of the 20th Century has all but gone away, HD is on our smart phones, and 4K displays are just around the corner. The older 4:3 TV, as a receiver and display monitor for picture information, did a valiant job, but it suffered from a peculiarity known as **domestic cutoff**. The TV set actually "cut off" or did not display the outer edges of the original video or filmed image at the top, bottom, left, and right sides of the screen. This area of lost picture information was roughly 10% in from the edge of the source material. Content creators knew that this cutoff would eventually happen, so they framed their shots within what is called the **safe action zone** (Figure 7.3). Most HD display technologies, and certainly streaming videos on computer and handheld media monitors, do not suffer from this same limitation.

To help with this, many cameras will have a line, corner marks or an overlay grid on the viewfinder or monitoring screen that shows where this safe action area exists around the edge of the full image frame. When composing your shots, you should keep in mind that important information or action should not take place in this outer edge of the frame. While taking account of this extra screen area, be aware of appropriately compensated headroom and look room as well. If you record images of signs or other written materials, make sure to place them fully visible within the frame away from the edges. There are often markings on the viewfinder known as the **safe title** area for just such a purpose. In general, regardless of your camera format, it is a good practice to keep all important action and composed visual elements well within the safe action zone (Figure 7.4). Most video editing software will also have the option to display similar action and title safe grids in the playback monitors, so any questionable framing may be double-checked by the editor.

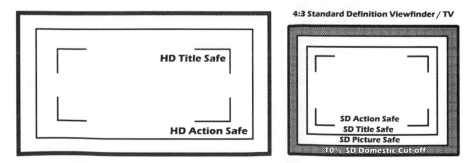

FIGURE 7.3 The safe action line helps keep important visual information away from the edges of the frame in both 16:9 and 4:3 images.

FIGURE 7.4 This lower third title is placed just inside the picture safe line.

How to Manually Focus a Zoom Lens

Any auto-focus camera lens should do all of the focusing "on-the-fly" as you set your shot's framing. If your camera is equipped with a manual focus zoom lens there is an easy way to achieve best focus on your subject.

The main things to remember are:

- Check the focus of the camera's eyepiece/viewfinder and verify it is set to your vision
- Select the framing for your shot with subjects in place, etc.
- Set your aperture wide to allow more light into the viewfinder system
- Zoom in on your subject (set lens to maximum focal length and magnify the object you wish to be in sharp focus)
- Set focus (on the eyes if a human face is your subject)
- Reset focal length to select shooting frame
- Set aperture for desired exposure

How to Manually Focus a Zoom Lens

Always Have Something in Focus

You will find it beneficial to have something within your frame in focus. The human visual system, when working correctly, always allows you to see some plane of space around you in proper focus. You have the luxury of automatic focus shifting – meaning that you can be focusing on something two inches away from your eye one moment and then focusing on an object very far away the next moment. Cameras have either manually focused lenses or auto focus controls that guess at what object you would like to have in focus. The center-weighted or "face recognition" auto focus settings can be helpful when you are first starting out, but controlling your focus manually is usually preferred. You get greater creative control that way.

The main lesson about focus is to have something important to the shot in focus at all times. Humans do not see "out of focus" by design (unless you require prescription corrective lenses and do not wear them). We do not like to watch blurry images because it goes against our nature. Our eyes and brains try to make it sharp when it cannot be made sharp, and we reject it. That is why a viewer might overlook bad framing or flat lighting, but any out-of-focus (blurry or soft focus) shot stands out like a sore thumb. Of course, there are special cases and allowances for creative uses of blur. Perhaps the shot is a subjective POV and the camera represents the altered perceptions of an inebriated or semiconscious character. Music videos, commercials, and experimental films often play with radical focus shifting and blurred imagery as well.

As an example, let us say that your frame has one female character in a close-up shot. If the depth of field of the shot is shallow enough, only the woman is in focus and the background is blurry. Creatively, this helps keep the attention of the audience on the woman and not on other objects behind her in the frame. However, if the woman fully exits frame and the focal plane does not alter, then the background will remain blurry and the audience is left watching an empty blurry frame until the next shot cuts on to the screen. It is a good practice to **rack focus** to the background as soon as the character fully exits the frame. This way the audience is watching the woman (in focus) leave the frame and then their eyes can immediately rest on the background, which has come into sharp focus. There is no awkward feeling or moment of confusion on the part of the viewer. This is critical, especially just before a cut to a new shot or new scene. The quick, smooth shift in the plane of critical focus to the background gives the viewer's eye something to focus on as the shot ends (Figure 7.5).

FIGURE 7.5   A series of shots illustrating a focus shift racking from the foreground to the background.

Control Your Depth of Field

You should always be aware of your depth of field (DOF) – the range of objects seen to be in acceptable focus within the depth of your shot. The DOF can be controlled (made greater or smaller) and shifted within the film space (closer or further from camera). Remember that the nature of optics will provide you with only one **critical plane of focus** in front of the camera's lens. Whatever lives exactly at that distance from the camera will be in sharpest focus. The DOF operates around this one critical focus plane and its depth (in distance from camera) is segmented into two unequal parts. The first segment (roughly one-third the overall area of good focus) falls before the critical plane, and the second segment (roughly the remaining two-thirds of the good focus depth) falls just behind the critical focus plane.

If you know the several variables that can affect the DOF then you will always know how to control it.

LIGHT—When you use lots of light, either from the sun or from large film lighting fixtures, you will need to close down the **iris** of the lens in order to achieve proper exposure. The smaller iris opening (or higher f-stop number) optically causes a larger depth of field. This is why many daylight exterior shots provide you with sharp focus on almost all objects – from very near to the camera out to infinity. **Deep focus** techniques can be used on interior film sets, but you have to bathe the space with very large quantities of light to achieve this.

When you shoot in very dark spaces the lens iris must be opened up very wide, letting in as much light as possible in order to capture a properly exposed image. This wider opening of the lens aperture causes a shallow DOF. You must be cautious when shooting in low light conditions because it is more difficult to keep the important objects within your frame in proper focus, particularly when there is movement towards or away from the lens. If your shooting environment is bright (sunny) and you wish for a more shallow DOF, then you could employ neutral density filtration (either to the lens or electronically in your camera) to set that wider lens aperture.

FOCAL LENGTH—The optics of the camera lens also play a role in how much DOF you get to use. Wide angle lenses, or lenses set to a short focal length such as 10 mm, will offer a greater DOF. Long focal length lenses, set to 75 or 100 mm or more, will generate a much more shallow DOF.

CAMERA-TO-SUBJECT DISTANCE—The DOF increases when your subject (and critical plane of focus) is far away from camera. The DOF decreases when your subject (and the critical plane of focus) is very close to the camera. Macro-photography (capturing images of small objects very close to the lens) exhibits this same phenomenon. Your lens may have a macro setting, or you could employ close-up filters (+diopters). Product shots and TV commercial work can use these to great effect.

SIZE AND SENSITIVITY OF THE RECORDING MEDIUM—The sensitivity of your video camera's digital imager and its size play a factor in the depth of field calculation.

It will now be rather simple to imagine a scenario for either a very large DOF or a very narrow one. Placing the camera far away from a subject, with a wide angle lens setting and lots of light, will generate a very large DOF. Placing camera rather close to your subject, with a long focal length lens in very dim lighting, will generate a rather shallow DOF. Use these guidelines when you wish to keep your subject in focus but blur out your foreground or background objects (Figure 7.6).

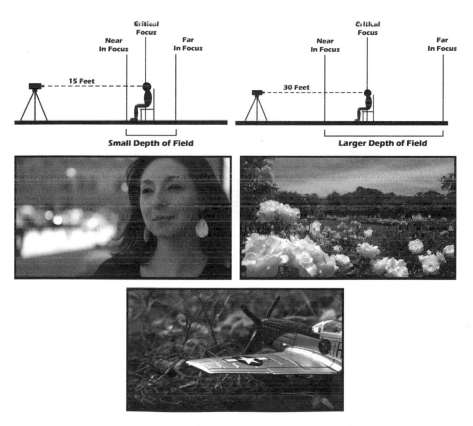

Control Your Depth of Field

FIGURE 7.6   A shallow depth of field directs an audience to look where the focus is. A larger DOF creates a deeper area within the film space that also appears in sharp focus allowing an audience to see both near and far. Macro or close up cinematography can yield a very shallow DOF of just a few mm or inches.

Be Aware of Headroom

An important part of your compositional considerations should always be headroom – how much or how little space you allow at the top of the frame for a person's hair or hat, etc. Too much headroom will force the eyes and face of a subject too low in the frame. Too little headroom will raise them too high in the frame or simply look wrong due to the chopping off of the forehead and so forth. If you have to err in one direction, however, you should have slightly less headroom.

Why? Well, when you give too much and force the face lower in the frame, you also force the mouth and chin lower. As the person speaks it is very likely that the bottom of the chin and jaw will break below the bottom edge of the frame in a CU shot. The top of the human head does not traditionally move, so it is safer to lose that above the top edge of frame. This keeps the chin and jaw fully visible in the frame as the person speaks (Figure 7.7). Consistent headroom across shots in mirrored coverage shots of a fictional narrative dialogue scene is also important. As the editor cuts back and forth between characters, the headroom of each shot stays relatively consistent, keeping the viewer's eyes engaged roughly at the same height in the frame.

The "talking head" subject being interviewed for a documentary also requires a consistent treatment of headroom. While shooting a long question-and-answer period for a documentary, it is important that the camera operator maintain correct headroom throughout the shoot. The editing may call for shots to be placed in any order, and if there is largely differing headroom among the shots it may look awkward when cut near one another in the final piece. As a final important tidbit about shooting "talent" for a documentary, try not to reframe drastically while the subject is speaking. Very slight pans and tilts may be necessary to keep proper framing as the subject moves around in his/her seat, but you should not drastically alter your focal length or focus while the subject is giving the answer to a question. If you do, it will most likely make that portion of the visuals unusable for the editor. You should wait until the subject stops speaking and then reframe and adjust focal length and focus.

FIGURE 7.7 Always aim for proper headroom in your shots.

Shooting Tight Close-Ups

If you need to shoot a tight close-up or an extreme close-up of a human face, mouth, or hands, be very clear with your talent exactly how constrained the framing really is. This enables them to better judge the limitations of their possible on-camera movements for such a tight shot. A close-up is going to be achieved with either very close camera proximity to talent or via a rather long focal length lens on a camera slightly farther away. In either case, the resulting frame represents a magnification of the person's face or hands and therefore the entire screen will be filled with that information.

With such extreme magnification, the slightest movements of the talent can "break frame" (move beyond the edges of the established frame border), alter good composition to bad, change critical focus within the depth of field, and so forth. Typically, your goal would be to have talent move as little as possible on these very close shots. If action is needed, be very precise with how little movement is really required and communicate that clearly to the talent. You may even choose to show them physically what you need by demonstrating it yourself.

There is an old expression concerning an actor's performance that says, "Less is more." This holds very true when photographing the close-up shots. With the entire face filling the frame, slow, subtle movements and minor changes in facial expressions yield a very effective performance. The human audience, attuned to watching faces for emotional cues, can make a very powerful connection with the actor in close-up.

Projects destined for television, computer, or mobile device screens can benefit from having more MS to MCU shots than media distributed for the large cinema screens. The closer shots display more important narrative information and the magnified visual details "read" better on the smaller display screens.

When you are planning your shots for coverage, incorporate the "Choker" and XCU shots of "details" with discretion. If they fit your overall visual style for the project, have a place in the narrative, and provide important details to the audience, then they will fit in with your other shot types. If not, they have the potential to be too "big" and run the risk of standing out as visual anomalies within your project.

Documentaries and other non-fictional filmmaking involve many "**talking head**" interview close-up shots. You will find that the MS and the MCU might be the tightest shots

FIGURE 7.8   It is easy to "break frame" or lose focus when dealing with human subjects in BCU and XCU shots.

you wish to get. A CU or especially a "Choker" might be too intimate when listening to a scientist or historian discussing factual information (remember the meaning of implied proximity between the image size and the audience). However, an audience might not mind a very tight close-up in an emotional documentary about a cancer survivor. Here, the personal connection feels more appropriate.

Shooting Tight Close-Ups

Ensure an Eye Light

It has been a long-standing practice in portraiture (painting, still photography, motion pictures) to include what some people call the **eye light, catch light,** life light or eye twinkle in your subject's eyes. This point of light, visible in the talent's eyes, causes a twinkle and helps draw your audience into looking more closely at the face and eyes of the subject. Having light reflected off the eyes implies the spark of life. Having no eye light can imply that the character is dark, evil, duplicitous, is no longer living, or, as in a horror film, might be a vampire, zombie, or robot.

Due to the moist surface and curvature of the human eye, any light source in front of the subject will reflect off the eye and be recorded in the image. A medium shot may be the most distant shot where the small point of light in the eye can be "read" or be visible to the audience. While recording any of the close-up shots it would be beneficial to have some light source set up near the axis of the lens for giving your talent the eye light — it may be your key source, if appropriate, or a special light, like a large softbox put there just for the catch light glint.

Whether you are using a point source, a soft source, a bounce, or the sun, the important thing is to make sure that the reflection in the eye shows the light source coming from the correct direction of other known light sources in the film world. Because most lighting fixtures in reality and in film worlds are above the head of the people, the reflection would be in the middle to the top hemisphere of the human eye as seen through the camera's lens. In certain instances, as with a desk lamp, phone or computer screen, or water reflection, the eye's twinkle light may come from below and be visible in the bottom half of the eye. In the end, because the eyes are so important, it is almost always a good idea to give them as much attention as you can in all your shots, even just for reasons of good exposure (Figure 7.9).

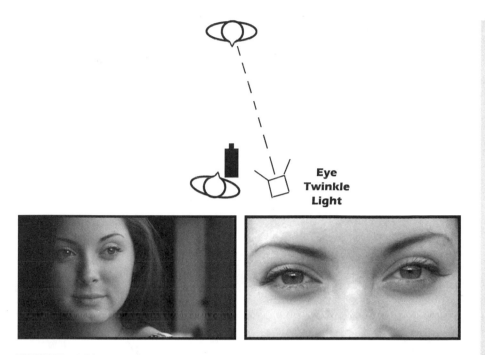

FIGURE 7.9 A light source placed along the axis of the lens will help generate an eye light or twinkle on the recorded image.

Try to Show Both Eyes of Your Subject

The eyes of your subject act as a magnet for the eyes of the viewer and much of the emotional or mental state of the character is conveyed via the eyes in a close-up shot. So, if it fits your story, you would be well served to make sure the eyes are easily visible. We have already discussed the use of the **eye light** or **catch light** to bring attention to the eyes, but we should mention that a **3/4 profile** shot is also a highly desirable blocking/camera angle to cover the individual in the closer shots.

The 3/4 profile allows the camera lens to see and record both eyes of the subject. This same angle on the subject would work for an over-the-shoulder shot as well, but you may have to play with the physical distance between the actors in order to get the framing correct. If you wanted to quickly change an over-the-shoulder shot into a clean single close-up in 3/4 profile, you would have to ask the actor whose back is to camera to step back a few paces in order to clear the frame. Keeping that now out-of-frame actor nearby will maintain the eye-line of the actor being recorded in the CU (see diagrams in Figure 7.10).

Remember that a straight-to-camera shot will reveal both eyes, and if the eyes remain off the axis of the lens, then you have a clear view of how the person looks. If the talent looks directly into lens then the shot becomes entirely a subjective shot, which is less appropriate for drama and more appropriate for news reporting. A full profile shot is also a specialty shot. Only one side of the subject's face is visible and the one eye that is visible cannot really be "looked into." The audience stays separated from the subject's thoughts or feelings, but if this framing begins a pan over to what the character is looking at then the initial profile is a motivator for conveying new visual information to the audience. Of course, you should use any talent position or camera angle that you feel is appropriate to your story, provided it conveys your meaning or makes visible your intended information. The 3/4 profile is just a very solid approach to shooting closer shots and it will not disappoint the audience.

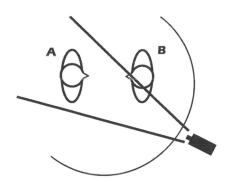 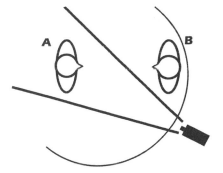

Character A Over-The-Shoulder 3/4 Profile   **Character A 3/4 Profile MCU**

FIGURE 7.10   The diagrams illustrate how to turn an OTS into a clean single shot by having the "shoulder" talent step back and out of frame. These examples show a full face, 3/4 profile and full profile shot of the subject. Use the most appropriate angle for the shot in your story, but remember to favor your subject's eyes as much as possible.

Try to Show Both Eyes of Your Subject

Be Aware of Eye-Line Directions in Closer Shots

An eye-line traces across film space to unite the subject's gaze to some object of interest. Whether the object of interest is another person, a picture frame, a car outside of a window, or a menacing cloud in the sky does not matter. What does matter is the direction in which the actor's eyes look when you cover them in a medium shot or closer. Head placement and the resulting direction of the subject's gaze are easy to "fudge" in a wide shot because we have greater context in the film space. Close shots reveal more detail of the subject's head and eye alignment but remove the greater context of the film space, and a keener emphasis on eye-line direction is needed.

Generally, when filmmakers look at the talent through the camera's lens they will have to gauge how accurate the eye-line of the actor is. Does it match the direction of the eye already established in the wider shots? Will it match up with the corresponding shot of the object being "seen?" Because close-up shots magnify the features, it may be necessary to modify the actual direction an actor is looking. The important thing is to ensure that the eye-lines for all concerned characters match in their individual shots. The angle or direction of the gaze will often just not look correct and you will have to talk the talent into the right eye-line. Experienced actors can pick a spot and "hit" their eye-line marks off camera easily. In certain situations it can be helpful if someone behind or around the camera holds a tracking object, such as their closed fist, in order to get the talent to establish the new and correct eye-line for your closer shots (Figure 7.11).

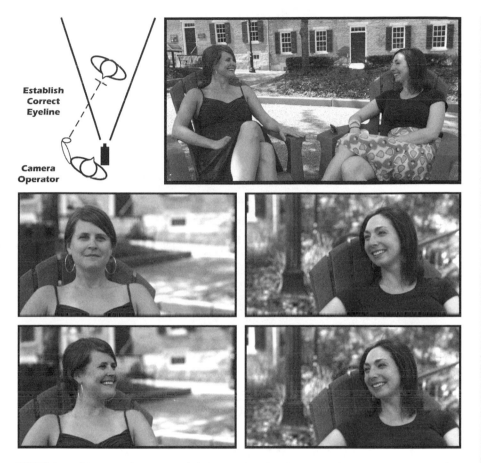

FIGURE 7.11   Talent's eye-line must match from wide shots into closer shots. You may have to talk the talent into establishing a new object of interest on set for a better eye-line. This eye-line is first off its "mark" and then corrected

Be Aware of Eye-Line Directions in Closer Shots

Follow Action with Loose Pan and Tilt Tripod Head

Much of what you record with your shots will involve objects or talent in motion. Whether you are framing a medium shot or a medium close-up, you could run the risk of having the action on screen bump the edges of frame or even break out beyond the boundaries of your frame – usually left, right, or top. It is best to keep all major action away from the edges of your frame, but there will be times where action covers more ground on set or location and you will need to follow the movements of your subject. This certainly happens with sports coverage, but it may be as subtle as tilting up slightly when your actor sits up tall in his seat when his character gets a brilliant idea.

Most tripod heads (where you mount the camera) are equipped with pan and tilt capabilities and therefore pan and tilt locks to help keep them stable. When the camera operator is asked to follow action and reframe "on the fly," it is best to have a better quality tripod head and camera support. The more professional equipment allows for smoother and more stable panning and tilting actions. The goal of the camera operator is to maintain good framing; if the talent is moving, such as someone pacing the floor, playing tennis, or dancing, it is wise to keep the pan and tilt locks loose. This allows for smooth, minor adjustments of the camera angle as the action unfolds during the take. This reframing happens all the time, but it is done so smoothly and unobtrusively that it is most often not noticed by the audience. You should aim to do the same (Figure 7.12).

FIGURE 7.12 A camera operator must be ready to reframe during the recording of action to maintain proper composition.

Follow Actior with Loose Pan and Tilt Tripod Head

Shooting Overlapping Action for the Edit

Remember, it is your job during production to provide the appropriate shots to the editor so that the visual elements will make sense and cut smoothly in the final product. When you have to shoot an action from two or more angles and you do not have the luxury of operating more than one camera, you will have to make the talent repeat the same action over and over again for each take at each camera position. Overlapping action is the action performed by the talent that is visible from each different camera angle covering the shots for a scene. You need to record this overlapping action in each shot so that the editor will have good and varied choices for creating an "action edit" or a "continuity edit." (Learn more about editing practices in our companion text, *Grammar of the Edit.*)

Wide shots and medium shots may call for more overlapping action coverage due to their inclusion of more visual elements. Closer shots will not normally require as much overlapping coverage because they tend to highlight details that are magnified on the screen and not as much movement can be recorded for matching from one shot to the next — although matching the movement and speed of head turns in CU shots is rather important for smooth continuity action edits.

Continuity of Action

Most filmmakers value performance over continuity and many will encourage their talent to perform similar but not identical movements, alter the scripted lines, or emote in various ways from shot to shot and take to take. This approach can work well if the performance is there in all coverage shots, but, if not, the continuity mismatches will be a nightmare during the editing process.

Matching Speed of Action

Your scene calls for a subject to walk up to a closed door, turn the knob, open the door, and walk through into the next room. You decide to cover the action from an MLS and an MCU on one side of the door and an MS on the other. The actions performed by the talent in the MLS and MS should be of similar speeds (walking up to the door and opening the door and walking through). However, there may be need for a modification to the speed of execution on the part of the actor while performing the close-up shot of the hand turning the doorknob. Closer shots of overlapping action should have the movements performed at a slightly slower speed.

A hand traveling into a close-up shot of a doorknob will appear to move much faster across the screen because the screen is only showing the magnified detail of the door-knob and the moving hand. As experienced by the audience, the larger object covers more screen space in a faster time. In wider shots, when more of the comparative film space is visible, the movements of an object or action can appear slower even though the rate of progress is the same. So, for proper continuity, you may wish to shoot the close-up insert shot with a slightly slower movement of talent. At your discretion, per-haps shoot another take at "normal" speed so that the editor will have both choices (Figure 7.13).

FIGURE 7.13   Talent movements in CU shots or tighter should be performed slightly slower so, when magnified across the entire screen, they appear normal when compared to the rate of movement in the wider shots of continuous action.

Overlapping Too Much Action

There is a danger in shooting too much overlapping action on each camera setup. For economy of time, money, and energy in both production and post-production, it is wise to be judicious with your choices of how much or how little overlapping action will need to be captured from each unique camera angle. Too little will provide the editor with inadequate options for cutting the continuity edit. Too much may allow a greater choice but can come at the added expense of more time and money being spent on get-ting the extraneous coverage that may never be used during the edit.

Storyboards and Shot Lists

Whether you are producing a short film, a music video, a 30-second commercial, or even an animation, you would benefit from creating storyboards, overheads, and shot lists before the first day of production begins. **Storyboards** are small drawings that map out what the framing and composition will be for each shot that you want to record. The pictures act as templates for the eventual real set-ups you make, like a comic book version of the motion picture. Storyboards also allow you to see how the various shots necessary to cover the action will edit together once you enter the post-production phase. The drawings help get everybody involved in the creation of the actual images on the same "visual page." Animatics (animated storyboards) have become popular as a modern pre-production tool but require additional software technologies beyond a pencil and paper.

Overheads can be simple "bird's-eye view" diagrams that map out where on the set you will place camera, talent, lighting fixtures, etc. They help get the crew ready to place the right things in the right places when you get to location or arrive on set. Finally, **shot lists** are a way to account for all of the various shots that you will need to accomplish to get the coverage for a scene. The list is often labeled per scene number with separate letters representing each unique camera angle on action (i.e., Scene 1-B, Take 1). Creating storyboards and shot lists will be accomplished before the physical shooting actually begins, during the period referred to as **pre-production** (Figure 7.14).

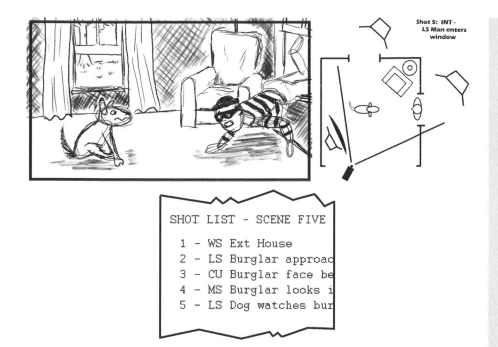

SHOT LIST - SCENE FIVE

1 - WS Ext House
2 - LS Burglar approac
3 - CU Burglar face be
4 - MS Burglar looks i
5 - LS Dog watches bur

Shot 5: INT -
LS Man enters
window

FIGURE 7.14 An example of a storyboard, an overhead schematic, and a shot list.

Aim for a Low Shooting Ratio

It should be clear that not every frame shot during production makes it into the final edit of the project. Bad takes, beginnings and endings of shots, coverage not required, and overlapping actions not used by the editor will end up on the "cutting room floor" (an expression from film editing days when the unwanted outtakes of the physical plastic strips of emulsion film were thrown on the floor of the edit room).

The **shooting ratio** is the relationship between the amount of visual material recorded during production and the amount of material that makes it into the final edited version. The overall shooting ratio is represented by two numbers separated by a colon (:). As an example, if you used one good take in the final edit, but shot seven different versions of that take, then your shooting ratio for that one shot would be 7:1. People have based this ratio on different criteria (film footage, takes, tape stock, etc.) but TIME is probably the most predominant factor. If you shot 30 hours of material for a one-hour program, then you have a 30:1 shooting ratio.

Scripted fictional narratives will often have a lower shooting ratio because each shot should be well planned ahead of time. Documentaries may have a larger shooting ratio due to the lack of scripting to action and interviews. Wildlife, travel, and especially multi-camera "reality" television shows can have huge shooting ratios. It is not always easy to predict what the shooting ratio of a project will become, but it is a good idea to at least generate a best guess ratio when planning your shoot. Budgets are not always about money. Time is a very important factor during production and post-production, so the fewer takes you have to roll on the more time is saved all around. A low shooting ratio with a good variety of shot coverage can be a winning combination for everyone (Figure 7.15).

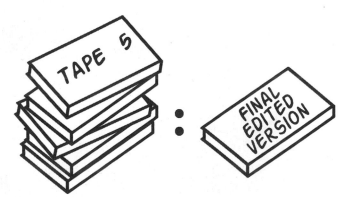

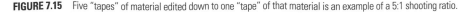

FIGURE 7.15 Five "tapes" of material edited down to one "tape" of that material is an example of a 5:1 shooting ratio.

Frame for Correct "Look Room" on Shots that Will Edit Together

You need to record a simple scene of two people facing each other having a conversation. In addition to a wide two-shot, your coverage calls for clean singles with medium close-ups. When you compose for the MCU of Character A on the left, you might place their head along the 1/3 "line" on frame left, allowing them to look across the empty space over to frame right. The "answering" shot of Character B is mirrored in its composition, with B's head on frame right looking across the void to frame left. This composition mimics what the wider two-shot had already established regarding the empty space in between the two characters. The eye-lines of the subjects trace back and forth across the empty space in between and, as a result, the audience will do the same when the two MCU shots are edited together. The direction of the "gaze" is maintained and followed across the cut.

This same technique can be used between a person and any object at which they may look. In one shot, a person frame left may be looking off frame right at some object. When you record the answering shot of that object, it should be placed over on frame right in order to allow the appropriate space for look room. When these two shots are cut together, the eye-line traces across to screen right on shot one and continues that direction in shot two until the viewer's eye rests upon the object of interest. It would be rather awkward to frame people or objects such that when they are cut together they appear to butt up against one another, as in Figure 7.16.

FIGURE 7.16 It is important to follow lines of attention and allow for proper look room space when composing closer shots of people and objects that will be cut together.

Shoot Matching Camera Angles when Covering a Dialogue Scene

With a traditional approach to shooting a simple dialogue scene you would most likely begin by covering the wide or establishing shot, moving the camera for a tighter two-shot, then getting one character for his over-the-shoulder and clean single, and finally "turning around" and getting the same tighter shots for the remaining character. Working this way, you set the scene for the audience and also allow for the talent to settle in and match their lines and actions better. Your goal should be to use the same camera distance, camera height, lens focal length, depth of field, and the same or very similar lighting for each character. The framing and composition of the single close-up shots and any OTS should mirror one another.

The important lesson for the new filmmaker to remember is that although the close-up shots may be shot last, they should be thought about ahead of time to check for how they will be physically set up in that environment. Will there be room for the camera to move to get the shots? Will there be any problems with background objects? Will lighting or depth of field pose any issues? Before you set everything and shoot the wide, it can be a good idea to quickly walk through the other camera set-up positions and check for possible "gotchas."

As usual, how things eventually edit together helps dictate how they should be originally recorded. When you cover the two individuals talking in this simple scene, their close-up shots and over-the-shoulder shots should match or mirror one another. This way, when the editor gets to cut the scene together, the viewer sees the wide shot and understands the overall scene's lighting and character placement in the film space. Then, when closer shots are cut back to back, the audience is given matching "mirrored" shots and knows how to place these individuals within the larger film space outside the CU frame. If you have covered the two characters with different camera heights, lenses, depths of field, or drastically different lighting, then there will be noticeable visual incongruity in the edited scene. Mismatched shots cut in a back-and-forth fashion could confuse and possibly annoy the viewer because the information being presented is not harmonious.

This sequence of mirrored coverage is often called **shot-reverse-shot**. The coverage shots for one character are shot all the way through into the closest framing and then camera and lighting can switch over to cover the shots for the remaining character.

In our example, the first MCU is shot from +45 degrees around the 180 degree arc and, eventually, the other character is covered in an MCU from −45 degrees (see Figure 7.17). You get matching imagery, and the shot-reverse-shot cycle is available for the edit.

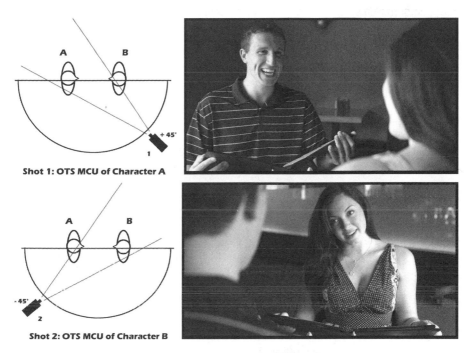

Shot 1: OTS MCU of Character A

Shot 2: OTS MCU of Character B

FIGURE 7.17 Shoot matching shot-reverse-shot coverage for traditional editing choices.

Shoot Matching Camera Angles when Covering a Dialogue Scene

Ways to Cross the 180 Degree Line Safely

We know that when shooting coverage for a scene, the camera should normally stay on one side of the set or location within the established 180 degree arc. We do this so that when the various shots of that scene's coverage are edited together, the screen direction of movements and the eye-lines of characters match the established spatial relations found in the wider master shot. There may be times when you wish to move the camera around the set and get new angles on action from the opposite or "incorrect" side of the axis of action. This can be done, but there are some special ways to do it without it being jarring to the viewing audience.

Talent movement (blocking changes) within the shot will establish a new axis of action for each new direction the subject faces. Once a new line exists, the camera is free to reposition.

If the movement of talent provides the motivation, then a mobile camera (handheld, Steadicam, dolly, etc.) can cross over the action line during the continuous shot. The original 180 degree line is established with the first wide shot, but the line is then changed and updated as the camera moves to follow the movement of the subject around the set.

If you establish the line in the wide shot and then move the camera to the farthest extreme along the arc without going over the line, you will have created a neutral shot for use during the edit process. Because this extreme location along the arc "sits on the fence," you would then be free to fall to the other side of the line and shoot from the new side. The new line is established after the neutral shot and allows the audience to reset their spatial understanding of the film space.

You may also try to use a **cutaway** shot to a related object or person within the same film space. If you provide shots from both sides of the action line, but you have also recorded cutaways or insert shots for the editor, then the cutaway can break the spatial attention of the viewer and the next shot may be shown from the far side of the original axis of action. The majority of the film space and the blocking of the subjects will be established in the wider shot, so the visual break of the cutaway creates an easier transition to the new action line for the audience. You could even shoot another reestablishing shot of the wide scene from a different angle (Figure 7.18).

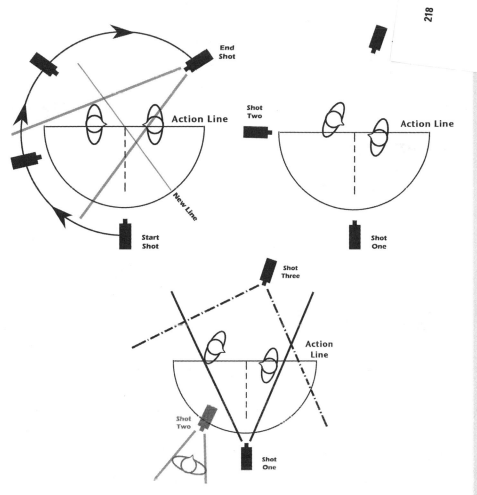

FIGURE 7.18 Ways to move the camera across the 180 degree line safely while shooting coverage for a scene

Place Important Objects in the Top Half of Your Frame

We normally view things from the top down (pages of a book, a web site, a person walking towards us, etc.) and, in many cultures, from the left to the right. This is no different when viewing a motion picture. Filmmakers have taken advantage of this phenomenon and created meaning around an object's placement within the frame. Objects (including people's heads) that are placed in the top half of the frame receive more attention from the viewer. The objects are said to have more "weight" or visual presence and are assigned a greater importance within the scene or story. Objects placed lower in the frame tend to have less "weight," have less visual presence, and are seen as less important in the story.

An example is a wide two-shot where a more powerful character stands frame left over the seated figure of the less powerful character on frame right. An up/down power dynamic is created (Figure 7.19).

This does not mean that you should never put important objects in the lower half of your frame, but the top half/bottom half guideline does come into play quite often. Some key factors in choosing your composition should be the object's importance in the narrative, the size (proximity) of the object, its focus and its illumination, and, of course, its position within the frame. Think about how the viewing audience will look at your frame on screen. How will they digest the visual information that you present to them? Many significant objects will be placed at the top, but interesting compositions that use the entire frame can also challenge the viewer. You can compel the viewer's eyes to roam the image looking for that item of interest. You may wish to experiment and put all the main subjects of a story at the bottom of the frame and see what kind of reaction you get from an audience.

FIGURE 7.19 Objects placed higher in the frame hold more visual "weight" or importance. A viewer's eye is trained to look there first.

Be Aware of the Color Choices Made Throughout Your Project

Color choices can be very important to a motion picture. A particular color can take on meaning in your story – red could be a warning or indicate passion, whereas blue could symbolize a cold or uncaring individual, a sterile environment, or could even represent freedom found in the air or water. Even if you do not take your color scheme that far into thematic meaning, the color choices that are made for set dressing, costumes, and make-up will have an effect on how the shots get recorded and how visible certain objects might be. For instance, you may not wish to put a subject clothed in all dark clothing in front of a shadowy or dark-colored wall for the fear that she will get "lost" in the sea of darkness. Or maybe that is precisely what you wish to do.

There is a science to color and light and you should certainly explore more of that on your own [see suggested internet and book references in Appendix A]. Just be aware that bright colors and warmer tones will tend to appear closer to a viewer (as though they were popping off the screen), whereas darker colors and cooler tones appear to be farther away as if they were receding into the background. This phenomenon could help you create particular areas of visual attention in your compositions by juxtaposing bright and dark color areas within your sets and wardrobe (Figure 7.20). An Art Director or Production Designer often works on such details and collaborates with the film's director and DP to help establish an overall "look."

Beyond the colors of paint and fabrics, you can also apply colored **gels** to light fixtures in order to create color washes across people and environments – most commonly seen as blue for cool moonlight at night and orange for warm interior night lights. These work especially well together within the same lighting scheme. There are also color-altering processes that you can use during the post-production phase of a digital video project. These color treatment effects may even include **desaturation** where you remove much (or maybe all) of the color information from your source material.

FIGURE 7.20 The colors or tones of wardrobe and set dressing can play a major role in your image creation. Beware of combining dark clothes with dark backgrounds.

Keep Distracting Objects out of the Shot

Many of you have seen a live news report on location when a passer-by waves vig-
orously at the camera from behind the standing reporter. The out-of-place movements
distract our attention away from the main point of the report and the connection to the
story is lost. A small crew on a live news report cannot do much to prevent these distractions, but any not-live-to-air shoot should allow for some control over the set. Take
the time to verify that the frame is clean and that no objects, either moving or stationary, might prove to be a visual distraction for the viewing audience.

The main goal is to keep the composition strong. Any object that has noticeable movements or bright colors or an odd shape can compromise the good composition by acting
as an eye magnet to the viewer. If you shoot a CU of a person's head, make sure that
no strange lines, shapes, or objects come "out" from behind their head. This can have
a comical effect when done intentionally, but, for the most part, frame these shots so
that no distracting objects either obscure the face in the foreground or "grow" out of
the head or body from the background. The same can be said for any "talking head"
interview CU shot for a documentary. Active TV sets, computer monitors, and even
windows to the outside world can draw the viewer's eye away from the main subject.
Either do not incorporate these items in the shot or blur them out through creating a
very shallow depth of field (Figure 7.21).

FIGURE 7.21   Try to keep your frame clean and free of distracting objects, especially near the heads of talent.

Keep Distracting Objects out of the Shot

Beware of Continuity Traps While Shooting a Scene

A filmmaker needs to be aware of many continuity concerns while shooting coverage for a scene — matching dialogue delivery, action or motion, framing, camera angles, eye-line, and so forth. There may be many things, however, beyond the basics that can cause a continuity headache. The important thing is to be observant and thorough. Continuity issues can make the post-production process difficult, so try to avoid them during production (Figure 7.22).

Continuity traps tend to be objects on set or around the shooting location that will change over time. Shooting all of the coverage for a particular scene or event can take a long time, so these continuity traps will appear to change (sometimes drastically) from one shot to the next and back again when the coverage is edited together. These secondary continuity errors may not be as noticeable as actor movement or eye-line matching but they are still potential sources of audience annoyance. Any time the audience is reminded that they are watching an artificially crafted motion picture experience you run the risk of losing them and their positive attention.

Continuity traps to watch for:

1) Be aware of functional clocks or large watches that will reveal the passage of time when shooting chronologically but will cause a continuity issue when the scene is edited.

2) The same goes for the movement of the sun. Either bright sunshine or the resulting shadow movement will jump around from shot to shot during the edited piece. You may not have any control over the sunlight, but you could structure your shooting schedule around it or change the framing so that it does not become an issue. Dawn and dusk may bring about issues of streetlights and car headlamps in use when none should be on.

3) Any background activity, such as an active TV set, people, and cars, should be either removed or made to do the same thing in each medium or close-up shot you need to take that may involve their participation.

4) Finally, audio concerns should be addressed, such as airplanes, automotive vehicle sounds, telephones ringing, refrigeration and HVAC units, and especially noncontrollable music from any source around your location. All of these could potentially pose a threat to smooth editing.

FIGURE 7.22   Be aware of continuity traps (both visible and auditory). The clock and the street musicians may not help your edited shots.

Use the Depth of Your Film Space to Stage Shots with Several People

Simple shots of one or two persons allow ample screen space to compose their blocking and placement within the frame. When your shot must contain a larger number of people you will have to find creative ways to layer the multiple subjects into the depth of the film space. The foreground, middle ground, and near background become a combined zone where persons can be blocked or staged to fit within the frame. As seen through the camera's lens, the bodies of the people will have a slight overlap, but the faces will mostly be clearly visible and discernible.

The actual blocking will depend on the physical space of the set or location, the set dressing or furnishings within the space, and the size of the individuals. For groups of six to ten people you may need to have some sitting and some standing and all at different distances from the camera's lens. If the group is larger or needs to be a crowd, there will eventually be a point where an overlap of faces will occur and most will not be discernible. In that event, place the most knowable or important people nearer to camera so the audience can still see their faces and recognize them for who they are. It is not often desirable to have one or more characters whose head is turned away from camera, but you might find that to have all heads facing the same direction looks awkward, unnatural, or too subjective. When you finally know the variables on the day of shooting, you should quickly experiment with the best blocking options that take advantage of the depth of the film space. Raising the camera height "above the crowd" (a slightly higher angle shot) will also show the staging of bodies deep into the set, and more faces may be seen this way (Figure 7.23).

FIGURE 7.23   Use the depth of the film space to help stage the bodies when more people must occupy the frame.

Use the Depth of Your Film Space to Stage Shots with Several People

In a Three-Person Dialogue Scene, Matching Two-Shots can be Problematic for the Editor

By staging three people standing across the width of the frame in a wide shot, you establish the position and spatial relations among the people. For this example, let us label the person on screen left as character A, the person in the middle as B, and the person frame right as C. You would normally continue to get coverage of the scene by moving in for the two-shot. In this case, you could get a two-shot of A and B and you could get a two-shot of B and C. The issue arises during the edit session.

In two-shot #1, character A will be frame left and B will be on frame right, but in two-shot #2, character B will be frame left and C will be frame right. If you cut #1 next to #2, you will clearly see character B jump from frame right to frame left. This may prove rather distracting to a viewing audience. Although you should shoot both two-shots mentioned earlier, you also need to shoot single close-up shots of all three characters so that the editor will have the best possible shot options when the cutting process begins (Figure 7.24).

FIGURE 7.24   Two-shots in a three person dialogue scene will not cut together well as the central figure jumps from one side of frame to the other. Give the editor better options by also shooting clean singles of all three characters.

In a Three-Person Dialogue Scene, Matching Two-Shots can be Problematic for the Editor

Zooming During a Shot

The optical shifting through multiple focal lengths that a zoom lens allows is not possible with our human eyes. The scaling of magnification is alien to our visual processing and stands out from 'normal' cinematography. As the **angle of view** runs from wide to narrow, a "zoom in" simply magnifies the center of the wider frame when the camera is locked down on the tripod head. That new, center framing at the end of your zoom in may not be what you want your final frame to be, so you should keep loose pan and tilt locks on the tripod to allow for easier reframing during the shot. Be aware that these changes in the focal length will alter the perceived perspective observed by the audience (wide = exaggerated distance / narrow = compressed space). The depth of field will also be affected by the FL changes, so be conscious of your focus marks.

There was a time when zooms in fictional narrative films were considered "amateurish" or "hokey" (like "snap zooms" from the 1970s kung-fu movies). Today, they are used to great effect in a highly stylized fashion in science fiction and action/adventure movies and even video game "cinematics" animation design. Because of their frequent use by amateurs using camcorders (think of that easy access to the W/T toggle switch) zooms are often incorporated into POV video shot by a character in a feature film, TV show, or music video. The viewing public has also grown quite accustomed to zooming shots when presented in news stories or photojournalist documentaries where the camera must remain further away from the action for safety reasons.

You may find that a focal length change during a shot with a moving subject is required to maintain your desired composition. Combining the focal length change with a panning or tilting action that follows the moving subject may hide the zoom in or zoom out. The camera's reframing helps cover the more visually distinct optical shift of the zoom factor. You can also "hide" a zoom with its speed of execution. Very, very slow zooms can be incorporated into a very long take, such as an engaging dialogue scene, where the focal length change is so subtle over time that it is not really noticed by the engrossed audience member (Figure 7.25).

**Shot 1 Part A:
Neutral Wide Angle
at Ground Level**

**Shot 1 Part B:
Tilt Up and Zoom In
at Same Time**

FIGURE 7.25 "Hiding" a zooming lens movement within a pan or tilt is often very effective. Framing and focal length changes are made at the same time to alter composition and perspective.

Zooming During a Shot

Motivate Your Truck-In and Truck-Out Dolly Moves

It is commonly accepted that camera movement during a shot is motivated by the staged action being covered – meaning, as things move in the shot, the camera can move along with them. This holds true for dolly shots that either push into a set or pull out of it. This practice is often called trucking or tracking.

Usually the motion of any object (a rolling ball) or any subject (a delivery boy) is ample motivation to truck in. The object moves into the depth of the shot so the camera follows, seeking out more detail and more information. This pushing in and exploring is natural to the audience because it replicates what a human might do in order to follow action and see more detail – get closer to the item or area of concern. It is an investigative expression of coverage.

Trucking out, however, is a less "natural" movement. The reverse motion of the truck out implies a person leaving a scene walking backward – not something that humans are likely to do on a regular basis. If a subject or object is moving toward the camera and the filmmaker wishes to truck out in order to keep the subject or object in frame, then that provides the motivation for the camera move. This is often called leading the subject. Because a truck out usually reveals larger or longer areas of the film space yet to be seen by the audience, it can be a useful tool in creating suspense (where is the character taking us? – what is he seeing behind us?), in relating new story information, and revealing the consequences of another's actions. Therefore, you are likely to find a truck out at the end of a scene or sequence or at the end of an entire motion picture. The truck out provides a visual overview of where a subject has been and sets up a possible reveal for new plot points and visual data (Figure 7.26).

FIGURE 7.26   Talent movement can motivate truck-in and truck-out dolly moves.

Allow the Camera More Time to Record Each Shot

We all know that time and money are very important to all motion picture projects no matter what the medium, format, story, or type of event being shot. Most often the ultimate goal is to pass on all production video to the edit team and have them piece together the final presentation. It is very important that you provide the post-production crew with as much usable visual material as possible, which means making sure that each take of each shot has plenty of start-up time and plenty of completion time.

It is wise to get the camera "**rolling**" before any critical action happens. This allows all equipment the time required to get up to operating "**speed**" and it gives the talent and crew time to settle. Rolling camera (starting the record process) before "Action!" is called also provides the editor with critical extra frames at the **head** (or beginning) of the shot. She or he can then potentially use these extra video frames to pad out the timing of the shots during the edit or even create a longer video transition effect in the editing software. It is a common pitfall of new filmmakers to start recording as they call out "Action!" and as a result they often miss some very critical frames at the start of the shot. This holds especially true for tape-based capture but still applies to digital media file video as well.

A similar process should be followed at the end of the shot. As the filmmaker calls "Cut!" the camera should be allowed a few more seconds of recording time. This ensures that all necessary action is captured by the camera and also provides that critical extra footage at the **tail** (or end) of the shot for the editor to play with. Getting into the practice of rolling early and cutting a bit late will help you win friends for life on the editing team (Figure 7.27).

HOW TO "CALL THE ROLL"

1. "LOCK IT UP!"
2. "EVERYONE SETTLE. THIS IS FOR A TAKE."
3. "ROLL SOUND" - IF RECORDING SEPARATELY
4. "SPEED" - FROM THE SOUND MIXER
5. "ROLL CAMERA"
6. "ROLLING" - FROM CAMERA OPERATOR
7. VOICE / PICTURE SLATE (SCENE & TAKE)
8. "MARKER"
9. CLOSE THE SLATE CLAP STICKS - 'CLACK!'
10. PAUSE A MOMENT OR TWO
11. "ACTION!"
12. ACTION BEGINS
13. ACTION ENDS
14. PAUSE A MOMENT OR TWO
15. "CUT!"
16. STOP DEVICES RECORDING PICTURE/SOUND

FIGURE 7.27   Rolling the camera early and stopping it late will ensure the extra "padding" footage often needed during the edit. Slating shots will help identify them during postproduction. If you wish, use this method to be thorough.

Allow the Camera More Time to Record Each Shot

Allow Actions to Complete Before Cutting Camera

There may be many occasions where this practice is neither possible nor prudent, but, for the most part, it should be followed because it makes a great deal of sense. It is the job of the editor to decide when to cut into a shot and when to cut out of a shot. The production crew should cover all of the action in each shot so that the editor has that footage from which to make his or her best choice while cutting the scene.

If an actor is to walk out of frame, let him/her walk fully out of frame and allow the empty space to be recorded for a short while. The same goes for a car, plane, dog, and so forth. Allow the exit action to complete and let the camera run for a bit longer – a second or two. These extra frames can be of particular importance if the editor decides to create a dissolve or fade or some other transition that will imply the passage of time before the next shot. If the action calls for something to fall, a door to close, or a person to round the corner of a building and disappear from view, then let all those actions complete in the shot before you cut camera. As discussed earlier, the static end frame of a pan or tilt will also provide the opportunity for the recorded action to be completed at the end of the camera move (Figure 7.28).

You may also occasionally see the camera trail off from an action and move its attention/framing onto a neutral background. After covering an action fully or partially, perhaps it tilts up to the sky, or down to the ground, or simply comes to a rest on some other nearby but unrelated object or background element in the scene. This treatment implies that the action is ongoing but gives the editor a clean neutral frame to cut away from and into the next shot or scene.

FIGURE 7.28 Allow actions to complete before stopping the camera.

Use Short Focal Length Lenses to Reduce Handheld Camera Shake

The **field of view** or angle of view that a lens provides depends on its focal length. A wide lens – a lens that is set to a short focal length such as 10 mm – captures a larger field of view and therefore creates an image that shows more of the environment in front of the camera. When you see more of the environment, objects in that space tend to appear smaller. If the camera were to move or shake slightly while recording a wide shot, as with a handheld camera, the smaller objects in the frame do not travel very far because of the relative distances they have to traverse in the wider image. The larger distances between objects and their relationship to the horizon line and the edges of frame will help them appear more stable if the camera experiences a minor shake or wobble.

Conversely, a lens set to telephoto – a long focal length such as 100 mm or more – captures a much narrower field of view. This lens setting magnifies details of a narrow slice of the environment, and the objects within the frame are enlarged. These magnified objects will have less distance to travel around the frame before they hit an edge or leave the frame altogether. Also, a shallow depth of field usually accompanies the long FL, so focus issues become heightened. This is why a handheld camera with a long focal length lens is likely to create an extremely shaky and motion-blurred image. Magnified objects in a narrow field of view make even small movements appear like large shifts in spatial stability. As a result, try to use short focal lengths when you need help stabilizing handheld camera coverage (Figure 7.29).

FIGURE 7.29   A wider lens angle provides more stability if the camera shakes during handheld recording.

Beware of Wide Lenses when Shooting Close-Up Shots

You may use any lens you like if it suits the shot and the story. You should be aware, however, of what a lens will do for your image in both a positive way and, potentially, a negative way. We all understand that wide lenses capture a large field of view and that they tend to have a larger depth of field. The curvature of the optics involved can also exaggerate the perspective when the subject is close to the camera. The shorter the focal length, the more exaggerated the warped perspective. Extreme versions of this optical phenomenon are called "fish-eye" lenses.

If you set your lens to the shortest focal length and reduce the camera-to-subject distance in order to get a close-up shot, you will most likely encounter this warped perspective exaggeration. The individual's nose will appear larger and perhaps bulbous, almost poking out at the camera, whereas the ears and the remainder of the head will appear to recede from the camera. Background objects, if visible, will also appear much smaller than they would with longer FLs.

This treatment is often used for a comic effect or when one wishes to show a "nightmare" state of consciousness. For normal CU work, however, you may be better served to use a longer focal length setting on your lens and move the camera further away from talent. Much like still photographers who use longer lenses to take portraits, you can reduce the exaggerated perspective of the subject by "flattening" the recorded space. The reduced depth of field of the long FL may also help isolate the facial features and bring more attention to the CU, while the background blurs (Figure 7.30).

FIGURE 7.30   Wide lenses in close can distort facial features in a CU. A longer focal length from slightly farther away can help keep the "portrait" perspective normal.

Shooting a Chromakey

When you watch a meteorologist deliver the weather report in front of a large radar image showing swirling patterns of cloud movement, you are seeing the result of a **chromakey**. You may be more familiar with the terms green screen or blue screen. These names refer to the same process whereby a certain color (chroma) is "keyed out" or removed from a video image. Post-production software is used to select that particular color (most often green or blue) and turn it invisible while the remaining pixel data in the image is untouched. This layer of "keyed" video becomes the foreground element (the weather person) or top layer in a composite. Then, some other video image (clouds on radar) is placed on the layer below to become the visible background of the new composited video image.

Although you could "key" any color in your video clips, the colors green and blue are most often used because they are two colors whose ranges of hues are not normally present in the skin or hair of human beings. Be advised that green- and blued-eyed people will have their eyes disappear if you use the same color for your chroma-screen color.

Lighting your foreground object should be done with the same care as you would use when lighting any subject for a motion picture project. Matching the lighting of the composite environment is sometimes desired if you are truly going for that special effect to trick your audience. If at all possible, you should have certain light fixtures just to use on your talent and another set of dedicated lighting fixtures to illuminate the chroma-screen in the background.

The main things to remember are:

- Keep the screen as smooth and flat as possible
- Illuminate the chroma-screen with uniform lighting (same light levels) across all the screen visible in your shot; the screen does not need to be very bright, just uniformly lit
- Keep your foreground subject far enough in front of the green screen so that there are no shadows of any kind cast on the chroma-screen
- If using a 16:9 widescreen camera, then you may mount the camera frame vertically to maximize the vertical resolution of the HD imager (shoot with portrait aspect ratio)

FIGURE 7.31   A simple green sheet (smooth, flat, and evenly lit) can serve as a chromakey screen. The result of pulling the key in post-production.

Shooting B-Roll, 2nd Unit, and Stock Footage

Depending on the genre and budget of your motion picture project, you may have a need for additional visual material beyond the principal photography.

If you are creating a work of non-fiction (especially a documentary, corporate promotional video, or even a how-to or process video) it is important to schedule time and resources to acquire B-Roll. B-Roll can be any visual material that "shows" something related to the topic of the program you are constructing. It is often used by the editor of the video to "cut away" from the main interviews or to pad out the timings between voiceover segments. Examples could be video of a corporation's headquarters, a busy factory's assembly floor, signage, trains pulling into a station, or shoppers in line at a store – whatever may be related to the topic of the main video.

On fictional narrative and long-form non-fiction, there often arises the need for visual materials that will be used in the final edit but are not part of the main scenes, interviews, or events recorded by the primary production crew. On films with larger budgets, the **2nd Unit** is another team that goes to precise locations to record exterior views, aerial views (helicopter or airplane), or driving shots and so forth. This imagery can be used as establishing shots, cutaways, or background plates for process shots or special visual effects shots. It will be very important to acquire this footage using the same format camera, or possibly even a higher resolution imaging device, to maintain or match the look and quality of the original production video.

Another option available to filmmakers is the acquisition of stock footage, archive film, or still photography for use in a new project. As the original material may not be of the same format, it will be important to create a workflow plan so the copies you access can be used in your final edit. Often payment for usage is required, or certainly a full credit needs to be given to the organization that contributes the archive materials.

Shooting B-Roll, 2nd Unit, and Stock Footage

Shooting a Talking Head Interview

Depending on the genre of and your chosen visual plan for your motion media project, there could be innumerable methods to frame, light, and record an interview subject. If you capture the person saying the things they have to say, then the job would appear to be accomplished successfully. Certain basic approaches to covering the "talking head" interview for documentaries have worked well for decades, so perhaps you would like to start here and diverge when it suits your "story."

A traditional approach is:

- Seat your subject in a quiet room, with few distractions. The chair should not swivel, rotate, or recline.
- If you, the filmmaker, are asking questions, then sit with your head very close to camera lens. Subject's eye-line will go to you consistently, near lens but not into lens.
- If you can record two channels of audio, use a body mic (lavalier) for clear, clean subject voice and a boom mic for voice plus ambience.
- Expand camera-to-subject distance if possible so you can frame a medium shot to medium close-up with a longer focal length. This helps with flattened portrait perspective and a shallower depth of field.
- Subject should be seen in 3/4 front profile composition either frame left or frame right, with appropriate head room and look/nose room.
- Allow space at bottom of frame for "lower-thirds" identification graphic added in post.
- A three-point lighting set-up is a good place to start. Try a soft key and fill with a hard kicker back light on opposite side from key. Key side of face away from lens. If you do not like it, use whatever lighting you have as is appropriate for your documentary's visual design.
- Exposure should be lower, so a shallow depth of field can help blur out the background of your "set." Audience then watches "in-focus" interviewee's face.
- Always ask the interviewee to say and spell his or her full name at the beginning of the recorded interview.
- Ask open-ended questions that require explanations and not simply "yes" or "no" answers.

FIGURE 7.32   An example of shooting an interview.

During Documentary Filming, Be as Discreet as Possible

When you are on location shooting documentary footage it can become very challenging to acquire the shots that you need without raising a lot of attention toward yourself and your crew. You will most likely attain the best results by remaining discrete, being respectful, and working quickly. As a crewmember working on any project it would be wise to remain discrete and efficient, but these working practices might get you more mileage when working in foreign or potentially hostile environments.

You should, first of all, obtain all required permissions, certificates, releases and waivers so that you can shoot at these locations legally. Your goal is to observe and record, not intrude or stage the events. The more people who are aware of who you are and what your purpose is, the more likely you are to get negative attention or simply have people behave differently than they normally might. The advancements in equipment – small digital video and audio recorders – will help you keep your "footprint" smaller, allowing for more discrete operations. Film emulsion cameras still tend to be a bit bulkier, and their rarity causes more curiosity in onlookers. Remember to obey all local laws and respect the privacy of individuals who do not wish to be a part of your project.

Chapter Seven – Review

1. Slate the head of your shots.

2. Communicate clearly with talent before and during production.

3. Frame action within camera viewfinder's Safe Action lines and frame signage or titling within Safe Title zone.

4. Manually focus a zoom lens at longest FL on subject you wish to see clearly.

5. Always have something in your frame in focus.

6. Control your depth of field through choices of FL, aperture, and camera to subject distance.

7. Be aware of headroom in your frame.

8. Use close-up shots when you want your audience to pay more attention and make either an intellectual or an emotional connection with the subject on screen.

9. It is most often appropriate to place an eye light or catch light so that your talent's eyes glint.

10. Try to show both eyes of your subject: 3/4 front profile is a good place to start.

11. Be aware of eye-line directions in closer shots.

12. Follow action with loose pan and tilt tripod head.

13. Record some overlapping actions during each coverage shot so the editor may cut on action movements within the frame during a scene.

14. Storyboards and shot lists help with organization and efficiency during production.

15. Be aware of your shooting ratio to save time and money.

16. Frame for correct "look room" across the cut on shots that will edit together.

17. Shoot matching camera angles of subjects when covering dialogue for a scene.

18. Plan accordingly to cross the 180 degree line safely when shooting coverage for a scene.

19. Place important objects in the top half of your frame.

20. Be aware of the color choices made throughout your project.

21. Keep distracting objects out of the shot and away from talent's head.

22. Be aware of continuity traps while recording coverage for a scene.

23. Use the depth of your film space to stage shots with several people.

24. In a three-person dialogue scene, matching two shots can be problematic for the editor.

25. Understand when and how to perform a zoom during a shot.

26. Motivate your truck-in and truck-out dolly moves.

27. Allow the camera more time to record each shot at head and tail.

28. Allow all actions to complete before cutting camera.

29. Use short focal length lenses to smooth handheld camera movement.

30. Be aware of very wide lens distortion when shooting close-up shots near to talent.

30. Light chromakeys with even illumination, no shadows, and no matching hue in the FG.

31. Remember to shoot B-Roll and other supporting visual materials for your project.

32. Three-point lighting, MS to MCU and 3/4 profile offer a good start to creating a traditional Talking Head interview.

33. During documentary shooting, be as discreet as possible

Chapter Seven – Exercises & Projects

1. Practice recording close-up shots of non-human subjects – signs, cars, plants, books, chairs, whatever. Make sure that you account for head room and look room and maintain all items of interest within the safe picture/safe title zones.

2. If your video camera has a zoom lens, practice zoom/pans and zoom/tilts and zoom/pan/tilts. Does it make a difference if the focal length change is motivated or unmotivated? Could you achieve a similar effect by moving the camera instead?

3. Go to a friend's house or take them to some public space in your community. Ask him or her questions about himself or herself and how they relate to the space where they are. Take note of the responses and then, after the interview, go and record B-Roll and inserts that will be useful for the editing process.

4. Using a handheld camera (with a wider focal length), practice following a moving subject from the back, leading from the front, and "crabbing" along from the side in profile. Which is easiest/most difficult to accomplish and why? Think of scenarios when you might wish to use each type of handheld "dolly." (Safety note: always have a spotter moving with you when operating camera by hand so no one falls or gets hurt – especially if you are walking backwards or sideways.)

Chapter Seven – Quiz Yourself

1. What documents can you prepare during pre-production that will help you set up the necessary shots quickly on the given shoot day?

2. Describe two ways in which you can "cross the line" safely when recording coverage for a dialogue scene.

3. What are the key visual cues that let you know a shot is achieved with a zoom and not a dolly move?

4. Why is it suggested to run the camera before calling "action" and for a few seconds after calling "cut?" Who will thank you the most for doing this on all takes?

5. What is the process of "Calling the Roll?"

6. How can you effectively control the depth of field for your camera/lens while recording on your own film set?

7. What is the danger in recording a tight close-up with your widest lens angle very near to the subject's face?

Chapter Eight
A Few Words of Advice

- Know the Rules Before You Break the Rules
- The Reason for Shooting is Editing
- Your Shots Should Enhance the Entire Story
- Involve the Viewer as Much as Possible
- Take Pride in the Quality of Your Work and Your Set Etiquette
- Know Your Equipment
- Be Familiar with Your Subject
- Understand Lighting – Both Natural and Artificial
- Study What Has Already Been Done

This book has presented some of the basic rules of visual grammar in filmmaking, defined a number of different shot types, and offered some basic working practices. None of this material is carved in stone and much of it is open to interpretation. Different people may call things by different names or choose to approach things in slightly different ways. Elaboration, experimentation, and blatant subversion have given rise to many new and interesting approaches to creating and conveying entertainment and information over the years. However, no matter what the technology or what the material to be presented, at the bottom of all the innovation would still lie the basic guidelines of globally accepted visual communication and cinematic language.

This summation chapter offers some additional food for thought and advice.

Know the Rules Before You Break the Rules

Contrary to popular belief, not all rules were made to be broken. Just as there are rules to sporting games, we have discovered in this book that there are rules that govern the production of motion pictures. The grammar of the shot – the film language – has evolved over the last 100 plus years but the basic tenets and guidelines have remained the same. As a result of this standardization of imagery, creators the world over are able to tell stories – or show stories – that are understood by a very wide audience. As with your own written language, you can read the images and comprehend what is going on in the motion picture presentation.

You can imagine then, if the rules of written language were not followed, there would be many people who could not read and comprehend what the words on the page were supposed to mean. The same holds true for the motion picture. Follow the established rules and guidelines of film grammar and you should find that the widest possible audience would understand the imagery and comprehend what you are attempting to convey via the visual elements of the "story" – regardless of whether it is a fictional narrative, a documentary, a news report, or an animated cartoon.

There is always room for experimentation and innovation; just be judicious with when, how much, and on which type of motion media project you let it loose. When you break the rules before you know the rules, you are taking certain risks with the project. If it is all your own, then so be it and go for it, but if you are using other people's money, time, and resources, it might be wise to start from an informed base of cinematic conventions. When you start with the basic rules and guidelines and build upon them in creative ways, you will most likely meet with more acceptance and success, but you won't know until you start to do it for yourself. So get out there and put them into practice. Learn more by doing more.

The Reason for Shooting is Editing

Unless you are shooting coverage at a live telecast, your goal in recording motion images will be to pass along the best possible visual material to the editor. The raw visual pieces are generated during film production but the real story isn't told until the final cut is made. If you create excellent individual shots at the expense of the story's editorial needs, then you have done a great disservice to the entire motion picture project. If it does not cut, then the problems started much earlier than post-production.

The film production process, no matter how simple or how elaborate, is never an easy undertaking. The potential for mistakes is always present. Numerous stresses, unplanned events, or last-minute changes can always happen. A good solution to alleviating as many of these potential headaches as possible is solid pre-production. Shot lists, storyboards, set/location overhead floor plans, and, of course, a strong understanding of film language will go a long way in helping you generate visually interesting and informative imagery that serves your story.

Well beyond talent performance, you must also make sure that your shots are technically acceptable for the edit. Have you matched angles, camera distances/heights, focal lengths, and lighting schemes on your coverage for a scene? Have you followed action until it completes? Is there good focus on all the right planes within the complex shot? Many aspects of the overall project must be planned and executed correctly for the final product to be as good as it possibly can be. So remember to think about what you are shooting and understand how it will be used during the edit.

Please don't use the expression, "We'll fix it in post" as an excuse for bad preparation and shoddy work during production.

Your Shots Should Enhance the Entire Story

The basic shot types discussed in this book will be able to provide you with the basic building blocks for shooting coverage of any motion picture event. If you do not move beyond the visual basics for recording a news report, a sporting event, or a documentary, then you may still show your audience a worthwhile experience. The simple film language provides all of the visual information necessary to clearly show the story's factual content. It has traditionally been the scripted fictional narrative film that allows for more experimentation in the imagery. Your shot compositions, talent blocking, lens choices, camera angles and movement, and so forth have the potential to support, underscore, and enhance the story being told or highlight, in special ways, the characters who populate that story. The filmmaker may find more freedom in creating visual expressions that stimulate and engage the audience. The images should be used to augment the narrative and the characterizations.

As a quick and easy example, let us say that two roommates have just found out that the third did not pay the rent on time. The wide establishing shot shows all three characters (A, B, and C) standing together. The characters, location, and scene are set from this first shot. Then you move in for the coverage. You record a clean single CU on character A, but only one medium close-up 2-shot for both B and C to appear on screen together. As we experience tensions between A and the team of B and C, then the cutting between shots of A by herself and B and C grouped together can enhance the narrative by physically showing A as a loner/outsider and B and C together as a unified team "against" their roommate.

FIGURE 8.1 The single shot of A keeps her isolated from the union of B & C in their two-shot.

Involve the Viewer as Much as Possible

Motion pictures really are a participatory experience. It might seem as though most people just sit and watch, but what usually happens when they are viewing good material is that they are actively engaged on many levels. Certainly, they should follow the story, but they will also experience many emotions and have physical reactions and responses to the actions viewed on the screen. What you show to the audience, how you choose to show it, and when it gets shown, are rather important factors in the success of a motion picture.

One of the main goals of most visual works of storytelling is to keep the viewer engaged. There should always be a need to pay attention. If there is no direct involvement for the majority of a motion picture then it is more likely to be seen as boring by the disinterested viewer. Of course, everyone has different tastes, and different stories call for different treatments of picture, sound, and pacing in the edit. All works should have a way to involve the viewer's senses, brain, and emotions. The visual elements are all within your control as a filmmaker, so at least make a concerted effort to cover all the important information – and figure out a way to do it creatively.

Remember, on the most basic level, when you show a new shot to the audience they are going to scan it for information and, if given time in the editing, they are going to appreciate it for all the aesthetic qualities that are incorporated into its frame: composition, lighting, color, focus, movement, and so on. Most modern audiences are very well acquainted with the visual grammar of film language. They can comprehend the important facts presented in the visuals very quickly. From one shot to the next, they are constantly scanning for, observing, and digesting visual information, which generates a sense of expectation within the viewer. If you fail to provide the audience with the appropriate information when they expect to see it, then you run the risk of losing them.

Motivating your shots is extremely important as well. There has to be a reason for the shot to exist. What information does it convey? Can an image "tell" more about the story to the viewing audience than spoken words? When it comes to a fictional narrative (scripted storytelling), "**show, don't tell**" is an excellent rule to follow and it should especially appeal to the more visually minded filmmakers.

As an example, let's consider the following scenario. A wide shot shows a college graduation ceremony in progress. A medium shot shows a young woman accepting her college degree on the stage. She expectantly looks out to the parents in the audience.

A close-up of her father shows that his eyes are tearing up with pride and happiness. The wide shot sets the scene and motivates the exploration of who is getting her degree. The medium shot of the young woman answers that question. Then, her eyeline out to the crowd motivates the CU of the father. His CU reveals new data about his emotional state. Each shot conveys new information, helps progress the narrative, and motivates each successive shot as well.

Take Pride in the Quality of your Work and your Set Etiquette

This guideline applies to both how you shoot your coverage and how you behave as a member of a motion picture crew. The artifice behind shooting is that in the ideal world your camera should be unnoticed by the viewing audience. It is often said that if an audience member notices a shot then it has become a bad shot. If your handheld shots are too shaky, your horizon lines are always a bit askew, the focus is off just a bit on the main object of interest, the dolly moves are filled with bumps and jiggles, or your zoom is not smooth, then it is highly likely that your audience will notice these issues and be taken out of the viewing experience. Rather than being engaged, informed, or entertained, they will, instead, be too aware that they are viewing a poorly shot motion picture.

As a filmmaker, it is very important for you to exhibit a high level of professional behavior. You need to keep your "behind the lens" actions and movements to a minimum during shooting. You could wear dark clothing to help blend in (be less visible in reflective surfaces) and not be a distraction to the talent performing in the scene. Always be courteous to all people involved in the project. Keep a cool head and get the shot – once you get it, move on. A good shooting pace keeps your talent and crew fresh and motivated to work hard. Don't blame others if you encounter problems, but work together to find a quick solution. Try not to schedule very long shoot days. If you have an exterior shoot planned and the weather turns foul, you should have an alternate interior shoot ready to go as a backup – some call this a "cover set." A professional demeanor, a low profile, and an efficient working style will go a long way in sustaining positive results on the shooting set.

Know Your Equipment

It is imperative that the members of a film crew be well acquainted with their equipment. Lighting, grip, audio, and camera are some of the key departments of concern during production. Whether it is the latest high-resolution digital video camera, a pocket camcorder or a mobile phone, the camera operator and other members of the camera department crew must know as much as possible about the device and all of the accessories. Experience is a great help here, but if you are a newer user, then reading the manuals will be a good first step, as would asking questions of other, more knowledgeable users of the equipment. Before the first day of shooting, you should make time to play with the equipment, build it, take it apart, and handle it so you know how it feels, sounds, moves and responds. Shooting tests for image quality and walking the media through a post-production workflow will be very informative.

Preparation goes beyond just being familiar with the equipment. You should be accountable for all of the parts as well. Make sure that you have all the pieces of gear that you need and that they are functional and clean. Charge all batteries the night before your first shoot day and remember to pack them when you leave for the job. Know your lenses. Understand their capabilities and make sure they are clean. Have all required cables, filters, and any extra tools. When you are in a studio or, especially, on location, designate an area strictly for camera department equipment and ask that other personnel stay clear. Keep your camera gear organized and in its cases whenever possible so that you know exactly where to go when you need something. On film sets, there is very little tolerance for time and money lost to easily avoided errors.

Be Familiar with Your Subject

As someone new to filmmaking, you should make the time to familiarize yourself with the material in the project during pre-production. Whether it is a documentary being made or a fictional narrative story being told, or a music video being shot, you should know the subject matter, the persons involved, and what the goals of the production will be. Read the entire script if you can get your hands on a copy. Understand the tone of the piece – dark, heavy, light, happy, etc. Be as familiar as possible with the locations, perhaps through a "tech scout" where you examine the location for access, electrical supply, sun passage, sound issues and so forth. Anticipate the needs of crew members and performers while watching for opportunities to make the entire production better. Good preparation of this kind will put you more at ease while shooting and allow you to work more efficiently should something go amiss.

Understand Lighting – Both Natural and Artificial

Anyone involved in creating good visuals for a motion picture project, whether it is something for television, movies, or the internet, should have a solid understanding of lighting and how to best use it for their shooting. One can spend a lifetime mastering the science behind light and color and also the nuances behind manipulating it correctly for use on film sets. Everybody starts somewhere in that learning process, so you should not delay in your own training. Composing great shots or pulling off wild dolly moves is certainly a positive thing, but without the appropriate lighting, all of it could be moot.

It is essential that you understand the basics of lighting – hard light, soft light, motivated light, bounced lighting, top lighting, practical set lighting, and so forth. You need to understand that there is lighting used just to get exposure (enough to record your image) and there is lighting for creative purposes. You may highlight certain characters or keep others in silhouette. Have overall high key flat lighting, or create strong **Chiaroscuro** with low key lighting. You may also wish to use certain colors that have particular meanings for your story. With all this light around your film set, it is very important to check your camera lens for **light flares** – lights that have their beams pointing into the lens. This errant light falling into your lens can cause flares or flashing on the image. This can be done creatively, but you will most often not wish for this to happen by accident.

When sunlight can be used, it can often save a great deal of time and money. However, as we all know, the sun is always "moving." As the Earth rotates on its axis, the sun appears to arc across the sky. This results in an ever-changing play of light and shadow across the world. When you are using natural sunlight as your primary light source, you should be aware that it will be different in just a matter of minutes to a few hours, depending on the time of year and your location around the globe. No matter where you are shooting, you should take some time to familiarize yourself with the availability and course that the sun will take across the sky – and, yes, there is an app for that. Part of your responsibility is to plan the best locations and best times of day when the sun can be used to its best illuminative and cinematic advantage. It might be midmorning, noon, or the "golden hour." Knowing about light and lighting is a critical part of anyone's motion picture training.

Study What Has Already Been Done

A large part of learning how to make motion pictures is knowing that you should really study what has already been done. Conducting research is an easy, informative, and entertaining way to prepare for almost any shoot. You may watch movies, television programming of all kinds (sit-coms, documentaries, cartoons, dramas, news shows, music videos, reality, etc.), experimental or avant-garde films, and even animations and video games. The web is a great resource for video clips that are available whenever you wish. Your goal is not to replicate precisely what others have already achieved, but to find **inspiration** and create new approaches to visual communication for yourself.

Many visually creative people (filmmakers, graphic designers, illustrators, screenwriters, etc.) also turn to art history for ideas, inspiration, and education in particular practices. Paintings, especially, can be a very rich source of compositional studies, color schemes, use of light and shadow, focus, texture, and so on. As everyone working on the motion picture could see a print of a particular painting or review a series of paintings from a particular artist, the works become a very visual way to relate ideas about color palettes or mood or subject matter. Sculpture, photography, architecture, textiles and so forth become excellent resources and references for the many people involved in creating the numerous visual elements that go into the making of a motion picture. Studying these art forms and sharing your findings with others will lead to a successful collaboration on the film set [see some suggested art and film history web sites in Appendix A].

In Conclusion

The key lesson in all of this material about "The Shot" is that recording motion images, whether with a high-end digital video camera or a smart phone, is not always a matter of simply pointing and shooting. Of course, one can take that approach and it may do well for recording birthday parties and holidays or even a particular kind of "informal" program. Any professional grade project that is worth doing is worth doing well, which means that you may have to employ a fair amount of proven cinematic language.

This book has introduced you to many of the basic practices, techniques, and guidelines for creating effective imagery that can build a solid motion picture experience for an audience. As you work on projects you will become more knowledgeable. You will get better at selecting the parts of this special language that suit your needs and the needs of your particular characters and story. Not every shot type, camera move, or lens angle will fit into the visual style that you plan for each project. Your goal over time is to develop an ever-expanding tool set and an ever-growing collection of references and resources so that you move from being a person with an idea to an artful and effective visual communicator using the full power of film language.

When you know the grammar of your shots, your shots will tell the story. Thank you.

Appendix A
Helpful Resources for the New Filmmaker

Web Sites

http://www.cinematography.com/

http://www.cinematography.net/

http://www.theasc.com/

http://www.precinemahistory.net/

http://www.joyoffilmediting.com/

http://ace-filmeditors.org/

http://www.artoftheguillotine.com/

http://filmmakeriq.com/

http://www.videomaker.com/

http://www.dofmaster.com/

http://www.filmcontracts.net/

http://www.wga.hu/index1.html

http://www.googleartproject.com/

Books

Cinematography: Theory and Practice
Image Making for Cinematographers and Directors, 2nd Edition
By Blain Brown
(Focal Press, 2011)

Voice & Vision
A Creative Approach to Narrative Film and DV Production, 2nd Edition
By Mick Hurbis-Cherrier
(Focal Press, 2011)

DSLR Cinema
Crafting the Film Look with Video, 2nd Edition
By Kurt Lancaster
(Focal Press, 2012)

The Visual Story
Creating the Visual Structure of Film, TV and Digital Media, 2nd Edition
By Bruce Block
(Focal Press, 2007)

Motion Picture and Video Lighting
2nd Edition
By Blain Brown
(Focal Press, 2007)

Light Science and Magic
An Introduction to Photographic Lighting, 4th Edition
By Fil Hunter, Paul Fuqua, Steven Biver
(Focal Press, 2011)

The Art Direction Handbook for Film
By Michael Rizzo
(Focal Press, 2005)

If It's Purple, Someone's Gonna Die: The Power of Color in Visual Storytelling
By Patti Bellantoni
(Focal Press, 2005)

The Screenwriter's Roadmap
21 Ways to Jumpstart Your Story
By Neil Landau
(Focal Press, 2012)

Directing
Film Techniques and Aesthetics, 5th Edition
By Michael Rabiger, Mick Hurbis-Cherrier
(Focal Press, 2013)

Changing Direction: A Practical Approach to Directing Actors in Film and Theatre
Foreword by Ang Lee
By Lenore DeKoven
(Focal Press, 2006)

Directing the Story
Professional Storytelling and Storyboarding Techniques for Live Action and
  Animation
By Francis Glebas
(Focal Press, 2008)

The Technique of Film and Video Editing
History, Theory, and Practice, 5th Edition
By Ken Dancyger
(Focal Press, 2010)

FilmCraft: Editing
By Justin Chang
(Focal Press, 2011)

Make the Cut
A Guide to Becoming a Successful Assistant Editor in Film and TV
By Lori Coleman, Diana Friedberg
(Focal Press, 2010)

Appendix B
Essential Crew Positions for Motion Picture Production

Screenwriter – The person who writes the screenplay, which is either an original idea or an adaptation of an existing property. Not typically involved during the production or post-production phases of the project.

Director – The person in charge of interpreting the story and characters from the screenplay. Generally turns the written words into selected shots. Works with actors to achieve desired characterizations. Collaborates with many other members of the production and post-production teams.

Director of Photography/Cinematographer (DP or DOP) – The person in charge of creating the overall "look" of the film. Chief member of the camera department. Works with director to select the shots. Creates the lighting scheme for each set-up. Collaborates with Electric, Grip and Art department heads. Often consults on color correction and grading during post-production.

Art Director – The person in charge of the design and construction of the film sets. Collaborates closely with the director, DP, Gaffer and Carpentry team.

Gaffer – The person in charge of the Electrical department. In consultation with the DP, chooses and sets the lighting fixtures that illuminate the film's sets or locations. Responsible for achieving the desired look and levels of light for exposure.

Key Grip – The person in charge of the grips. Works closely with the DP and Gaffer to get the necessary support equipment (for camera and lighting) placed for each shot.

Camera Operator – The person in charge of running the camera. Responsible for ensuring proper framing and double-checking focus during a shot. Sometimes starts and stops the recording process of the camera as well.

Camera Assistant – The person responsible for all camera equipment (bodies, lenses, accessories, batteries, media, etc.). Ensures that everything is clean, cabled, and running correctly. During the take, usually follows focus. Also, often, the keeper of the camera report and logs.

Sound Mixer – The person in charge of running any audio recording equipment on set. Maintains good levels of sound during recording. Coordinates best microphone placement with the set Boom Operator.

Boom Operator – The person in charge of holding or rigging a microphone from a boom pole (telescoping rod that supports the sensitive microphone suspended over the actors as they speak).

Grip – Member of the Grip department. Grips have many responsibilities and are capable of performing many tasks on a film set that involve moving and supporting things.

Dolly Grip – A Grip specifically assigned to build, maintain, and move the camera dolly around the film set. May set up and level any tracks or rail needed for the dolly move.

Electric – Member of the Lighting department. Responsible for running the power lines of electricity to all departments on a film set. Hoists, strikes, angles the film lights on set.

Assistant Director – The person on the crew responsible for setting and maintaining the production schedule. The A.D. will verify with all departments that they are ready for a take, call the actors to set for the Director, and call the roll to begin the recording process for a take.

Editor – The person, during post-production, responsible for editing picture and sound elements into the final story that will be experienced by the audience.

Glossary

180 Degree Line—The imaginary line established by the sight lines of subjects within a shot that determines where the 180 degree arc of safe shooting is set up for the camera coverage of that scene. Traditionally, one would not move camera to the opposite side of this action line because it would cause a reversal in the established screen direction when the shots are edited together. See also 180 Degree Rule, Axis of Action, Sight Line.

180 Degree Rule—In filmmaking, an imaginary 180 degree arc, or half circle, is established on one side of the shooting set once the camera first records an angle on the action in that space. All subsequent shots should be made from within that same semicircle. Since screen direction, left and right, for the entire scene is already established, the camera may not photograph the subject from the other side of the circle without causing a reversal in the screen direction.

30 Degree Rule—A cousin to the 180 degree rule, this rule suggests that when recording coverage for a scene from differing camera angles within the film set, the camera should be moved around the 180 degree arc at least 30 degrees from one shot to the next in order to create enough variation on the angle on action so that the two different shots will edit together and appear different enough in their framing. A focal length change between set-ups will also help.

4:3—The aspect ratio for standard definition television. Four units wide by three units tall – more square in its visual presentation than the high definition 16:9 video display.

50/50—A profile 2-shot, typically in a medium shot or closer, where both subjects look across the screen at one another – used especially in dialogue scenes.

Act (noun)—Much as with stage plays, in long form programming (feature films or episodic television, etc.) the "story" is broken down into several major sections known as acts. In fictional narrative filmmaking, a story will traditionally have three acts – loosely termed the set-up, the confrontation, and the resolution.

Action—What the director calls out to signify that the acting for the shot being recorded should begin.

Aesthetics—A way of creating and analyzing art and art forms for their beauty.

Angle of Incidence—The angle from which incident light falls upon a film set. A single lighting fixture directly overhead will have a 90 degree (from horizon) angle of incidence.

Angle of View—The field of view encompassed by the light-gathering power of a camera's lens. A wide angle lens has a wide angle of view. A telephoto lens has a more narrow angle of view on the world.

Angle on Action—The angle from which a camera views the action on the film set.

Answer Shot—see Matching Shots.

Aperture—In motion picture equipment terms, the aperture refers to the iris or flexible opening of the camera lens that controls how much or how little light is used to expose the image inside the camera. A wide aperture or iris setting lets in a larger amount of light. A smaller aperture lets in less light. On many camera lenses, the aperture can also be fully "stopped down" or closed all the way for total darkness on the image.

Artificial Light—Any light generated by a man-made device such as a film light, a desk lamp, or a neon sign.

Aspect Ratio—The numerical relationship between the dimensions of width and height for any given visual recording medium. In the example 16:9, the first number, 16, represents the units of measure across the width of a high definition video frame. The second number, 9, represents the same units of measure for the height of the same frame.

Atmospherics—Any particulates suspended in the air around a film set or location, such as fog, mist, or dust, which will cumulatively obscure the distant background or "catch" and "show" the light in the air.

Attention—The direction in which a subject looks within the film space. The attention of a subject may be drawn by another subject, an inanimate object, or anything that attracts his/her gaze. An imaginary line connects the eyes of the subject and the object of his/her attention. An audience member will trace this line in order to also see what the subject is observing. See also Sight Lines.

Axis of Action—The invisible line created by talent sight lines that helps establish which side of the action the camera can record coverage for that scene. The camera should not be moved to the opposite side of this action line because it will cause a reversal in the established screen direction. See also 180 Degree Rule, Sight Line, Imaginary Line.

Back Light—A light used on a film set placed behind an object but pointed at its back side. It generally serves to help separate the object from the background by providing a rim or halo of light around the edges.

Background—The zone within a filmed frame that shows the deep space farther away from camera. The background is often out of focus, but serves to generate the ambience of the location.

Binocular Vision (Human Visual System)—Having two eyes located at the front of the head. The slight distance between the two eyes causes the human to see nearby objects from two distinct vantage points. The brain then combines the two distinct images into one picture where the overlapping elements take on a three-dimensional aspect.

Blocking—The movement of talent within the film space and the corresponding movement, if any, of the camera in order to follow the actions of the moving talent.

Boom Arm—Deriving its name from the armature on a sailing ship's mast, a boom arm is used to swivel and extend the camera's placement in order to get sweeping shots or keep the camera buoyant without a tripod directly beneath it.

Break Frame—When an object being recorded accidentally moves to the edge of the frame and falls outside the visible area of the image.

B-Roll—Any visual material acquired for a project (especially news, documentary, and reality) that visually supports the main topic of discussion but does not include important human subjects. Often used to "mask" edits in interviewee's answers or commentary when used as a cutaway on the picture track.

Camera Angle—The angle at which a camera views a particular scene. Camera angles can be based on horizontal camera positioning around the subject or vertical camera positioning below or above the subject.

Camera Person/Camera Operator—The person, man or woman, who physically handles the camera during the shooting, whose main responsibility is to maintain proper framing and composition and to verify good focus.

Camera Set-up—A place on the film set where a camera is positioned to record a shot. Each time the camera is physically moved to a new position it is considered a new camera set-up. The camera set-up is often associated with a particular shot from the shot list for scene coverage.

Camera Support (Tripods, etc.)—Any device or piece of film equipment that is used to support the motion picture camera. Tripods, dollies, and car mounts are all examples of various kinds of camera support.

Canted Angle—See Dutch Angle.

Catch Light—See Eye Light.

Charge-Coupled Device (CCD)—The electronic light sensor built into many video cameras whose job is to turn light wave energy into electronic voltages, which get recorded as brightness and color values on a tape, hard drive, or memory card in the camera.

Chiaroscuro—Italian for clear/dark, the term is used in the visual arts to talk about the high contrast ratio between light areas of a frame and dark areas. Filmmakers, as well as painters, use this technique to show or hide certain visual elements within their frames.

Clean Single—A medium shot to a close-up that contains body parts of only one person even though other characters may be part of the scene being recorded.

Close-Up Shot—Any detail shot where the object of interest being photographed takes up the majority of the frame. Details will be magnified. When photographing a human being, the bottom of frame will just graze the top part of their shoulders and the top edge of frame may just cut off the top part of their head or hair.

CMOS (Complementary metal-oxide semiconductor)—A type of image sensor used in many smaller devices such as cell phones and consumer digital cameras.

Color Temperature—Often referenced on the degrees Kelvin scale, color temperature is a measurement of a light's perceived color when compared to the color of light emitted from a "perfect black body" exposed to increasing levels of heat. The color temperature for film lighting is generally accepted as around 3200 degrees Kelvin. Noontime sunlight is generally accepted as around 5600 degrees Kelvin. The lower numbers appear "warm" orange/amber when compared to "white," and the higher numbers appear "cool" blue.

Composition—In motion picture terms, the artful design employed to place objects of importance within and around the recorded frame.

Continuity—In motion picture production terms: (i) having actors repeat the same script lines in the same way while performing similar physical actions across multiple takes; (ii) making sure that screen direction is followed from one camera set-up to the next; (iii) in post-production, the matching of physical action across a cut point between two shots of coverage for a scene.

Contrast—The range of dark and light tonalities within a film frame.

Contrast Ratio—The level of delineation between strong areas of dark and strong areas of light within a film frame as represented in a ratio of two numbers: Key + Fill:Fill.

Coverage—Shooting the same action from multiple angles with different framing at each camera set-up. Example: A dialogue scene between two people may require a wide shot of the room, a tighter two-shot of both subjects, clean singles of each actor, reciprocal over-the-shoulder shots favoring each actor, cutaways of hands moving or the clock on the wall, etc.

Crane—Much like the large, heavy machinery used in construction, a crane on a film set may raise and move camera or have large lighting units mounted to it from high above the set.

Critical Focus—As with the human eye, there can be only one plane or physical slice of reality that is in sharpest focus for the motion picture camera. The plane of critical focus is this slice of space in front of the lens that will show any object within that plane to be in true focus. Example: When recording a person's face in a medium close-up, their eyes should be in sharpest focus, in which case the plane of critical focus is at the same distance away from the lens as the actor's eyes.

Cross the Line—Based on the concept inherent to the "action line" or 180 degree rule, this expression refers to accidentally moving the camera across the line and recording coverage for a scene that will not match established screen direction when edited together. See also Jump the Line.

Cutaway—Any shot recorded whose purpose is to allow a break from the main action within a scene. The editor may place a cutaway into an edited scene of shots when a visual break is necessary or when two other shots from the primary coverage will not edit together smoothly.

Daylight Balance—Emulsion film stock and video cameras may be biased toward seeing the color temperature of daylight as "white" light. When they are set this way, they have a daylight balance.

Degrees Kelvin—The scale used to indicate a light source's color temperature, ranging roughly from 1000 to 20,000 degrees. Red/orange/amber colored light falls from 1000 to 4000 and bluish light falls from 4500 on up to 20,000.

Depth—The distance from camera receding into the background of the set or location. The illusion of three-dimensional deep space on the two-dimensional film plane.

Depth of Field (DoF)—In filmmaking terms, the DOF refers to a zone, some distance from the camera lens, where any object will appear to be in acceptable focus to the viewing audience. The depth of field lives around the plane of critical focus, but rather than being centered equally, it appears one-third in front of and two-thirds behind the point of critical focus. Any object outside the DOF will appear blurry to the viewer. The DOF may be altered or controlled by changing the camera-to-subject distance or by adding light to or subtracting light from the subject and adjusting the lens iris accordingly.

Desaturation—In filmmaking, the removal of colors (hues) from an image such that only grayscale values (blacks, grays, whites) are left in the pixels of the image.

Digital Zoom—A camera/lens function which digitally enlarges an image based on a magnification of the existing pixel data by the camera's processor. The result is often blurry or "pixelated" due to this expansion of limited picture information. A digital blow-up. Differs from an optical zoom, which uses glass lenses to record an actual magnified image of a distant object.

Direct Address—A subjective style of recording motion pictures where the subject looks (and speaks) directly into the camera lens. Used in news reporting, talk shows, game shows, etc.

Director of Photography (DP, DoP)—The person on the film's crew who is responsible for the overall look of a motion picture project's recorded image. He or she primarily creates the lighting scheme but may also help in planning the angles, composition, and movement of the camera as well as design details such as color palettes and object textures.

Dirty Single—A medium shot to a close-up that contains the main person of interest for the shot but also contains some visible segment of another character who is also part of the same scene. The clean single is made "dirty" by having this sliver of another's body part in the frame.

Dolly—Traditionally, any wheeled device used to move a motion picture camera around a film set either while recording or in between takes. A dolly may be three or four wheeled; ride on the floor or roll (with special wheels) along straight or curved tracks; have a telescoping or booming arm that lifts and lowers the camera.

Domestic Cutoff—The outer 10% of analog-transmitted picture information that is cut off at the outside edges of a cathode ray tube television set and not viewable by the in-home audience. Although not as common in the digital age, this phenomenon should be taken into account when composing shots for a project that will be broadcast on television or viewed as a standard definition DVD. Videos encoded for web playback will display full frame.

Dutch Angle/Dutch Tilt—In filmmaker terms, any shot where the camera is canted or not level with the actual horizon line. The "Dutch angle" is often used to represent a view of objects or actions that are not quite right, underhanded, diabolical, or disquieting. All horizontal lines within the frame go slightly askew diagonally and, as a result, any true vertical lines will tip in the same direction.

End Frame—Any time the camera has been moving to follow action, the camera should come to a stop before the recorded action ceases. The editor may use this clean, static frame to cut away from the moving shot to any other shot that would come next. In a filmed sequence, viewing moving frames cut to static frames can be a jarring visual cut, and this static end frame helps prevent this visual glitch.

Establishing Shot—Traditionally the first shot of a new scene in a motion picture. It is a wide shot that reveals the location where the immediately following action will take place. One may quickly learn place, rough time of day, rough time of year, weather conditions, historical era, and so on by seeing this shot.

Exposure—In motion picture camera terms, it is the light needed to create an image on the recording medium (either emulsion film or a video light sensor). If you do not have enough light you will underexpose your image and it will appear too dark. If you have too much light you will overexpose your image and it will appear too bright.

Exterior—In film terms, any shot that has to take place outside.

Eye Light—A light source placed somewhere in front of talent that reflects off the moist and curved surface of the eye. Sometimes called the "catch" or "life" light, this eye twinkle brings out the sparkle in the eye and often informs an audience that the character is alive and vibrant. Absence of the eye light can mean that a character is no longer living or is hiding something, etc.

Eye-Line Match—When shooting clean single coverage for a scene with two or more people, the eyes of the two characters should be looking off frame in the direction of where the other character's head or face would be. Even though the actors may not be sitting next to one another as they were in the wider two-shot, the eye-line of each "looking" at the other must match from shot to shot so that there is consistency in the edited scene.

Fill Light—A light, of lesser intensity than the key light, used to help control contrast on a set but most often on a person's face. It is "filling" in the shadows caused by the dominant key light.

Film Gauge—In the world of emulsion film motion pictures, the physical width of the plastic film strip is measured in millimeters (i.e., 16 mm, 35 mm). This measurement of film width is also referred to as the film's gauge.

Film Noir—A term generated by French film critics of the late 1940s to describe the visually and thematically dark motion pictures created in Hollywood from the early 1940s to the late 1950s. Meaning, "black film," the term typically applied to black and white, gritty crime-dramas that used a very low-key lighting design.

Film Space—The world within the film, both that which is currently presented on screen and that which is "known" to exist within the film's manufactured reality. Diegesis.

Fish-Eye Lens—A camera lens whose front optical element is so convex (or bulbous like the eye of a fish) that it can gather light rays from a very wide area around the front of the camera. The resulting image formed while using such a lens often shows a distortion in the exaggerated expansion of physical space, object sizes, and perspective – especially with subjects closer to camera.

Focal Length—The angle of view that a particular lens can record. A number, traditionally measured in millimeters (mm), that represents a camera lens' ability to gather and focus light. A lower focal length number (i.e., 10 mm) indicates a wide angle of view. A higher focal length number (i.e., 200 mm) indicates a narrower field of view where objects further from the camera appear to be magnified and fill more of the frame.

Focus—The state where objects being viewed by the camera appear to be sharply edged, well defined, and show clear detail. Anything out of focus is said to be blurry.

Following Focus—If a subject moves closer to or further away from camera but stays within the film frame, often the camera assistant or camera operator must manually control the focus of the recording lens in order to keep the moving subject in clear, crisp focus. If the subject at the plane of critical focus moves away from that plane and outside the corresponding depth of field, he/she will get blurry unless the camera assistant follows focus.

Foreground—The zone within a filmed frame that starts near the camera's lens but ends before it reaches a more distant zone where the main action may be occurring. Any object that exists in the foreground of the recorded frame will obscure everything in the more distant zones out to the infinity point.

Foreshortening—In the visual arts, it is a way that three-dimensional objects get represented on the two-dimensional plane. When pictured from a certain view or perspective, the object may appear compressed and/or distorted from its actual shape; the closer end will appear larger and the farther end will appear smaller.

Fourth Wall—In fictional narrative filmmaking, this term means the place from where the camera objectively observes the action on the film set. Because it is possible for the camera to record only three of the four walls within a film set without moving, the fourth wall is the space on set where the camera lives and it is from that privileged place where it observes the action. "Breaking the fourth wall" means that talent has directly addressed the camera lens and therefore the audience.

Frame—The entire rectangular area of the recorded image with zones of top, bottom, left, right, center, and depth.

Front Lighting—Any lighting scheme where lights come from above and almost directly behind the camera recording the scene. Talent, when facing toward the camera, will have an overall even lighting, which often causes flatness to their features but may also smooth out surface imperfections.

Glossary

Geared Head—A professional piece of camera support used on dollies, cranes, and tripods that has two spinning geared wheels that allow for very fluid vertical and horizontal movements of the camera. The camera operator must crank each gear wheel manually in order to maintain the appropriate framing during tilts or pans.

Gel—Heat-resistant sheet of flexible, thin plastic that contains a uniform color. Used to add a "wash" of color on a film set. Example: When the feeling of sunset is required for a shot, one can place an orange/yellow gel between the lights and the set to give the impression of a warmer sunset color.

Genre—A French term meaning a category within some larger group. In film, the term genre applies to types of movies such as comedy, drama, action, western and so forth.

Golden Hour—The moments just after direct sunset but before the ambient light in the sky fades to nighttime darkness. Filmmakers often appreciate the visual quality the soft top light of dusk creates on exterior scenes; sometimes called Magic Hour.

Grip—A film crew member whose job it is to move, place, and tweak any of the various pieces of film equipment used for support of camera and lighting units, or devices used to block light, among other duties. A special dolly grip may be used to rig the dolly tracks and push or pull the dolly or camera during the recording of a shot.

Handheld—Operating the motion picture camera while it is supported in the hands or propped upon the shoulder of the camera operator. The human body acts as the key support device for the camera and is responsible for all movement achieved by the camera during the recording process.

Hard Light—A quality of light defined by the presence of strong, parallel rays being emitted by the light source. Well-defined, dark shadows are created by hard light.

Head—A common film term for the beginning of a shot, especially during the post-production editing process.

Headroom—The free space at the top of the recorded frame above the head of the talent. Any object may have "headroom." Too much headroom will waste valuable space in the frame, and not enough may cause your subject to appear cut off or truncated at the top.

High Angle Shot—Any shot where the camera records the action from a vertical position higher than most objects being recorded. Example: The camera, looking out a third-floor window of an apartment house, records a car pulling into the driveway down below.

High Definition (HD)—A reference to the increased image quality and wider frame size (16:9) of the digital video format. The increase in vertical line resolution per frame (720 or 1080) increases the sharpness and color intensity of the playback image. All HD formats use square pixels.

High Key Lighting—A lighting style in which a low contrast ratio exists between the brightly lit areas and the dark areas of the frame. Overall, even lighting gives proper exposure to most of the set and characters within it. There are no real dark shadow regions and no real overly bright regions.

HMI—A film lighting fixture whose internal lamp burns in such a way as to emit light that matches daylight/sunlight in color temperature (5500–6000 degrees Kelvin).

Hood Mount—A device used to mount a tripod head and camera to the hood of a motor vehicle such that the occupants of the vehicle may be recorded while the vehicle is in motion. Often a large suction cup is employed to help secure the camera rig to the hood.

Horizon Line—The distant line that cuts across a film frame horizontally. It is used to help establish the scope of the film space and helps define the top and bottom of the film world.

Imaginary Line—The invisible line created by talent sight lines that helps establish what side of the action the camera can record coverage for that scene. The camera should not be moved to the opposite side of this action line because it will cause a reversal in the established screen direction. See also 180 Degree Rule, Sight Line, Axis of Action.

Interior—In film terms, any shot that has to take place inside.

Iris—In motion picture equipment terms, the iris refers to the aperture or flexible opening of the camera lens that controls how much or how little light is used to expose the image inside the camera. Some modern video cameras use an electronic iris that controls the amount of light automatically. Most high-end HD and emulsion film lenses use an iris of sliding metal blades that overlap to make the aperture smaller or wider. A marked ring on the lens barrel can manually control the size of the opening.

Glossary

Jib Arm—A piece of motion picture camera support equipment that allows the camera to move around a central fulcrum point, left/right/up/down/diagonally. It may be mounted onto tripod legs or on a dolly.

Jump Cut—An anomaly of the edited film when two very similar shots of the same subject are cut together and played. A "jump" in space or time appears to have occurred, which often interrupts the viewer's appreciation for the story being shown.

Jump the Line—Based on the concept inherent to the "action line" or 180 degree rule, this expression refers to moving the camera across the line and recording coverage for a scene that will not match the established screen direction when edited together.

Key Light—The main light source around which the remaining lighting plan is built. Traditionally, on film sets, it is the brightest light that helps illuminate and expose the face of the main subject of the shot.

Kicker Light—Any light that hits the talent from a ¾ backside placement. It often rims just one side of the hair, shoulder, or jaw line.

Legs—An alternate name for a camera tripod.

Lens Axis—In motion picture camera terms, it is the central path cutting through the middle of the circular glass found in the camera's lens. Light traveling parallel to the lens axis is collected by the lens and brought into the camera that is exposing the recording medium. One can trace an imaginary straight line out of the camera's lens (like a laser pointer) and have it fall on the subject being recorded. That subject is now placed along the axis of the lens.

Light Meter—A device designed to read and measure the quantity of light falling on a scene or being emitted from it. Often used to help set the level of exposure on the film set and, consequently, the setting on the camera's iris.

Line—The imaginary line that connects a subject's gaze to the object of interest being viewed by that subject. Example: A man, standing in the entry way of an apartment building, looks at the name plate on the door buzzer. The "line" would be traced from the man's eyes to the name plate on the wall. The next shot may be a close-up of the name plate itself, giving the audience an answer to the question, "what is he looking at?"

Locked Off—The description of a shot where the tripod head pan and tilt controls are locked tight so that there will be no movement of the camera. If there were a need to make adjustments to the frame during shooting, the pan and tilt locks would be loosened slightly for smooth movement.

Long Shot—When photographing a standing human being, their entire body is visible within the frame and a large amount of the surrounding environment is also visible around them. Sometimes called a wide shot.

Look Room/Looking Room/Nose Room—When photographing a person, it is the space between their face and the farthest edge of the film frame. If a person is positioned frame left and is looking across empty space at frame right, then that empty space is considered the look room or nose room.

Low Angle Shot—Any shot where the camera records the action from a vertical position lower than most objects being recorded. Example: The camera, on a city sidewalk, points up to the tenth floor of an office building to record two men, suspended with rigging, cleaning the windows.

Lower Thirds—A title or graphic that appears as a superimposed visual element across the bottom lower third of the screen. Usually used to identify a person or place in a factual news piece or a documentary interview.

Low Key Lighting—A lighting style in which a large contrast ratio exists between the brightly lit areas and the dark areas of the frame. Example: Film noir used low key lighting to create deep, dark shadows and single-source key lighting for exposure of principal subjects of importance.

Matching Shots (also known as Reciprocating Imagery or Answering Shots)—When shooting coverage for a scene, each camera set-up favoring each character being covered should be very similar if not identical. One should match the framing, camera height, focal length, lighting and so forth. When edited together, the "matching shots" will balance one another and keep the information presented about each character consistent.

Medium Shot—When photographing a standing human being, the bottom of the frame will cut off the person around the waist.

Middle Ground—The zone within the depth of a filmed frame where, typically, the majority of the important visual action will take place. Objects in the middle ground may be obscured by other objects in the foreground, but middle ground objects may then also obscure objects far away from camera in the background.

Monocular Vision (Camera Lens)—A visual system in which only one lens takes in and records all data. The three-dimensional aspect of human binocular vision is not present in the monocular vision of the film or video camera.

MOS—A term applied to shots recorded without sound. It should be noted on the clap slate and on the camera report and camera log. Although originating in the early days of sync sound emulsion film production, it may be used on any project where a camera records the visual images and a separate device records the audio signal. The post-production team knows not to search for a sync sound clip that corresponds to that "MOS" picture clip.

Motivated Light—Light, seen on a film set, that appears to be coming from some light source within the film's pretend world.

Natural Light—Any light that is made by the sun or fire; non-manmade sources.

Negative Space—An artistic concept wherein unoccupied or empty space within a composition or arrangement of objects also has mass, weight, importance, and is worth attention. Used to help balance objects within the frame.

Neutral Density Filter—A device that reduces the amount of light entering a camera (density), but does not alter the color temperature of that light (neutral). It is either a glass filter that one can apply to the front of the camera lens or, with many video cameras, a setting within the camera's electronics that replicates the reduced light effect of neutral density glass lens filters.

Normal Lens—A camera lens whose focal length closely replicates what the field of view and perspective might be on certain objects if those same objects were seen with human eyes.

Objective Shooting—A style of filmmaking where the talent never addresses the existence of the camera. The camera is a neutral observer, not participating actively in the recorded event but simply acting as a viewer of the event for the benefit of the audience.

Overexposed—A state of an image where the bright regions contain no discernible visual data but appear as glowing white zones. The overall tonality of this image may also be lacking in true "black" values so that everything seems gray to white in luminance.

Overheads—Drawings or diagrams of the film set, as seen from above like a bird's-eye view, that show the placement of camera, lighting equipment, talent, and any set furnishings, etc. These overheads will act as a map for each department to place the necessary equipment in those roughed-out regions of the set.

Overlapping Action—While shooting coverage for a particular scene, certain actions made by talent will have to be repeated from different camera angles and framings. When cutting the film together, the editor will benefit from having the talent making these repeated movements, or overlapping actions, in multiple shots so that when the cut is made it can be made on the matching movement of the action across the two shots.

Over the Shoulder (OTS)—A shot used in filmmaking where the back of a character's head and one of his shoulders create an "L" shape in the left/bottom or right/bottom foreground and act as a "frame" for the full face of another character in the middle ground opposite the first character. This shot is often used when recording a dialogue scene between two people.

Pan—Short for panoramic, the horizontal movement, from left to right or right to left, of the camera while it is recording action. If you are using a tripod for camera support, the pan is achieved by loosening the pan lock on the tripod head and using the pan handle to swivel the camera around the central pivot point of the tripod in order to follow the action or reveal the recorded environment.

Pan Handle—A tripod head with a horizontal pivot axis which allows for the panning action of the camera either left or right. The pan handle is a stick or length of metal tubing that extends off the tripod head and allows the camera operator to control the rate of movement of the camera pan by physically pushing or pulling it around the central axis of the tripod.

Point of View (POV)—In filmmaking terms, any shot that takes on a subjective vantage. The camera records what one of the characters is seeing. The camera sits in place of the talent, and what it shows to the viewing audience is supposed to represent what the character is actually seeing in the story. It can help an audience relate to that character because they are placed in that character's position.

Point Source—A light source derived from a specific, localized instance of light generation/emission. A non-diffused light source.

Post-production—The phase of motion picture creation that traditionally happens after all of the action is recorded with a camera (also known as production). Post-production can include picture and sound editing, title and graphics creation, motion effects rendering, color correction, musical scoring and mixing, etc.

Practical—A functional, onset lighting fixture visible in the recorded shot's frame that may actually help illuminate the set for exposure. Example: A shot of a man sitting down at a desk at night. Upon the desk is a desk lamp whose light illuminates the face of the man.

Pre-production—The period of work on a motion picture project that occurs prior to the start of principal photography (also known as production). Story development, script writing, storyboards, casting, etc. all happen during this phase.

Prime Lens—A type of lens that has only one focal length.

Principal Photography—The recording of motion images that involve the major talent of a production during the primary dialogue and/or action scenes contained in the script.

Production—The period of work on a motion picture project that occurs while the scenes are being recorded on film or video. This could be as short as a single day for a commercial or music video or last several months for a feature film.

Proscenium Style—In theatre as well as motion pictures, this is a way to stage the action such that it is seen from only one direction. The audience or, in film's case, the camera views and records the action from only one angle.

Pulling Focus—Camera lenses that have manual controls for the focus will allow a camera assistant or camera operator to move the plane of critical focus closer to the camera, therefore shifting the distance of the zone that appears to be in sharp focus within the depth of the frame. This is often done to shift focus from one farther object in the frame to one closer object within the frame.

Punch-In—When two or more separate shots of differing frame sizes cover the same subject along the same camera axis.

Pushing Focus—Camera lenses that have manual controls for the focus will allow a camera assistant or camera operator to move the plane of critical focus further away from the camera, therefore shifting the zone of what appears to be in sharp focus within the frame's depth. This is often done to shift focus from a near object in the frame to one further away.

Racking Focus—During the recording of a shot that has a shallow depth of field, the camera assistant or camera operator may need to shift focus from one subject in the frame to another. This shifting of planes of focus from one distance away from the camera to another is called racking focus.

Reveal—Any time that the filmmaker shows new, important, or startling visual information on the screen through camera movement, talent blocking, or edited shots in post-production. The reveal of information is the payoff after a suspenseful expectation has been established within the story.

Rim Light—Any light source whose rays "rim" or "halo" the edges of a subject or an object on the film set, often placed somewhere behind the subject but directed at him.

Rule of Thirds—A commonly used guideline of film frame composition where an imaginary grid of lines falls across the frame, both vertically and horizontally, at the mark of thirds. Placing objects along these lines or at the cross points of two of these lines is considered part of the tried and true composition of film images.

Safe Action Line—Related to the domestic cutoff phenomenon, the safe action line is found on many camera viewfinders and is used to keep the important action composed more toward the inner region of the frame. This prevents important action from being cut off.

Scene—A segment of a motion picture that takes place at one location. A scene may be composed of many shots from different camera angles or just one shot from one camera set-up.

Screen Direction—The direction in which a subject moves across or out of the frame. Example: A person standing at the center of frame suddenly walks out of frame left. The movement to the left is the established screen direction. When the next shot is cut together for the story, the same person should enter the frame from frame right, continuing their journey in the same screen direction – from the right to the left.

Glossary

Shooting Ratio—The amount of material you shoot for a project compared to the amount of material that makes it into the final edit. Example: You shoot fourteen takes of one actor saying a line, but only use one of those takes in the final movie. You have a 14:1 shooting ratio for that one line of dialogue.

Shot—One action or event that is recorded by a camera at one time. A shot is the smallest building block used to edit a motion picture.

Shot List—A list of shots, usually prepared by the director during pre-production, that acts as a guide for what shots are required for best coverage of a scene in a motion picture project. It should show the shot type and may follow a number and letter naming scheme (e.g. Scene 4, Shot C, or simply 4C).

Shot–Reverse–Shot—A term applied to an editing style where one shot of a particular type (medium close-up) is used on one character and then the same type of shot (medium close-up) is edited next to show the other character in the scene. You see the shot, "reverse" the camera angle, and see a matching shot of the other character.

Side Lighting—A method of applying light to a subject or film set where the lights come from the side, not above or below.

Sight Line—The imaginary line that traces the direction in which a subject is looking on screen; sometimes called a line of attention. Sight line also establishes the line of action and sets up the 180 degree arc for shooting coverage of a scene.

Silhouette—A special way of exposing a shot where the brighter background is correct in its exposure but the subject (in the MG or FG) is underexposed and appears as a black shape with no detail but the hard edge "cutout."

Slate—(noun) The clapboard used to identify the shot being recorded. Often the name of the production, director, DP, the shooting scene, and the date are written on the slate. (verb)—Using the clapboard sticks to make a "clapping" sound, which serves as a synchronization point of picture and sound tracks during the edit process.

Soft Light—Any light that has diffused, non-parallel rays. Strong shadows are very rare if one uses soft light to illuminate talent.

Spreader (Tripod)—The three legs of a tripod are often attached to a rubber or metal device in order to keep the legs from splaying too far apart while the heavy camera sits atop the tripod head. This three-branched brace allows for greater stability, especially as the tripod legs are spread further and further apart to get the camera lower to the ground.

Staging—The placement of talent and objects within the film set.

Standard Definition—A reference to the normal image quality and frame size of most televisions around the world during the twentieth century. Limitations in broadcast bandwidth, among other technological reasons, required a low-resolution image (525-line NTSC or 576-line PAL) of the 4:3 aspect ratio for television reception in the home.

Start Frame—Any time the camera needs to move in order to follow action, the camera should begin recording, stay stationary for a few moments while the action begins, and then start to move to follow the action. The start frame can be useful to the editor of the film so that the shot will have a static frame to start on at the beginning of the cut. Static frames cut to moving frames can be a jarring visual experience and this static start frame may help prevent this from occurring.

Sticks—(i) An alternate name for a camera tripod. (ii) The clapboard or slate used to mark the synchronization point of picture and sound being recorded.

Storyboards—Drawings often done during pre-production of a motion picture that represent the best guess of what the ultimate framing and movement of camera shots will be when the film goes into production. These comic book-like illustrations act as a template for the creative team when principal photography begins.

Subjective Shooting—A style of filmmaking where the talent addresses the camera straight into the lens (as in news broadcasting) or when the camera records exactly what a character is observing in a fictional narrative, as with the point of view shot.

Tail—The common film term for the end of a shot, especially during the post-production editing process.

Tail Slate—Often used while recording documentary footage, a tail slate is the process of identifying the shot and "clapping" the slate after the action has been recorded but before the camera stops rolling. The slate is physically held upside-down to visually indicate a tail slate.

Take—Each action, event, or dialogue delivery recorded in a shot may need to be repeated until its technical and creative aspects are done to the satisfaction of the filmmakers. Each time the camera rolls to record this repeated event is called a "take." Takes are traditionally numbered, starting at "one."

Taking Lens—The active lens on a motion picture or video camera that is actually collecting, focusing, and controlling the light for the recording of the image. On certain models of emulsion film motion picture cameras there can be more than one lens mounted to the camera body. Most video cameras have only one lens, which would be the "taking" lens.

Talking Head—Any medium close-up shot or closer that frames one person's head and shoulders. Usually associated with documentaries, news, and interview footage.

Three Point Lighting—A basic but widely used lighting method where a key light is employed for main exposure on one side of talent, a fill light for contrast control on the opposite side, and a back light for subject/background separation.

Tilt—The vertical movement, either down/up or up/down, of the camera while it is recording action. If using a tripod for camera support, the tilt is achieved by loosening the tilt lock on the tripod head and using the pan handle to swing the camera lens up or down in order to follow the vertical action or reveal the recorded environment.

Timecode—A counting scheme based on hours, minutes, seconds, and frames used to keep track of image and sound placement on videotapes, digital media files, and editing software.

Tracks/Rail—Much like railroad tracks, these small-scale metal rails are used to smoothly roll a dolly across surfaces, either inside or outside, in order to get a moving shot.

Tripod—A three-legged device, often with telescoping legs, used to support and steady the camera for motion picture shooting. The camera attaches to a device capable of vertical and horizontal axis movements called the tripod head, which sits atop the balancing legs.

Truck In/Out—Moving the camera into set or pulling camera out of set, usually atop a dolly on tracks. Also known as tracking in and tracking out.

Tungsten Balanced—Film and video cameras may be biased toward seeing the color temperature of tungsten lamps (aka, film lights) as "white" light. When they are set this way, they have a tungsten balance at approximately 3200 degrees Kelvin.

Two-Shot—Any shot that contains the bodies (or body parts) of two people.

Underexpose—A state of an image where the dark regions contain no discernible visual data but appear as deep black zones. The overall tonality of this image may also be lacking in true "white" values so that everything seems gray down to black in luminance.

Vanishing Point—A long-established technique in the visual arts where opposing diagonal lines converge at the horizon line to indicate the inclusion of a great distance in the image's environment. It is an illusion used to help represent three-dimensional space on a two-dimensional surface.

Video Format—A video combines recorded electronic voltage fluctuations or digital bit data that represent picture and sound information. Video cameras are manufactured to record that data onto a tape or memory card in a particular way. The shape, amount of data, frame rate, color information and so forth that gets recorded are determined by the technologies inside the video camera. Examples include NTSC-525 line, PAL, HD-1080i, HD-720p.

Visible Spectrum—The zone in electromagnetic energy waves that appears to our eyes and brains as colored light.

Voice Slate—A practice used at the head of a shot after the camera is rolling and before the director calls "action." Often, a camera assistant will verbally speak the scene and take number so as to identify audio data that may be recorded separately from the picture.

Workflow—A plan or methodology that maps the flow of picture and sound data from the production through numerous post-production phases and ultimately to a finished product that is distributed for viewing. Managing a clear digital mediafile workflow is very important to the efficient completion of any project.

Zoom Lens—A camera lens whose multiple glass lens element construction and telescoping barrel design allow it to gather light from a wide range or field of view and also from a very narrow (more magnified) field of view. The focal length of the lens is altered by changing the distances of the optical elements contained within the lens barrel itself. Most modern video cameras have built-in optical zoom lenses that can be adjusted from wide to telephoto with the touch of a button.

Glossary

Index

Note: 'f' following a page number indicates a figure.

action, 267; allowing actions to complete before cutting camera, 234; axis of action, 151–3, 268–9; continuity of, 208; excess overlapping, 209; matching speed of, 208–9; overlapping action, 208, 209, 281; using pan and tilt tripod head for following, 206, 207f

action line, 151–3; see also axis of action; imaginary line; 180 degree line

acts, 144, 145f, 267

aesthetics, 5, 268

amateur videos, 169

angle of incidence, 131, 268

angle of view, 228, 235, 268

angles on action, 45, 268

animatics, 26

ANSI rating, 116

answering shots, 57, 69, 157–9; see also matching shots

aperture, 103, 104, 117, 268

archive film, 241

art directors, 219, 265

art history, 259

artificial light, 114–5, 258, 268

ASA rating, 116

aspect ratio, 4, 5–7, 268; 4:3 aspect ratio, 267; see also frame size

assistant directors, 266

atmosphere/atmospherics, 93–4, 268

attention, 150, 268

audience, what to show your audience, 3

Auto Focus, 103

axis of action, 151–3, 268–9; see also action line; imaginary line; 180 degree rule; sight lines

background, 90–1, 269

back light, 128, 129f, 132–3, 269

basic shots, 11–21, 22f; big close-up shots, 12f, 20; bust shots, 18; choker shots, 12f, 20; close-up shots see close-up shots; extreme close-up shots, 12f, 22f; extreme long shots, 12f, 13; extreme wide shots, 12f, 13; full shots, 15; long shots see long shots; medium close-up shots see medium close-up shots; medium shots, 8–9, 12f, 17, 22f, 279; very long shots, 12f, 14, 37f; very wide shots, 12f, 14, 37f; wide shots see wide shots

BCU see big close-up shots

big close-up shots, 12f, 20

binocular vision, 76, 269; see also human visual system

bird's-eye view, 58

blocking, 166, 269

blue, 219

blue screen, 238

books for filmmakers, 261–3

boom arm, 176, 269

boom operator, 266

booms, 178f

break frames, 17, 269

breaking the fourth wall, 38, 275

b-roll, 240, 269

bust shots, 18

camera(s), 2, 4; allowing actions to complete before cutting camera, 234; allowing enough time to record each shot, 232; handheld cameras, 168–9, 175; rolling camera, 232, 233f

camera angles, 45–61, 269; 3/4 back view, 53; 3/4 view, 51; 360 degrees method, 46–7, 48f; camera position method, 50–4; clock face method, 49, 50f; frontal view, 50, 51f; full back view, 53–4; horizontal, 46–54; matching, 214–5; profile view, 52; vertical, 54–61

camera aperture, 103, 104, 117, 268

camera assistants, 101, 180, 186, 265

camera in motion, 168–74

camera lenses, 95–105; fish-eye lenses, 100, 274; lens focus, 101–3; lens perspective, 97–101; normal lenses, 280; prime lenses, 96, 282; prime vs zooms, 95–6; taking lens, 286; wide angle lenses, 98, 236; zoom lenses see zoom lenses

camera movement, 168–74; equipment, 175–81

camera operators, 2, 101, 180, 265, 269
camera person, 2, 265, 269
camera position method, 50–4
camera set-up, 270
camera shake, 235
camera support, 168, 270
camera-to-subject distance, and depth of field, 194–5
canted angle *see* Dutch angle
catch light *see* eye light
charge-coupled devices (CCDs), 114, 270
chiaroscuro, 258, 270
choker shots, 12f, 20
chromakey, 238, 239f
chrominance, 116
Cinemascope, 6
cinematographers, 265
clean single, 270; *see also* dirty single
clock face method, 49, 50f
close-up shots, 10, 12f, 19, 22f, 198–9, 270; big close-up shots, 12f; examples of, 12f; extreme close-up shots, 12f, 22f; eye-line directions, 204, 205f; medium close-up shots, 12f, 22f; wide lenses and, 236
CMOS (complementary metal-oxide semiconductor), 114, 270
color(s), 126–7, 219; correcting or mixing colors on set, 115
color balance, 114
color saturation, 126
color temperature, 113, 270
communication, with talent, 188, 189f
complementary metal oxide semiconductor (CMOS), 114, 270
composition, 33–74, 271; camera angles, 45–61; definition of, 33; framing human subjects, 35–7; look room, 40–1; rule of thirds, 42–3, 44f; subjective versus objective shooting styles, 38–9; three-shot, 70–1; two-shots, 62–9
continuity, 271; of action, 208; of performance, 146; of screen direction, 147–9; traps, 222, 223f
contrast, 124, 271
contrast ratio, 130, 271
cool light, 113
coverage, 23, 271
cover set, 255
Cowboy shot *see* medium long shots
crab, 177

crab dollies, 177, 179f
cranes, 181, 271
crane shots, 181
crew positions, 265–6
critical plane of focus, 194, 271
crossing the line, 154–5, 271; *see also* jumping the line
CU *see* close-up shots
curved lines, 87, 88f
cutaway shots, 216, 271
cutting camera, allowing actions to complete before cutting camera, 234

daylight balance, 114, 272
deep focus techniques, 194
degrees Kelvin, 113, 272
depth, 272
depth cues, 92–4; atmosphere, 93–4; object size, 92–3; overlapping, 92
depth of field (DOF), 101, 103–5, 272; camera-to-subject distance, 194–5; controlling, 194–5; focal length and, 194, 228; illumination and, 119, 120f, 194; shallow, 235; size and sensitivity of the recording medium, 195
depth of film space, 89–90; background, 90–1; foreground, 89, 90f; middle ground, 90; to stage shots with several people, 224, 225f
desaturation, 126, 219, 272
developing shots, 180
diagonal lines, 82–7
dialogue scenes: matching camera angles, 214–5; matching two-shots in three-person dialogue scenes, 226, 227f
digital zoom, 272
direct address, 38, 272
directional light, 121
direction, lines of, 150
director of photography (DP or DOP), 265, 272
directors, 265; art directors, 219, 265; assistant directors, 266
direct-to-camera two-shots, 65–6
dirty single, 68–9, 273; *see also* clean single
distracting objects, 220, 221f
documentary filming, being discrete during, 244
dollies, 176–7, 178f, 273
dolly grips, 266
dolly shots, 230, 231f
domestic cutoff, 190, 273
DSLR HD video cameras, 103
Dutch angle, 82, 273

Dutch tilt *see* Dutch angle
dynamic shots, 165–83

editors, 266
electric, 266
ELS *see* extreme long shots
emulsions films: color balance, 114; frames per
    second, 167
end frames, 173–4, 273
equipment: camera movement, 175–81;
    knowledge of, 256
establishing shots, 13, 273
etiquette, 255
EWS *see* extreme wide shots
exposure, 117–9, 120f, 194, 273
exposure index (EU), 116
exposure time, 118
exterior, 274
extreme close-up shots, 12f, 21, 22f
extreme long shots, 12f, 13
extreme wide shots, 12f, 13
eye light, 200, 201f, 274
eye-line match, 160, 161f, 274
eye lines, direction in close shots, 204, 205f
eyes, subjects, 202, 203f
eye twinkle *see* eye light

face focus, 36
fast motion, 167
field of view, 235
50/50 profile 2-shots *see* profile two-shots
50-50 shots *see* profile two-shots
fill light, 128, 129f, 274
film gauge, 4, 274
filmmakers, 2
film noir, 274
film production, phases of, 27
film space, 274
filters, neutral density filters (ND filters),
    104, 118, 280
fish-eye lenses, 100, 236, 274
focal length, 95, 96, 274–5; and depth of field,
    194, 228; long, 235; short focal length to
    reduce handheld camera shake, 235
focus, 101–3, 180, 192, 193f, 275; Auto Focus,
    103; critical plane of focus, 194, 271; deep
    focus techniques, 194; face focus, 36;
    following focus, 103–5, 275; pulling focus,
    103–5, 282; pushing focus, 283; racking
    focus, 283

following focus, 103–5, 275
foreground, 89, 90f, 275
foreshortening, 56, 275
4:3 aspect ratio, 267
fourth wall, 38, 147, 275
frames, 147, 275; break frames, 17, 269;
    choosing, 4–5; end frames, 173–4, 273;
    headroom in, 35–7; placing important
    objects in the top half of, 218; start
    frames, 173, 285
frame size, 4; *see also* aspect ratio
frontal shooting, 50, 51f
front lighting, 131–2, 275
f-stop, 95, 96
full back view, 53–4
full shots, 15

gaffer, 265
gain control, 118
gaze, 150
geared heads, 175, 276
gels, 219, 276
general guidelines, 185–247
genres, 38, 276
God view (bird's eye view), 58
golden hour, 276
grammar, definition of, 2
Grammar of the Edit, 143
green screen, 238
grey scale, 117
grip equipment, 137
grips, 266, 276; key grip, 265

handheld camera, 168–9, 175
handheld camera shake, 235
hard lights, 121–2, 137, 276
HD *see* high definition
head of shots, 232, 276
headroom, 36–7, 196, 197f, 276
head shots *see* close-up shots
high angle shots, 56, 276–7; of an
    environment, 57–8; of an individual, 56;
    as a point-of-view, 57
high contrast images, 124
high definition, 5, 190, 277
high-end video productions, frames per
    second, 167
high key lighting, 125, 277
HMIs, 115, 277
hood mount, 277

horizon line, 78–80, 277
horizontal camera angles, 46–54
hues, 126
human subjects: cutting the face in half, 42f; framing, 35–7
human visual system, 84, 102, 110, 172, 269; and the illusion of the third dimension, 76; proper focus, 192; response to brightness, color and movement, 166; *see also* binocular vision

illumination, and depth of field, 119, 120f, 194
illusion of three-dimensions, 76–7
image capture, 167
imaginary line, 151–3, 277
IMAX®, 6
interior, 277
International Organization for Standardization (ISO), 116
interviews, talking head interviews, 198, 242, 243f
iris, 95, 194, 277

jib arm, 278
jibs, 181
jib shots, 181
jump cuts, 157, 278
jumping the line, 154–5, 278; *see also* crossing the line

Kelvin scale, 113, 272
key grips, 265; *see also* grips
key light, 128, 129f, 278
kicker light, 132, 278
knee shots (medium long shots), 12f, 16, 22f

LEDs, 115
legs, 176, 278
lens axis, 38, 278
lenses, 4, 54; fish-eye lenses, 100, 274; focus, 101–3; height, 54; normal lenses, 280; perspective, 97–101; prime lenses, 96, 282; and shooting close-up shots, 236; short focal length lenses to reduce handheld camera shake, 235; taking lenses, 286; wide angle lenses, 98, 236, 237f; zoom lenses *see* zoom lenses
life light *see* eye light
light(s), 109–41, 258; artificial light, 114–5, 258, 268; back light, 128, 129f, 132–3, 269; from behind, 132–3; controlling, 137; cool light, 113; and depth of field, 194; directional light, 121; as an element of composition, 110–1; as energy, 112; exposure and quality of, 117–9, 120f; eye light, 200, 201f, 274; fill light, 128, 129f, 274; front lighting, 131–2, 275; hard lights, 121–2, 137, 276; high key lighting, 125, 277; key light, 128, 129f, 278; kicker light, 132, 278; under lighting, 133, 134f; light meter, 278; low key lighting, 124, 125f, 279; motivated lighting, 130–1, 280; natural light, 114–5, 258, 280; point source lights, 121, 282; rim light, 132, 283; sensitivity and quality of, 116; set and location, 135–6; side lighting, 132, 284; soft light, 122, 123f, 137, 284; sources of, 133; three-point lighting method, 128, 129f, 286; top lighting, 133, 134f; warm light, 113
light flares, 258
lighting ratio, 130
light meter, 118, 278
light quality, hard versus soft, 121–2, 123f
lines, 78–87, 88f, 150, 151f, 278; curved lines, 87, 88f; diagonal lines, 82–7; of direction, 150; Dutch angle, 82; horizon line, 78–80; vertical lines, 80–1
location lighting, 135–6
locked off shots, 8, 279
long shots, 8, 12f, 15, 22f, 279; with proper headroom, 37f; with a single human subject, 9f; very long shots, 12f, 14
looking room *see* look room
look room, 40–1, 279; on shots that will edit together, 213
low angle shots, 58, 279; of an environment, 59–61; of an individual, 58–9; as a point-of-view, 59
low contrast images, 124
lower third titles, 191f, 279
low key lighting, 124, 125f, 279
LS *see* long shots
luminance, 116

macrophotography, 195
magic hour *see* golden hour
Manual Focus, 103
Master Scene Technique, 23–4
master shots, 23
matching shots, 146–9, 157–9, 160f, 279

MCU *see* medium close-up shots
medium close-up shots, 12f, 18, 22f; with eyes
    looking away from lens axis, 39f; with
    headroom, 36f
medium long shots, 12f, 16, 22f
medium shots, 8–9, 12f, 17, 22f, 279
middle ground, 90, 280
mid shot *see* medium shots
MLS *see* medium long shots
monocular vision (camera lens), 280
MOS, 187, 280
motion, camera in motion, 168–74
motion imagery, 2
motion picture, 2
motivated lighting, 130–1, 280
movement of subjects, 166
MS *see* medium shots
music videos, 169

natural light, 114–5, 258, 280
negative space, 40, 280
neutral angle shots, 55
neutral density filters (ND filters), 104, 118, 280
normal lens, 280
nose room, 40–1; *see also* look room

objective shooting, 38–9, 280
object size, 92–3
oblique angle *see* Dutch angle
180 degree line, 216, 217f, 267; *see also* axis of
    action; 180 degree rule; sight lines
180 degree rule, 151–3, 267; *see also* 180
    degree line
organization, 186
OTS *see* over-the-shoulder shots
overcranking, 167
overexposure, 118, 119f, 281
overheads, 210, 211f, 281
overlapping action, 92, 208, 281; excess of, 209
over-the-shoulder shots, 53, 158, 160f, 281;
    three-shots, 71; two-shots, 66–7, 68f

paintings, 259
pan, 169–72, 281; for following action, 206,
    207f; shooting the tilt and, 173–4; and
    tilt head, 175
pan handles, 175, 281
performance: continuity of, 146; quality of, 146
period pieces, 136
planning what to show your audience, 3

point of critical focus, 101
point-of-view (POV), 57, 59, 281; *see also*
    over-the-shoulder shots
point source light, 121, 282
post-production phase, 27, 282
power dynamic two-shots, 69
practicals, 135, 282
pre-production phase, 27, 210, 282
presentation speed, 167
prime lenses, 96, 282
principal photography, 27, 282
production designers, 219
production phase, 27, 144, 282
professional behavior, 255
profile two-shots, 62–3, 64f, 267
profile view, 52
proscenium style, 282
pulling focus, 103–5, 282
punch-in, 282
pushing focus, 283

quality, of performance, 146

racking focus, 283; *see also* pulling focus
railroad tracks, 83–4, 286
reciprocating imagery, 157–9, 160f; *see also*
    matching shots
red, 219
research, 259
resources for filmmakers, 261–3
reveal of information, 283
reverse view *see* full back view
rim lights, 132, 283
rolling camera, 232, 233f
rule of thirds, 42–3, 44f, 283
rules and guidelines, 250

safe action line, 283
safe action zone, 190
safe title area, 190
sandbags, 176
saturated colors, 126
scenes, 145f, 283; matching shots in, 146–9,
    157–9, 160f, 279
screen direction, 283; continuity of, 147–9;
    lines, 150
screenwriters, 265
script analysis, 25
script breakdown, 25
scripts, 25, 28–9

Script Supervisor, 23
SD *see* standard definition
2nd Unit, 240
sensitivity, of video camera digital imager, 195
set lighting, 135–6
set-up, 25
shooting: for editing, 143–63, 251; frontal
    shooting, 50, 51f; the pan and
    the tilt, 173–4
shooting ratio, 212, 284
shooting styles, subjective versus
    objective, 38–9
short focal length, 235
shot lists, 25–6, 210, 211f, 284
shot-reverse-shots, 214, 215f, 284
shots, 284; allowing actions to complete before
    cutting camera, 234; allowing enough time
    to record each shot, 232, 233f; bust shots,
    18; close-up shots *see* close-up shots;
    crane shots, 181; cutaway shots, 216, 271;
    developing shots, 180; direct-to-camera
    two-shots, 65–6; distracting objects, 220,
    221f; dolly shots, 230, 231f; dynamic shots,
    165–83; enticing the entire story, 252;
    establishing shots, 13, 273; frontal
    shooting, 50, 51f; full shots, 15; head of,
    232, 276; high angle shots *see* high angle
    shots; jib shots, 181; knee shots *see*
    medium long shots; locked off, 8; long
    shots *see* long shots; low angle shots *see*
    low angle shots; master shots, 23;
    matching shots in scenes, 146–9, 157–9,
    160f, 279; medium shots *see* medium
    shots; neutral angle shots, 55; reasons for
    different types of, 23–4; of several people,
    224, 225f; shot-reverse-shots, 214, 215f,
    284; slating shots, 233f; straight-to-camera
    shots, 202; tail of, 232; three-shots, 70–1;
    types, 8–10; very long shots, 12f, 14; very
    wide shots, 12f, 14; waist shots, 17; wide
    shots, 8, 9f, 12f, 15, 98
shutter speed, 118
side lighting, 132, 284
sight lines, 150, 284
silhouettes, 135, 284
size, of the camera digital imager, 195
slates, 186, 187f; noun definition, 284; verb
    definition, 284
slating shots, 233f
sliders, 177

slow motion, 167
soft light, 122, 123f, 137, 284
sound mixer, 266
speed, 232; presentation speed, 167
speed of action, 208–9
spreader, 176, 284–5
staging, 166, 285
standard definition, 5, 285
start frames, 173, 285
steadicam, 180–1
sticks, 176, 285
still photography, 241
stock footage, 240
storyboards, 26, 210, 211f, 285
straight-to-camera shots, 202
studying what has already been done, 259
subjective shooting, 285; versus objective
    shooting styles, 38–9
subjects: familiarity with, 257; in motion, 166;
    showing both eyes, 202, 203f
subtext, 34
sun, 121, 122
sunlight, 121, 122, 258
support, 176
synchronization, 186
syncing, 186

tail of shots, 232, 285
tail slate, 187, 285
takes, 26, 285–6
taking lens, 286
taking pride in the quality of your work, 255
talent blocking, 166
talent movement, 166
talking head, 198, 242, 243f, 286
telephoto, 235
30 degree rule, 155–7, 267
3/4 back view, 53
3/4 profile shots, 202
3/4 view (3/4/front, 3/4 profile), 51
360 degrees method, 46–7, 48f
3D video cameras, 76
three-point lighting method, 128, 129f, 286
three-shots, 70–1
tight close-up shots *see* big close-up shots
tilt, 169–72, 286; shooting the pan and, 173–4
tilt-pan, 170
tilt tripod head, for following action, 206, 207f
timecode, 186, 286
timecode syncing, 186

time, for the camera to record each shot, 232
top lighting, 133, 134f
tracking in, 177
tracking out, 177
tracks/rail, 83–4, 286
tripod heads, 175, 206
tripods, 175–6, 286
truck, 177–80
trucking in, 177, 230, 231f, 286
trucking out, 177, 230, 231f, 286
tungsten balanced, 114, 286
tungsten lighting, 114
two-button shots *see* medium close-up shots
two-shots, 62–9, 287; direct-to-camera, 65–6;
    dirty single, 68–9; over-the-shoulder
    two-shots, 66–7, 68f; power dynamic, 69;
    profile two-shots, 62–3, 64f, 267; in
    three-person dialogue scenes, 226, 227f

undercranking, 167
underexposure, 118, 119f, 287
under lighting, 133, 134f

vanishing point, 83–4, 287
vertical camera angles, 54–61
vertical lines, 80–1
very long shots, 12f, 14; with proper headroom, 37f
very wide shots, 12f, 14; with proper
    headroom, 37f

video format, 4, 287
viewers, keeping viewers involved as much as
    possible, 253–4
visible spectrum, 112, 287
VistaVision, 6
visual plans, 3
voice slates, 186, 287

waist shots, 17
warm light, 113
web sites for filmmakers, 261
white balance, 114
wide angle lenses, 98; shooting close-up shots
    with, 236, 237f
wide angle shots, 98
wide screens, 6, 7
wide shots, 8, 12f, 15; with proper headroom,
    37f; with a single human subject, 9f; very
    wide shots, 12f, 14
workflow, 5, 287
working practices, 185–247
WS *see* wide shots

XLS *see* extreme long shots
XWD *see* extreme wide shots

zoom lenses, 97, 287; digital zoom, 272;
    manually focusing, 191; zooming during
    shots, 228, 229f